Anglo-American Ceramics
Part I

Transfer Printed Creamware and Pearlware for the American Market 1760 - 1860

David and Linda Arman

For
Gladys W. Richards

ISBN:0-915438-02-X

The engraving appearing on the title page is taken from a painting by John R. Penniman (1783 - 1838) of Boston, Massachusetts, engraved by W. B. Annin for use as the frontispiece for Abel Bowen's book *The Naval Monument*, published in 1816.

Published by:
Oakland Press
P. O. Box 39
Portsmouth, RI 02871
Phone/Fax 401-841-8403
www.oaklandpublications.com
e-mail: info@oaklandpublications.com

"The bulk of our particular Manufactures you know are exported to foreign markets, for our home consumption is very trifleing in comparison to what are sent abroad, & the principal of these markets are the Continent & Islands of N. America. To the Continent we send an amazing qu.ᵗʸ of white stone ware & some of the finer kinds, but for the Islands we cannot make anything too rich & costly...." Josiah Wedgwood letter dated March 2, 1765[1].

Liverpool creamware pitcher with a finely executed portrait of the American ship VENILIA, with the name of her Captain, CALEB BATES, under the spout, sold at Robert Skinner's, Auctioneers and Appraisers, Bolton, Massachusetts on November 11, 1991 for $39,600.

[1] Wedgwood Archives E-18067-25. Josiah Wedgwood to Sir William Meredith, March 2, 1765. Used with permission of the Trustees of the Wedgwood Museum, Barlaston, Staffordshire, England.

Also by
David and Linda Arman

Historical Staffordshire: An Illustrated Check-list

First Supplement to Historical Staffordshire:
An Illustrated Check-list

Contents

Acknowledgements

We are most grateful for the help and patience of those who assisted us with the preparation of this book. Information has been gathered from both private collectors and museum professionals. Among the former, we would like to thank the following: Dr. and Mrs. Nicholas Bruno, Mr. and Mrs. Eugene Fleischer, Mr. Stephen Fletcher, Mr. and Mrs. Lance Keller, Mr. and Mrs. William Kurau, Mr. and Mrs. Bryan Lindberg and their daughter Bryanna, Mr. and Mrs. Jens Louv, Mr. J. Jefferson Miller II, Dr. and Mrs. Rexford Stark, Mr. S. Robert Teitelman and Mr. and Mrs. John Watson. As concerns the museum personnel, we can't thank Pat Halfpenny, Juliet Chase and Susan Newton of Winterthur enough for their assistance, along with Tony Lewis and John Pemberton of the Mariner's Museum, Alice Frelinghuysen at the Metropolitan Museum and Ann Smith and Raechel Guest of the Mattatuck Museum. Although we never met, we must thank Stella Beddoe, Keeper of Decorative Art at the Royal Pavilion Museums, Brighton, England and Myra Brown, Curator of Ceramics at the National Museums and Galleries on Merseyside, Liverpool, England. They both made the trans-Atlantic use of their fine collections quite easy. Also special thanks to Patrick Boxx for many of the fine photographs contained in this book.

Portions of the format we used for this book do not allow us to acknowledge the ownership of pieces shown in individual illustrations, therefore we have listed them below. When an illustration is shown in *italics*, this means that the ownership was as indicated, when this book was being researched, but in the interim, possession of the item has changed and the piece is also shown in it's present known collection without italics.

Albany Institute of History and Art, Albany, New York
Collection of the Albany Institute of History and Art

2.18a/b, A.12, C.1, C.23, E.5, E.6, J.34, V.1, W.1.

American Antiquarian Society, Worcester, Massachusetts
Courtesy of the American Antiquarian Society

A.19b, V.7b.

Arman Absentee Auctions/Collectors Sales and Services, Middletown, Rhode Island
Courtesy of Joseph Arman

1.5, 1.7, 1.10, 1.11, 1.12, 1.13, 2.1, 2.3, 2.4, 2.5, 2.12, 2.13, 2.14, 3.38, 3.55, 4.1, 4.4, 4.27 - 4.29, 4.48, 4.73, 4.76, A.4, A.22, A.24, A.30, B.8, C.12a, C.12b, C.14, C.19, C.25, C.29, E.3a, E.7, F.6, F.12, F.16, F.19, H.7, L.1, L.3, L.14a/b, M.21, O.1, P.8, P.20a, S.4, S.5, S.7, S.11, S.12, S.24, S.25, S.50, S.55, S.56, S.81, S.84, U.5, U.7a, V.4 - V.6, V.8, W.15, W.22b, W.27, W.28, W.31, W.40, W.41, W.43, W.47, W.59, 6.1, 6.3a-e, 6.7a-d, 6.12, AI.10, AI.12, AI.15 - AI.22, AI.45, AI.47 - AI.51, AIII.1, AIII.13, AIII.44 - AIII.46, AIII.52.

Brighton Museum and Art Gallery - Willet Collection Brighton, England
Reproduced by courtesy of the Royal Pavilion, Art Gallery and Museums

C.27, P.1, P.3, P.4, P.17, S.72, S.78, AI.13, AII.38b.

Dr. and Mrs. Nicholas Bruno

2.9, 2.10, 4.2, 4.17, 4.20, 4.47, C.16, D.7, G.1a, H.7, H.18, J.31a, S.42, U.6, Y.1.

Henry Francis Du Pont Winterthur Museum
Reproduced courtesy of Winterthur Museum, Delaware.

4.3, A.5, C.22, D.8, D.9, E.11, F.14, G1b, H.24, J.27, J.28, J.31b, J.32, L.15, L.24, L.29, M.19, N.6 - N.8, P.19, P.43, S.39, S.40, S.44, S.45, T.6, U.3, U.9a, W.3, W.22c, W.25, W.30b, W.32b, W.68, AIII.7, AIII.14, AIII.19, AIII.25, AIII.43, AIII.54a/b.

Mr. and Mrs. Eugene Fleischer

A.34, T.2, U.11.

Mr. Edward Gillette

4.30, H.9, J.4.

Mr. and Mrs. William Guthman

1.6a, 1.6b, P.15.

Mr. and Mrs. Arthur Gutman

4.5, 4.19, 4.42, M.14, S.14, W.66, 6.15.

Mr. and Mrs. Lance Keller

3.25, 4.24.

Mr. and Mrs. William Kurau

4.49, A.7, A.34, C.8a, C.8b, C.18, *D.11,* J.7, *U.11, W.2,* W.24.

Mr. and Mrs. Bryan Lindberg

1.8.

Liverpool Museum, Liverpool, England
Reproduced by courtesy of the National Museums and Galleries on Merseyside

S.73, T.1.

Mr. and Mrs. Jens Louv

1.14, 1.15, 2.6, 2.26, *4.2,* 4.6, *4.7, 4.9,* 4.18, 4.39, *4.47, 4.51,* 5.1, D.10, *G.1a, H.18, J.16,* L.18a, L.26, L.27, L.30, M.1, M.10, N.3, P.12, P.37, P.39, S.2, S.46 - S.48, S.51 - S.54, S.75, T.7, U.4, *U.6, W.2,* W.15a, W.21, W.45, *W.48,* W.51, 6.13.

The Maine Antique Digest, Waldoboro, Maine

A.17.

The Mariner's Museum, Newport News, Virginia
Courtesy of the Mariner's Museum

A.13, A.16, E.1, S.37, S.62b, S.63, S.64, 6.11a-c, 6.16, 6.17, AIII-18a-d.

The Mattatuck Museum, Waterbury, Connecticut
Reproduced Courtesy of the Mattatuck Museum

4.15, A.9, N.4.

The Metropolitan Museum of Art, New York, New York
Reproduced courtesy of the Metropolitan Museum of Art

P.27, W.61.

Peabody Essex Museum, Salem, Massachusetts
Courtesy, Peabody Essex Museum

5.3, 5.4, C.3, D.5, E.2, E.3b, G.2, H.1, H.21b, H.22, H.23, J.12, J.15, P.44, S.30, S.31a, S.43, S.69, W.58, W.69, 6.14.

Philadelphia Museum of Art, Philadelphia, Pennsylvania
Courtesy Philadelphia Museum of Art

2.16a/b, C.30.

Robert Skinner, Inc., Boston and Bolton, Massachusetts
Photographs courtesy Skinner, Auctioneers and Appraisers of Antiques and Fine Art, Boston and Bolton, Massachusetts.

iii, 1.2, 1.3, 1.4, 5.5, B.5, C.5, C.6, G.5, H.2, J.19, W.13, W.34, W.49.

Smithsonian Institution, National Museum of American History
Reproduced by courtesy of the Smithsonian Institution, Washington

A.3, A.25, B.6, B.13, D.6, F.5, F.9, H.13, J.20, K.1, M.16, P.16, P.23, P.25, P.46a/b/c, Q.2, S.38, S.41a, S.76, S.79, W.6, W.7. W.18c, W.33, W.50, W.52, W.62, W.63.

Dr. and Mrs. Rexford Stark

1.9, 1.17, 1.20, 1.21, 1.22a/b/c, 1.23, 1.24, 1.25, 1.26, 1.27, 2.11, 2.2, 2.8a/b, 2.17, 2.21, 2.23, 3.52, 4.6, 4.8, 4.13, 4.16, 4.21 - 4.23, 4.26, 4.31 - 4.34, 4.36 - 4.38, 4.41, 4.43, 4.45, 4.46, 4.50 - 4.53, 4.55 - 4.57, 4.70 - 4.72, 4.74, 4.76, 5.2, 5.6 - 5.8, 5.8c, 5.10, A.2, A.8, A.10, A.11, A.14, A.15, A.20, A.20b, A.21, A.24, A.29, A.32, B.1, B.2, B.4, B.7, B.12, C.2, C.9a/b - C.11, C.12c, C.13, C.26, C.28, D.3, D.4, E.7 - E.10, E.13, F.1, F.3, F.10 - F.12, F.17, H.4 - H.6, H.8, H.10 - H.12, H.14b, H.19, H.20, I.1, I.2, J.1 - J.3, J.5, J.8 - J.11, J.13, J.14, J.16, J.18, J.21 - J.26, J.29, J.30, J.36, L.8, L.11, L.12a, L.16, L.18b, L.20, L.23, M.3, M.4, M.7 - M.9, M.12, M.13, M.15, M.17, M.18, M.20, N.5, O.2, O.3, P.2, P.6, P.7, P.9 - P.11, P.13, P.14, P.20b, P.21, P.24, P.28a, P.30 - P.34, P.36, P.41, Q.1, S.1, S.6, S.10, S.17, S.19 - S.21, S.23, S.31b, S.34, S.35, S.59, S.61, S.62a, S.65, S.66, S.70, S.71, S.74, S.70, T.3, T.4, T.8, T.10, U.1, U.2, U.5, U.10, U.12, V.2, V.3, W.2, W.4, W.8, W.11, W.12, W.14, W.16, W.18a, W.19, W.20, W.23, W.32a, W.42, W.46, W.48, W.57, W.60, W.64, W.67, UNK2. AI.1 - AI.9, AI.11, AI.14, AI.23, AI.28, AI.37 - AI.39, AI.42 - AI.44, AI.46, AII.1 - AII.42, AIII.3, AIII.4, AIII.8 - AIII.12, AIII.15 - AIII.17, AIII.20, AIII.22, AIII.23, AIII.26 - AIII.42, AIII.47 - AIII.51.

Mr. S. Robert Teitelman

A.1, A.7, A.17, A.33, D.11, F.8.

Mr. and Mrs. John Watson

4.12, 4.54, A.23, *B.7, D.7,* F.17, *L.14a,* L.21.

Mr. Norman Wolfe

D.2.

Collection of the Authors

1.16, *1.17,* 1.18, 1.19, *2.2,* 2.7, *2.8,* 2.15, 2.19, 2.20, *2.21,* 2.24, 2.25,
2.27, 2.28, 2.29, 3.1, 3.2, 3.3, 3.4, 3.8, 3.9, 3.10, 3.12, 3.12a, 3.13, 3.15,
3.16, 3.17, 3.18, 3.22, 3.24, 3.26, 3.28, 3.30, 3.31, 3.33, 3.36, 3.37, 3.39,
3.41, 3.43, 3.44, 3.46, 3.47, 3.50, 3.54, 3.56, 3.57, 4.7, 4.9, 4.10, 4.11,
4.14, *4.21,* 4.25, *4.30,* 4.35, 4.40, 4.44, *4.49, 4.51,* 4.58, 4.59, 4.60 -
4.69, *5.8c,* 5.9, A.1, A.26,, A.28, A.29, A.31, *A.32, A.33, A.34, B.1,*
B.2, B.7, B.10, *C.15, C.17, C.18,* C.20, C.24, C.31, D.1, E.4, F.2, F.4,
F.7, H.3, *H.9,* H.14a, H.17, H.21a, I.3, *J.4, J.5,* J.6, *J.24, J.30,* J.35,
L.2, L.4 - L.7, L.9, L.10, L.12b, L.13, L.17, L.19, L.31, M.2, M.11,
M.13, *M.15,* N.1, N.2, P.22, P.26, P.29,, P.35, P.42, S.3, S.8, S.9, S.13,
S.15, S.16, S.18, *S.19,* S.22, S.26, S.28, S.29, S.32, S.33, S.36, S.49,
S.57, S.58, S.60, S.67, S.68a/b, S.77, S.82, T.5, *U.2,* U.7b, U.8, *U.11,*
W.5, *W.11, W.20,* W.22a, W.29, W.30a, W.35 - W.39, W.44, *W.48,*
W.54 - W.56, *W.60, W.64,* W.65, UNK1. 6.2, 6.4 - 6.6, AI.24 - AI.27,
AI.29 - 36, *AI.44,* AI.52 - AI.57, *AIII.4, AIII.15,* AIII.21b.

Various Private Collections

3.23, 3.34, 3.42, 3.45, 3.49, 3.51, 5.8b, A.19, C.7, E.14, F.15, G.3, G.6,
J.1b, M.6, V.7a, W.9, W.10, W.18b. AI.40, AI.41, AIII.5

C.C.I. - Computer Created Images

B.11, C.4, L.22, L.25, P.31, S.13, S.13b, S.83, AIII.2, AIII.6, AIII.21a,
AIII.24.

Foreward

This is the first of a three volume set which we intend to publish within the next five years. This trilogy will cover the American export market for English transferware from the beginning to the end, from Liverpool pitchers to the multicolored light transfer decorated tablewares. While modern products of the English ceramics industry continue to be popular in the United States to this day, it is the so-called "Historical" subjects which are the topics of these books. American historical subjects are found on English ceramics from the coronation of George III, through the end of our tragic Civil War. For one-hundred years, North America provided a ready market to the English potters and it was only after the end of the War between the States, that an American ceramics industry was able to successfully challenge the potteries of Staffordshire.

These books do not contain new material painstakingly researched by scholars over a period of time. The authors do not consider themselves "scholars", but rather, compilers. We have sought to record information as it became available during the thirty years we have bought, sold and collected historical ceramics. We were amazed at the results when we finally observed the completed product, which you now hold in your hands.

We should have realized, in the fifty years since Robert McCauley and Ellouise Larsen completed their books on Liverpool and Staffordshire, a lot has happened in the field. However, we were not prepared for the fact that the number of identified transfers in this specific field has almost *tripled,* from one-hundred seventy five views to the over five-hundred now recorded. And new, heretofore unknown transfers, are being recorded almost daily. Undoubtedly, this book will cause many collections to be examined a bit more closely, resulting in still more unrecorded transfers being discovered. This is an amazing fact, when one realizes that American collectors and dealers have been researching and writing about English transferware with American subject matter since 1878. English interest in this field has only been evident since the founding of that fine organization, The Friends of Blue, a scant twenty-five years ago.

We believe that in order for a person to become interested in collecting a given item, they must be aware of several different facts. First, they must know *what* is available to collect, what are the various subject matters covered by the collecting field? Secondly, they must know the frequency in which they will encounter specific items. Namely, what is rare and what is common. Third, the beginner must be able to compute the approximate value of each object, so that they are comfortable with the price they pay when they begin to acquire a collection. In order to accomplish this, they must be aware of the fourth piece of knowledge, the so-called nuances of value. It has been said that the valuation of a given antique, is perhaps the most difficult single item to learn for the beginning collector. In all of our publications, we have sought to place an approximate value on a piece, to guide the collector. Many relegate this practice as demeaning and more than one "scholar" has dismissed reference books that contain this information as mere "price guides." Obviously, we do not agree with this school of thought.

This volume is intended to help the beginning collector, who has little or no idea about transferware or historical ceramics. It will also be of use to advanced collectors, in that it will introduce them to many heretofore unpublished transfers with an American interest. There are some subjects which many will find mildly controversial. They have been placed here with the idea of starting a dialogue and serious research to ascertain certain facts. That, in a nutshell, is the true purpose of this book; to stimulate the interest in this exciting field of collecting and initiate additional research into the phenomenon known as Historical Transferware.

Introduction

In the last several years, English authors have produced many reference works dealing with the products of the English ceramic industry, and the extent of the export trade with North America. They have been quite diligent in their research of existing records of the factories which shipped millions of pieces of ceramics to North America in the period from 1760 through 1880. However, there is a gap in their records, since there does not seem to be much information for the critical period from 1780 through 1830. Also, these records do not specifically identify the subject matter of the decoration. In Neil Ewins' 1997 work, *"Supplying the Present Wants of Our Yankee Cousin.... Staffordshire Ceramics and the American Market 1775 - 1880*, the all too typical entry is similar to that of a Charleston, South Carolina merchant who advertised the following:

> **"Large Queen's Ware plates....**
> **Dessert Do....**
> **Large Blue & Green edge, do..**
> **Elegant Blue and White, Breakfast sets..."**[1]

The problem is obvious. What was the subject matter, if any, that decorated the pieces? "Blue and Green edge" is fine, but did they have a polychromed Seal of the United States in the center? Judging by the number of blue and green edged plates that have survived, more than just a few contained a central decoration. "Elegant Blue and White, Breakfast sets" does not give us a clue as to the subject matter of the transfer. Was it LANDING OF LAFAYETTE, DON QUIXOTE or MACDONNOUGH'S VICTORY? Once again, judging by the survivors, it could have been any of those three, or many others.

We, as has been the tradition with American authors in this field, base our ideas as to the extent and subject matter of the English export trade, on what has survived. We are indeed fortunate in this respect, since there has been a steady flow of published information in the period between 1878 and 1998, the one-hundred and twenty year period that Americans have researched this field. There have been three periods of intense interest in Historical Staffordshire in this Country. The first was the period around the beginning of the Twentieth Century, when the following references attempted to make sense of this popular ceramic, which was still in daily use. Many early authors make note of the fact they bought pieces of "crockery" right off the farmer's table. This first period of collecting brought us the following references:

> 1892, Alice M. Earle, *China Collecting in America*
> 1899, Edwin Barber, *Anglo-American Pottery*
> 1899, R.T.Haines Halsey, *Pictures of Early New York on Dark Blue Staffordshire Pottery*
> 1901 - 1904, Keramic Studio, *Old China* (magazine)
> 1903, N. Hudson Moore, *The Old China Book*
> 1916, Ada W. Camehl, *The Blue China Book*
> 1924, Mabel Smith, *Anglo-American Historical China*

These early volumes are invaluable, since they documented the series and views that were actually here! They are the basis of all the listings and research which followed. In these pioneering books, we find the first mention of transfers found not only on blue and white pearlware, but also Liverpool and Staffordshire creamware and pearlware. It is this period of time which is believed to be "pure", in the fact that collectors and dealers were not yet bringing items to America that were originally made for the English home market. "Pure", meaning that what was currently here was the result of the importation of ceramics to fill a need for inexpensive ceramic ware for daily use in the early 1800's, not brought in to fill a collector's market in 1900. It didn't last long, since this first china collecting craze created a tremendous market not only for the home market antique ware, but a market that Wedgwood, Rowland & Marcellus, Alfred Grey and others quickly filled with modern "Staffordshire" and a few notable fakes.

The second period of great interest took place in that ten year period between 1940 and 1950. Major collections passed through the auction block, fully documented in fine catalogues by Parke-Bernet, Anderson Galleries and others. Such familiar names as Laidacker, Larsen and McCauley built upon the knowledge of the earlier collectors/authors and brought forth a new generation of reference works:

> 1938, Sam Laidacker, *Standard Catalogue of Anglo-American China*
> 1938 - 1944, Sam Laidacker, *Auction Supplement to The Standard Catalogue of Anglo-American China*
> 1939, E. B. Larsen, *American Historical Views on Staffordshire China*
> 1939 -1956, Sam Laidacker, *The American Antiques Collector* (magazine)

1942, Robert McCauley, *Liverpool Transfer Designs on Anglo-American Pottery*
1950, E. B. Larsen, *American Historical Views on Staffordshire China (revised)*
1951, Sam Laidacker, *Anglo-American China, Part II* (other than American Views)
1954, Sam Laidacker, *Anglo-American China, Part I* (the American and Literary Views)
1955, Catherine Fennelly, *Something Blue*

That brings us to the third great period of interest in the field. Yes, we are now in the midst of yet another era of intense collecting in the field of English transferware. Now, it is not only an American phenomenon, but both the English and Canadians have joined in the pursuit of "old crockery". Most of the references we have already listed have been reprinted and many more have found their way to the collector's library. Excellent English authors have made a great impact upon this area of knowledge, spurred on by the founding of the Friends of Blue collectors' organization in 1973. True research, done by such respected authors as Geoffrey Godden, Alan Smith and David Drakard have provided the framework for additional information to be discovered. The current group of references include:

1969, W. L. Little, *Staffordshire Blue*
1970, R & V Wood, *Historical China Cup Plates*
1970, A. W. Coysh, *Blue and White Transferware 1780 - 1840*
1970, Alan Smith, *Liverpool Herculaneum Pottery*
1972, A. W. Coysh, *Blue-Printed Earthenware 1800 - 1850*
1973, Marian Klamkin, *American Patriotic and Political China*
1974, J. Jefferson Miller, *English Yellow-Glazed Earthenware*
1974, David and Linda Arman, *Historical Staffordshire*
1977, Geoffrey Godden, *An Encyclopedia of British Pottery and Porcelain Marks*
1977, David and Linda Arman, *First Supplement to Historical Staffordshire*
1978, Petra Williams, *Staffordshire Romantic Transfer Patterns, Cup Plates and early Victorian China*
1982, Coysh and Henrywood, *The Dictionary of Blue and White Printed Pottery 1780 - 1880 Volume I*
1983, Elizabeth Collard, *The Potter's View of Canada*
1989, Coysh and Henrywood, *Dictionary, Volume II*
1989, Lockett and Godden, *Davenport China, Earthenware and Glass 1794 - 1887*
1992, David Drakard, *Printed English Pottery*
1994, Pat Halfpenny, *Penny Plain, Twopence Coloured*
1995, J. B. Snyder, *Historical Staffordshire*
1996, Pollan et al, *Nineteenth Century Transfer-Printed Ceramics From the Townsite of Old Velasco, Texas*
1997, David and Linda Arman, *The China and Glass Quarterly Vol. 1 - 4.* (magazine)
1998, Friends of Blue Twenty-fifth Anniversary Exhibition, *True Blue, Transfer Printed Earthenware*

Just the sheer volume of new releases confirms the idea that we are in the midst of a third collecting boom. As we are completing the research for this book, there is a movement to start an American version of the Friends of Blue, The Transfer Collectors Club, which will advance the hobby of collecting not only blue and white, but also the other wares, such as Liverpool, Yellow-glaze and The Romantic light-colored transferware. This club will have a quarterly publication, which will further advance our collective knowledge. All indications seem to confirm that this is the latest period of heightened interest in this field of collecting.

That brings us back again to this series on transferware and especially the volume in front of you. While we have endeavored to use the finest computer technology available, unfortunately some of the photos are of rather poor quality. For this we apologize. Keep in mind that some of these were scanned off a twenty year old mimeographed sheet, that would *never* allow one to obtain a decent image. However, we made the decision that it was more important to illustrate even a poor image, than no image at all. Likewise as concerns the "CCI" (computer created images) encountered in Chapter Five. Some of our records only contained a poor Xerox copy of a transfer. Using the computer, we were able to recreate an exact image of what was on the copy. Not wanting to mislead the collector into mounting a search for the item illustrated, we felt we should identify these objects as not being in existence, except within the memory banks of our machine.

Also, we have been able to identify the potters who used many of the transfers found on the Liverpool and Staffordshire "whitewares". Our English counterparts feel they can attribute products on the basis of similarity of ceramic forms. That may be a very valid approach, however we feel you can make the same attribution on the basis of individual characteristics of the transfer itself. Whether either of these approaches will stand the test of time remains unknown, but we have used that which makes us feel comfortable. As concerns the valuation we have assigned the transfers, this is our opinion and should be used with that in mind.

Finally, a few minor points, the words creamware, pearlware and transferware can be spelled as single or compound words. For the sake of conformity we have adopted the single word basis as a personal preference. Likewise, it is quite a mouthful to describe the items in this book as "Liverpool or Staffordshire pitchers with a white body usually having black transfers." We think it much easier to use the term "whitewares" to denote this ware. We hope this usage will become more common with the passage of time. In the meantime, welcome to the newest addition to the vast amount of information concerning that lunacy called American Historical Transferware.

Notes

[1]Ewins, Neil, *"Supplying the Present Wants of Our Yankee Cousins..." Staffordshire Ceramics and the American Market 1787 - 1880,* 1997, The City Museum and Art Gallery, Stoke-On-Trent.

Chapter One
Political History
and
Ceramic History

Political History - The Colonial Period 1492 - 1760

Columbus established Spanish claims to the "New World" when he sailed the "ocean blue, in 1492." Close on his heels, establishing claims for their patrons, were **John Cabot** (1497 - England), **Henry Hudson** (1609 - Dutch/Swedes-English) and **Verrazano** (1524 - French). This set the stage for a three part, three-hundred year rivalry, which consumed the continent of North America and did not end until the Treaty of Ghent, in 1815.

It has been said that the Spanish came to North America because they wanted gold and converts to Spanish Catholicism. They came first, when Columbus established the settlement of Isabella on Hispaniola in 1496. By 1513, **Ponce de Leon** had visited Florida, **de Pineda** the Gulf Coast (1519), **Gordillo** had gone north to Cape Fear (1520) and **Gomez** had led an expedition Southward from Nova Scotia in 1524. Within a few years, their successors were destroying native civilizations and culture in the name of God, in a vast area from the tip of South America to the North American Southwest.

In 1562, French Huguenots made an unsuccessful attempt to colonize the area near the present Georgia - Florida border. One hundred years later they successfully settled in the north (Canada). Led by **Champlain**, the French wanted furs and religious converts. Controlling the great St. Lawrence River, the French explorers **Brule** (1623), **Nicolet** (1633) and **Groseillier** (1654-59) had made the Great Lakes and surrounding rivers totally French, and the northern fur trade a French occupation. The historic expeditions of **Jolliet** and **Marquette** in 1673 and **LaSalle** in 1682 brought the Mississippi and Ohio Rivers to the French and gave them unlimited access to the interior, which they named "Louisiana" for Louis of France.

The real "late-comers" to the colonization of this vast unknown continent were the English. They came for land. Not gold, not converts, not for the glory of God, but for land. They proved to have the greatest lasting power of them all, and proved to be the greatest danger to both the existing native societies and any other European colonials they encountered. After an abortive attempt at colonizing Virginia at Roanoke Island in 1584, the English returned twenty-three years later to Jamestown. Despite terrible losses among the earliest settlers, the English continued pouring people into the colony and made it economically viable with the introduction of tobacco cultivation. Assimilating the earlier Dutch-Swedish colonies located in the area of New York (1664), the English held most of the eastern coast by the beginning of the 18th century.

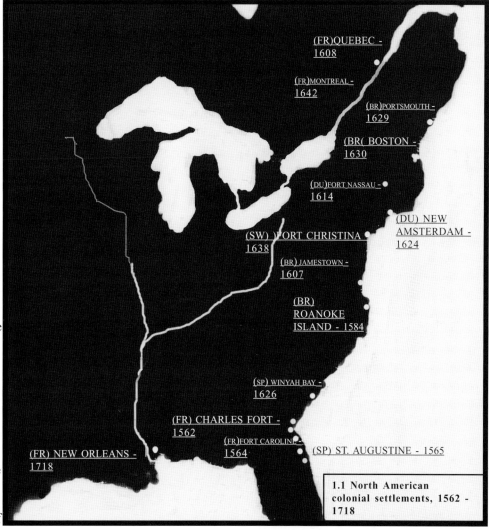

(FR)QUEBEC - 1608

(FR)MONTREAL - 1642

(BR)PORTSMOUTH - 1629

(BR(BOSTON - 1630

(DU)FORT NASSAU - 1614

(DU) NEW AMSTERDAM - 1624

(SW) FORT CHRISTINA 1638

(BR) JAMESTOWN - 1607

(BR) ROANOKE ISLAND - 1584

(SP) WINYAH BAY - 1626

(FR) CHARLES FORT - 1562

(FR)FORT CAROLINE 1564

(SP) ST. AUGUSTINE - 1565

(FR) NEW ORLEANS - 1718

1.1 North American colonial settlements, 1562 - 1718

With the French in the North and the Mississippi Valley, the Spanish in the South and Florida and the English along the Eastern coast, the stage was set for the great conflict over control of the Continent. These clashes ranged from isolated guerrilla attacks to major battles between European-style armies, fielded by the great powers of Europe. This conflict took place along the coast and in that area between the Appalachian Mountains and the Mississippi River. While North America was usually just a side-show to the great wars of Europe, it was in the North American colonies that the final and deciding scene was played. The Seven Years War, known in North America as The French and Indian War, was the final confrontation that ended the threat of France and it's Indian allies to the English colonies. With the end of the war in 1763, France was out of Canada and England was supreme. A weak Spain was temporarily in control of Louisiana, and the inhabitants of England's colonies suddenly found themselves free of any major threats.......except from the "mother" country, who now wanted partial remuneration for the costs of the preceding century of warfare. Thus, the Peace of Paris ended two-hundred and seventy years of conflict that started with Columbus' voyages. The colonial race in North America was finished, and the stage was set for the "shot heard 'round the world" that ultimately "turned the world upside down"; the successful revolt of the American colonies of Great Britain.

Ceramic History - The Colonial Period

Illustration 1.1 shows the North American continent as dark and foreboding. Put yourself in the place of the young men sent to the dismal outposts and settlements of Empire along the primeval coasts of Florida, Virginia or Maine. In the sixteenth and seventeenth centuries these places ran the gamut from small fortified trading posts, surrounded by disease, suspicious natives and hostile fellow Europeans, to the great citadels of Quebec and Havana. Think of the excitement caused by the arrival of a ship that would bring you news of the outside world, new colonists or items from "home".

Briefly, we will examine three outposts which have been excavated by teams of archeologists. This will enable us to obtain a small insight into the types of ceramics that found their way to North America.

The first such outpost is **Wolstenholme Towne** settled by 220

Englishmen in 1619, at the present site of Carter's Grove Plantation in Virginia on the James River. Consisting of a wooden stockade armed with a single cannon, this site and other adjoining sites were occupied from approximately 1620 through 1645. Excavated by Colonial Williamsburg, the "finds" were dramatic and are well-detailed by Ivor Noel Hume in *Discoveries in Martin's Hundred*. They included the first face-covering helmets (armor) to be found in North America, remains of several settlers killed in an Indian massacre in 1622, lead seals from bales of German fabric circa 1620 and the earliest known piece of locally manufactured European-style pottery, which is a slipware plate dated 1621[1]. It is the ceramic articles that most interest us, so we will concentrate on them.

Along with the dated slipware dish, other examples of locally potted items in the English manner were found, which indicates there was an extensive local output. Also found were a Rhenish (German) figural stoneware jug produced in the period 1610-1615, a Westerwald blue and grey stoneware jug from the Rhineland of the same period, a Spanish earthenware blue decorated bottle (1625-1645) and a Dutch "milk pot" of the same period. These items illustrate that these small and isolated settlements had commercial contacts with both England and the rest of Europe.

1.2 Above: Germanic stoneware figural jugs found at most seventeenth century North American archeological sites. 1.3 Below: English Delftwares similar to those found in the excavation of early eighteenth century Boston.

The second site is **Fort William Henry**, which was located at the present site of Pemaquid, Maine. Constructed in 1693 by the Royal Governor of Massachusetts, the purpose of the fort was to secure the area for English settlers from native tribes and the French. Four years after completion, the Fort was conquered and razed by the French, causing the quick evacuation of the British garrison. Thirty-three years later, the English returned and built **Fort Frederick** on the same location, and fortunately for future archeologists, the buried artifacts of the earlier inhabitants were not disturbed. The Fort was examined by archeologists from the State of Maine and the ceramic fragments revealed were of great interest.

The strata of the earlier Fort William Henry did show evidence that the garrison hurriedly evacuated, leaving behind many

1.4 English and Dutch Delftware similar to those items excavated in Fort William Henry, Wolstenholme Towne and Boston.

personal possessions. A large number of clay pipe bowls, wig curlers and German clay figures were discovered. Among the English ceramics found were a tin-glazed apothecary jar, sgraffito decorated bowls and yellow-glazed earthenware fragments. A German stoneware mug, an Italian bottle, a Spanish jar and a Rhenish figural jug (similar to those illustrated) were also unearthed. These remains could be accurately dated to be no later than August, 1696, when the Fort was destroyed[2]. Thus, for the second time, we are presented with the fact that a primitive, remote Imperial outpost had trade and contact with the commerce of Europe.

The third and final archeological excavation took place in **Boston** during the building of The Bostonian Hotel in 1981. Only a few ceramics were discovered at the mid-seventeenth century strata, but these were important because they showed that even at this early date, there was evidence of English Delft and Iberian Majolica. The unearthed items representing the later period of 1690 through 1720, reveal that Boston had a thriving local redware industry, plus large quantities of English ceramics such as Delft, tin-glaze, slip decorated earthenware and grey/blue stoneware. Also represented were quantities of Iberian utilitarian wares and the fancier French faience[3].

It becomes clear when examining the results of these excavations and others, that the inhabitants of New England, New France and New Spain considered themselves *Europeans*. Europeans, who were simply establishing an extension of their homeland in the North American wilderness. They returned to Europe to serve in their country's armies and after their service, many came back to North America. Although there were local ceramics industries established, they continued to purchase their finer possessions from the homeland. This practice, for the British Colonies, was made into law by the English Navigation Acts of 1660, which forced the colonials to purchase all their goods in England. This commercial pattern continued until the late 19th century, when the English potteries were finally successfully challenged by a native American ceramics industry.

Political History - North America 1760-1775

When we left the historical portion of this narrative, the French had left Canada and Spain held Louisiana. Pitt, the Elder, was harassing the French throughout the world, and the

British ruled in Canada, after the fall of Quebec in September, 1759. The English American colonies were finally at peace. Prosperity and growth were the norm. George III succeeded George II to the throne in October, 1760, and was crowned and married in September, 1761. Thus, America had a new king and queen.

Ceramic History - 1760-1775

The dual events of the coronation and marriage of the King

1.5 Queensware teapot by Josiah Wedgwood with a transfer of Queen Charlotte. Circa 1762.

coincided with the advent of transfer printing by the mercantile genius, Josiah Wedgwood. In partnership with John Sadler and Guy Green, Wedgwood produced transfer decorated creamware with portraits of both the King and Queen. Later, other creamware pieces would be decorated with transfers of THE DEATH OF WOLFE, WILLIAM PITT, THE MARQUIS OF GRANBY, JOHN WILKES and designs celebrating martial victories, such as the capture of Cuba in 1762[4]. The American colonists were affected by these events and there is no doubt that some of this early *historical* trans-

ferware was marketed in this country. Some Americans served in the English armed forces during the rout of the French and

1.6a This little creamware teapot is one of the earliest recorded pieces made for the American market. It is decorated in black enamel and refers to the hated Stamp Act, which was repealed in 1766.

Spanish from the West Indies. Others were so proud to be British, that they celebrated the victories by naming, among other things, their homes, after the battles or their heroes. No less a historical figure than Lawrence

Washington, named his estate Mt. Vernon, in honor of Admiral Vernon, with whom he had served in the Indies.

Political History - 1776 - 1815

Led by radical agitators such as Samuel Adams, his cousin John Adams, Patrick Henry and pamphleteers such as Thomas Paine, the American colonists resisted the attempts by the British Government to raise taxes from the seat of government in London. Isolated incidents of local unrest, led to armed resistance and

1.6b The reverse of 1.6a reflects the colonist's feelings toward the repeal of the Stamp Act.

finally a formal declaration of independence by the colonies in 1776. These colonies set about raising an army to meet the expected armed response from the English. George Washington was given sweeping powers to wage a war of resistance. Unfortunately, when a people revolt because of unrest due to taxation, it becomes rather difficult for the succeeding government to raise the necessary taxes needed to run that government and deploy the defending army. Basically, by force of personality and strength of character, Washington was able to keep his army intact (losing nine of twelve battles), until the French saw advantage in the supporting of their enemy's enemy, and came to the rescue of the fledgling Republic. **Yorktown** was evacuated by the defeated British army and the Treaty of Paris (September 3, 1783) ended the war. The English withdrew from the thirteen colonies, not really convinced they had lost the war. Many still thought of the inhabitants of their former colonies as "English."

The American experiment was "shaky" at best and disastrously weak in the face of French and Spanish territorial designs. Before any of these schemes could become operational, France was rocked by a

1.7 Armorial devices were not terribly popular in the early American Republic. In most cases, it is safe to assume that these were made for "home" consumption.

"true" revolution, that destroyed the Government, Church and Society. Revolutionary France, under the Directory, threatened England, and soon war between these two powers started anew. America's new government, under Washington and Adams, wanted no part in this new conflict, knowing their Country would be swallowed by the coming maelstrom. Without a navy, (the *Frigate Alliance*, the last ship remaining in the Continental Navy, had been decommissioned and sold several years earlier) and without a standing army, the Nation was basically defenseless. With withering opposition by Jefferson and the Democrats, first Washington and then Adams, sought to build an army and then a navy. The first years of Washington's presidency saw the Federal government challenged by rebellion in both

1.8 To judge by the number of religious subjects found today, these transfers were never terribly popular. However, they could be used for both the English and American consumer.

western Massachusetts and western Pennsylvania. In addition to these internal problems, the nation was also challenged by external forces. The British had never evacuated their western outposts, as agreed to by the Treaty of Paris. Agitating the Indians and plotting with Spain, England sought to regain the area surrounding the Great Lakes, and continue down the Mississippi to control New Orleans and thus stop the westward expansion of the Americans.

The French Revolution and it's government were the darlings of Jefferson and the Democrats. Plotting against the Federalists, the Democrats, with their political support based in the west, welcomed France's determination to resist Britain's plans to capture the Mississippi. Citizen Genet was received in Philadelphia as the new Ambassador from France, and he quickly set about plotting the demise of Spanish Florida and began sending armed American

1.9 A wonderful example of an underspout cartouche that was never filled in and now serves to illustrate how the potters could personalize stock designs.

4

1.10 The same cartouche as illustrated in figure 1.9, this made as a presentation piece for a certain SALLY CURRIER, with a date that undoubtably was special to her.

ships to sea, as French privateers, to disrupt British commerce. Meanwhile, both France and England decided that American cargoes were helping the enemy, so the navies of both combatant countries started seizing American merchant vessels.

The Federalist government of John Adams was so alarmed by the imminent threat of a French invasion, that it appointed ex-general/ex-president George Washington as General in charge of a 10,000 man (on paper only) American army. The tiny navy was sent to sea to protect American convoys. This quasi-war with France faded into insignificance with the self-destruction of the belligerent French government and the gradual ascent of Napoleon to the Imperial throne. However, during this brief period of hostilities, the *USS Constellation,* under the command of Captain Truxton, defeated the heavier gunned *L'Insurgeant,* and the army had a brief moment of glory when the English-backed Indians, led by Tecumseh, suffered a disastrous defeat by an American army led by Anthony Wayne at the **Battle of Fallen Timbers**.

Adam's presidency faded from history and America fell victim to the divisiveness of the two party political system, a concept which Washington had fought his entire life. By the dawn of the nineteenth century, Washington was dead and America was in mourning. Jefferson was President, and was attempting to reconcile his beliefs in the common man with the realities of governing. Overseas, the American Republic, as well as the nations of Europe, were paying tribute to the Tripolians for safe passage of it's citizens in the Mediterranean. This politically unpalatable situation ultimately led to the Marines assisting the Navy in the temporary pacification of the pirates of Tripoli. A future generation of young American naval officers received their

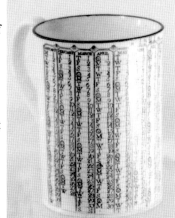

1.11 Sometimes the transfers were very practical, as is evidenced by this tankard decorated with the calendar for the year 1821.

1.12 World events, especially from the English view, were used as transfer subjects. Above: ENGLAND EXPECTS EVERY MAN TO DO HIS DUTY is the slogan found on this pitcher mourning the death of Admiral Lord Nelson. **1.13** Below: The reverse of the above pitcher, which is a depiction of the **Battle of Trafalger**, where in October, 1805, the French lost any hope of ever challenging English rule of the seas, and England lost her finest naval leader.

first "blooding" during the Tripolitan War, where a navy captain named Edward Preble gained national fame. Jefferson accomplished the real estate agreement of all time, when he purchased the Louisiana Territory from a cash-poor Napoleon I. Britain, fighting for her life, increased the harassment of American commerce and the impressment of American sailors, which caused Jefferson to place a commercial embargo on England in 1807. This presaged the coming War of 1812. Madison succeeded Jefferson,

taking up residence in the new federal city of Washington, and attempted to unite his country in the face of growing incursions by the warring belligerents in Europe. New England, led by the Governor of Massachusetts, Caleb Strong, wanted no part of a war against England. The Westerners, personified by a political militia general from Tennessee, named Andrew Jackson, were howling for British, Canadian and Indian blood. "Free Trade and Sailor's Rights" became the rallying cry for the war-hawks. Meanwhile, an American army, under the command of William Henry Harrison, defeated the Indian tribes at the **Battle of Tippecanoe** in 1811.

War was finally declared against Britain, and the Westerners immediately assumed that Canada was ripe for the plucking. This proved to be incorrect, so for the first year of the War, the

1.14 Above: When war was declared on France in May, 1803, the potters used this transfer to celebrate the patriotic fever sweeping the country. **1.15** Below: The reverse of **1.14** has a cartoon taken from a print by Fores, showing THE GOVERNOR OF EUROPE STOPED IN HIS CAREER. For more information about this particular transfer and pitcher, see Chapter Six - **Fakes and Reproductions.**

Ogdensburg and **Sackett's Harbor.** He eventually took command of the northern frontier, replacing an incompetent and treacherous James Wilkinson. With Brown in command and a young Winfield Scott as his deputy, the military fortunes of the Republic were reversed and the army won several notable victories, including many in joint operations with American naval forces. By late 1814, control of the Lakes was in the hands of the Americans. Incompetency and defeat were once again evident when the British defeated an American force composed of militia, regulars and naval personnel at the **Battle of Bladensburg,** Maryland in

American army, along the Canadian border, was plagued by incompetency and defeat. However, in October, 1812 and May,1813, a militia general from New York, successfully defended that State's borders twice against British incursions. Jacob Brown quickly earned a regular army Brigadier's commission for these victories at

August, 1814. The American forces were completely routed, leading to the name "The Bladensburg Races", which described the haste in which the Americans left the field of battle. National humiliation had to be endured when these same British forces burned the Federal City, supposedly in retaliation for the earlier burning of York, Ontario by an American army. Hatred for the Americans burned deep in the hearts of the British commanders, notably Admiral Cochrane, who viewed this American war as nothing more than "aid and comfort" to Napoleon.

The British force turned northward, and less than a month later, began the assault on Baltimore. This time the results were far more favorable to the Americans when the British commander, General Ross, was killed in the land attack and the British fleet failed to subdue Fort McHenry. The English then retired to the West Indies to regroup for their next adventure, the capture of New Orleans and the control of the Mississippi.

Strategically, the balance of power was rapidly shifting in favor of Britain. Napoleon had been conquered, thus releasing immense British military resources to be used to regain their lost American colonies. Although the Duke of Wellington had refused the command of these forces, his brother-in-law, General, Sir Edward Pakenham, arrived at New Orleans to take command of a large army composed of veteran regiments that had defeated the French. Against them was an American army, led by Andrew Jackson, entrenched behind a fortified line bristling with muskets and cannon. It was a slaughter of the English forces. Thousands of men died or were mutilated, and three British generals were killed, including Pakenham. The Americans reportedly lost three men. The British army had been mauled as never before, even when fighting Napoleon. The date was January 8, 1815.

The news of this resounding victory arrived in Washington City on February 4th. On February 11th, a British sloop of war, *HMS Favourite*, came into New York harbor under a flag of truce, to report that a truce had been signed at Ghent on Christmas day, 1814. The second war of American Independence was over, because Britain reluctantly conceded that her people would no longer support the war. American independence was assured, although none of her initial aims in going to war were achieved. Free trade was still at the mercy of the British navy and Canada was a secure part of the British Empire. Happily for the Americans, circumstances came to the rescue, as the peace in Europe opened the seas to all nations, and the opening of the

1.16 The American market imported a tremendous amount of "blue and green edged wares" from the potteries. When the National Seal was adopted by Congress in 1782, the potters used the motif in many forms on popular ware. This decoration probably continued to be placed on ceramics bound for America, well into the 19th century.

1.17 Blue edged plate produced for the American market for the 1840 Presidential campaign of William Henry Harrison. The British potters quickly adapted their designs to meet the current need - even if the celebrated event happened 29 years earlier, as in the case of Harrison's 1811 victory, heralded on the above plate.

Louisiana Territory gave the expansionists all the land they desired. The American Republic had become legitimate by the fact that she had stood up to the two world powers. Unsuccessful militarily at first, her successes in 1813 and 1814, gave her inhabitants the national character and self-confidence to develop their own vast resources. America turned her back on Europe and went about her "manifest destiny", much at the cost to her native inhabitants and her neighbors to the south.

Ceramic History 1776 - 1815

1.18 This creamware plate has a border of enamel berries and leaves surrounding a portrait of the late General Pike.

The extensive ceramic trade between the colonies and the home country was devastated by the Revolutionary War. Further tensions between the two countries and those caused by revolutionary France, combined to depress trade even more during the period leading up to and during the 1812 conflict. Not that the potters and their agents didn't try, but full trade was not regained until after the Treaty of Ghent. The political clamor from the "potteries" was one of many reasons the British government put a stop to this unpopular war. In the year 1795, and again in 1800, it is reported that Staffordshire exports to the United States were numbered at approximately ten million pieces in each year[5]. By 1808, during the escalating prewar tensions, this had fallen by over 60%, causing unemployment and unrest in Britain. On the other hand, with the Peace signed in 1815, America imported over twenty-two million pieces[6] of English ceramics in that single year alone.

Between 1783 and 1812, the English sought to meet the demand from America, calling for vast quantities of blue and green feather edge and transfer decorated earthenwares. The home market was purchasing creamware and pearlware decorated with designs taken from the various prints of the day.

1.19 GENERAL JACKSON THE HERO OF NEW ORLEANS decorates this plate, surrounded by a pink lustre border.

These reflected the popular views of the current social and political institutions, such as the church, the military, politics, the monarchy, marriage and various occupations. Most of these were not salable in America, so the English continued using contemporary engravings and prints of the day as their sources, except they switched to those subjects that were on prints popular in America. The adoption of a national Seal led to ceramics decorated with a variety of Eagles, some quite comical[7]. The death of Washington caused not only an outpouring of grief in America, but a comparable outpouring of ceramics bearing his likeness and lamenting his death, from the English potteries. The American political arena gave birth to an array of ceramic transfer portrait busts of Presidents named Washington, Adams, Jefferson, Madison and Monroe. Commodore Edward Preble and the assault on Tripoli graced many American tables, thanks to the Staffordshire and Liverpool potteries. After the War of 1812, a whole new pantheon of heroes were placed upon ceramics destined for America. By 1820, the entire panoply of English ceramics such as lustre, transfer and enamel decorated creamware and pearlware, yellow-glaze, figures and toys were being imported yearly, by the millions of pieces from "the potteries" to America. During this time, potters in America attempted to stem this British flood, but they were largely unsuccessful until the 1870's, when the native ceramics industry finally began to grow and prosper.

Political History and Ceramic History 1815 - 1852

America had turned inward after the end of the War of 1812. Her internal expansion, begun prior to that war, continued as the Americans fought both the Indians and the Spanish. The **Creek** and **Seminole Wars** ended with the Southern tribes physically removed to the Indian (Oklahoma) territory. Florida was taken from the Spanish. American settlers of Texas, a province of Mexico, revolted in 1835 and were later annexed by the United States. Provoked to war by the land-hungry Americans, Mexico suffered invasion and defeat by the American army led by a few old soldiers from the War of 1812, notably Jacob Brown, Winfield Scott and Zachary Taylor.

1.20 Left: One of the earliest pieces of American made historical ceramics is this redware tile, covered with a solid red-orange glaze and bearing an em-bossed standing figure of a man, titled **J.Q. ADAMS LIBERTY**. This was made for either the 1825 or 1829 presidential campaign. **1.21** Right: High quality plaque press-molded in the form of a picture frame and decorated in a mottled tan glaze. The bust of Zachary Taylor is also press-molded, applied to the frame and colored in a solid deep brown glaze. Made for the 1849 presidential campaign.

Although Winfield Scott would continue to serve his nation until 1860, for the purposes of this book on ceramics, the election of Zachary Taylor in 1852, marks the gradual decline and eventual end to the seventy-five year romance of the American public with that product of the English potteries we term Historical China.

American Historical Ceramics

As we have stated, the American ceramics industry did not become a threat to the British dominance of the market until the latter portion of the Nineteenth century. When we speak of the "ceramics industry", we are not referring to the stoneware and redware manufacturers who made the heavy, utilitarian wares typified by the multitude of greyish containers decorated in blue. Some of these potters did make an attempt to compete in the "historicals" market. This is evidenced by some of the pieces we have illustrated on the next few pages. In our opinion, only one company was successful in duplicating the wares that were flooding this country during the period from 1790 to 1840, and that was the American Pottery Manufacturing Company of Jersey City, New Jersey. The extremely rare hexagonal earthenware pitcher made for the presidential campaign of William Henry Harrison is exquisite. However, if the item's rarity in the twentieth century is any measure of it's popularity when new, this

1.22 a/b/c This American stoneware bank contains portrait busts of "Franklin", in the fur hat, William Penn, in the tricorn hat and George Washington. Tan to pale yellow-tan glaze.

1.23 Left: Finely made bank in the form of a log cabin, complete with a cider barrel near the door. Stoneware with a mottled tan and brown glaze made for the 1840 presidential campaign of William Henry Harrison. **1.24** Right: Extremely rare stoneware bottle in the form of "Toby Filpot" (a notorious English drunkard of the 19th century) astride a barrel. Barrel is impressed with printer's type spelling out " J. SMITH THE MORMAN PROPHE/T." Probably American, possibly English. **1.25** Below left: A slightly larger than life-size pitcher, in the form of a head with a military collar, decorated in a dark brown "Rockingham" glaze. Embossed "ROUGH AND READY" "GEN'L TAYLOR." American, circa 1849. **1.26** Below center: Earthenware pitcher with a thick overall chocolate brown glaze over a hexagonal body containing embossed Seals of the United States.

must have been a great marketing failure, because there are only seven or eight of these recorded. When compared to the amount of Staffordshire items for the same presidential campaign, it quickly becomes quite clear that this was not a "fast seller" in the United States of 1840. So, the native industry for dinner services continued to be totally dominated by the English manufacturers, well into the "flow blue" and ironstone period (1850 through 1880). Only in the 1880's, did the American pottery industry challenge the English, and drive them from the dominant sales position in the rapidly growing consumer market of North America.

That completes our condensed history of the colonization of North America and the ceramic precedents which have led us to this point in the late twentieth century. We have seen that English ceramics were valued and cherished, even at the earliest moments of the European settlement of the continent. We have also seen that as early as 1700, the potter was depicting the Monarchy and national heroes upon ceramics. These were made for both domestic and colonial consumption. With the advent of transfer printing, which coincided with the coronation of George III, it was much less costly for the potter to produce ceramics with the likenesses of the current crowned head or the current politician in favor. England's

1.27 Left: the American Pottery Manufacturing Company, Jersey City, New Jersey pitcher made for the 1840 campaign of Willian Henry Harrison.

governmental policy of insuring that only the "home" country would be the source for finished products, insured an acceptance of these products, even in the former colony of America. This carried over through the Revolution, the War of 1812, and continued until the late 1870's. This brings us to the sources of these ceramics, the sources of the transfers and the potters who made them, which we will discuss in Chapter Two.

Notes - Chapter One

[1] Hume, Ivor Noel, *Martin's Hundred*, 1991, University of Virginia Press and Alfred A. Knopf.

[2] Bradley, Camp and Sprague, *Unearthing New England's Past -Transplanted Europeans, Fort William Henry*, 1984, Scottish Rite Museum and Library.

[3] Bradley, James W., *Unearthing New England's Past - Urban Salvage, The Bostonian Hotel Site*, 1984, Scottish Rite Museum and Library.

[4] Drakard, David, *Printed English Pottery, History and Humor in the reign of George III 1760-1820*, 1992, Jonathan Horne Publications.

[5] Ewins, Neil, *"Supplying the Present Wants of Our Yankee Cousins..." - Staffordshire Ceramics and the American Market 1787-1880*, 1997, The City Museum and Art Gallery.

[6] *ibid*

[7] Arman, David and Linda, *The China and Glass Quarterly - Meet the Collectors - "What do you call a group of Eagles?"*, July/August, 1997, The Oakland Press.

Selected Bibliography - Chapter One

Freeman, Douglas Southall, *George Washington*, seven volumes, 1948-1957, Scribners.

Harwell, Richard, *Washington*, abridged version of the above, 1968, Scribners.

Leckie, Robert, *The Wars of America*, 1968, Harper and Row.

Lord, Walter, *The Dawn's Early Light*, 1972, W. W. Norton and Company.

Nevin, David, *1812*, 1996, Forge.

Smith, Richard Norton, *Patriarch*, 1993, Houghlin, Mifflin Company.

Chapter Two
Pots, Potters and Printers

The Potting Process

Creamware and Pearlware

European potters in the eighteenth century were obsessed with the idea of copying Chinese porcelain, which was considered to be the highest quality ceramic available. In order to accomplish this, they needed to produce a *white*, thin-walled product. After the middle of the century, certain potters, such as Josiah Wedgwood, Thomas Whieldon and Josiah Spode made improvements to the existing earthenwares, thus accomplishing these goals, which they named "creamware", (or in Wedgwood's case "Queens Ware"). This thin earthenware was dipped into a clear glaze, which, when combined with the natural impurities of the clay, gave the ware a "creamy" or pale yellow tint. Later, Wedgwood would experiment with a still whiter body and add a touch of cobalt to the glaze and name this product "pearlware".

Creamware is readily identifiable as a pottery having a cream-colored body and a perfectly clear glaze. On the other hand, pearlware has a pure white body and the glaze has a slight blue tint, especially on the underside of the base, where it has pooled during the potting process. These are essentially the two types of earthenware which will concern us in our study of historical ceramics for the American market.

Liverpool and Staffordshire

The ware which has been designated **Liverpool** is creamware, usually decorated with a black print, using the "transfer" method of decoration, which we will discuss shortly. The earliest transfer printing was applied on enamels and on soft-paste porcelain such as that produced by the Worcester and Bow factories in the mid-18th century. It was quickly adapted to the less costly earthenwares by John Sadler and Guy Green,

2.1 A **Liverpool** form pitcher with a black transfer of "BRITON'S GLORY THE SPINNING MACHINE" highlighted in ochre, green and blue enamel.

working with Josiah Wedgwood. The earliest transfers were

2.2 "MAJR. GEN'L BROWN NIAGARA" black transfer on a typical **Staffordshire** form.

applied over the glazes of the creamwares and pearlwares, a practice which continued well into the 19th century. It wasn't until 1783 that the technique of applying the transfer under the glaze was used for a majority of earthenwares. This underglaze process was used for all the blue printed transferwares of the 1820's, which we will discuss in volumes II and III of this trilogy.

Identifying Liverpool and Staffordshire Forms

Liverpool pottery usually has a creamware body and is readily identified by those distinctive forms which we will now discuss, and compare with the equally distinctive forms found on pearlware and creamware **Staffordshire** items. Figure 2.1 is that of the typical Liverpool creamware pitcher. This is recognized by the tall, slim form, with the gentle curving body and the pronounced spout and applied "ear-shaped" handle. Figure 2.2 is that of a typical Staffordshire pearlware or creamware pitcher, recognized by the round-bodied globular form, a pronounced neck and handle of varying designs.

Figure 2.3 is a typical mid-18th

2.3 Liverpool creamware teapot with a black transfer of "THE REVERAND JOHN WESLEY".

century **Liverpool** creamware teapot with a globular body, an ornately embossed spout and a handle formed to resemble a branch or twig. Figure 2.4 is a typical **Staffordshire** teapot of the

1820s with an oval body, plain spout and handle. Please note that we are emphasizing the use of the terms "**Liverpool**" and "**Staffordshire**". As you probably know, Liverpool is a port city in

2.4 **Staffordshire** pearlware teapot with a black transfer of "La Fayette Crowned In Glory" and "Cornwallis Surrendering His Sword at Yorktown".

England, while Staffordshire is a district roughly 150 miles north west of London, composed of the towns of Tunstall, Burslem, Hanley, Stoke-on-Trent, Fenton and Longton. However, for our purposes, a "**Liverpool**" shape pitcher will be a tall, slim form typified by figure 2.1, while a "**Staffordshire**" shape pitcher will bring to mind the globular form illustrated in figure 2.2. Thus, throughout this volume, these terms refer to **forms**. A very important point.

In figure 2.5, we illustrate a Liverpool creamware coffee pot and in figure 2.6, the form of a Liverpool bowl. You will note that we have not illustrated any comparable examples in Staffordshire pearlware or creamware. These are omitted because these forms will not be encountered until we begin our study of the blue transferwares of the 1820s.

2.5 **Liverpool** creamware coffee pot with a black transfer titled "The Tea Party."

2.6 Liverpool creamware punch bowl with a black transfer of "The Sailor's Farewell".

water, and apply this to the copper plate with pressure furnished by a hand-press. When subjected to the pressure of the press (while the potter used pieces of cloth to draw off the moisture), the colored lines of the copper plate were imprinted upon the paper. Step four: He would then trim the paper to the approximate shape of the ceramic object he wished to decorate. The fifth step occurred when the printed paper was placed on the ceramic object and the design was *transferred* from the paper to the ceramic. After drying, the piece was fired in an oven at a low temperature to remove the oil, and the sixth step of glazing took place, when the piece was dipped into the glaze (this describes *under* glaze printing. To perform *over* glaze printing, steps five and six would be reversed). The final operation was the firing of the piece at a high temperature of over 1000

2.7 Rare "Capitol At Washington" paper transfer printed from the original copper plate used by J. & W. Ridgway. Reprinted from the 1899 volume, *Anglo-American Pottery* by Edwin Atlee Barber.

The Process of Transfer Printing

As we stated earlier, we will now discuss the process of transfer printing on a ceramic body. Perfected in the early 1760's, this consisted of *transferring* an inked image, which had been engraved upon a copper plate, to a piece of paper and then to the ceramic. It was basically a seven step process. The first step was for the potter to choose a print of a scene or subject he felt would appeal to a certain market (such as a victorious American ship overwhelming a British vessel), and have an engraver cut the design onto a thin flat sheet of copper. Step two: The potter would then heat this copper plate and rub into it a mixture of oil and color, filling the engraved lines with this mixture. He would then wipe off the copper plate, leaving the colored oil mixture in the engraved lines of the design. Step three: He would then take a sheet of **paper** that had been treated with a mixture of soap and

2.8 Three forms of Liverpool creamware, all decorated with the same transfer of "The Seal of the United States" enclosed by a chain of the "Fifteen States".

degrees centigrade. This seemingly elemental process revolutionized the ceramics industry, and allowed the inexpensive mass production of ceramics that gave the middle class their first "china" tablewares.

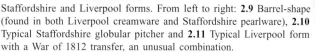

Staffordshire and Liverpool forms. From left to right: **2.9** Barrel-shape (found in both Liverpool creamware and Staffordshire pearlware), **2.10** Typical Staffordshire globular pitcher and **2.11** Typical Liverpool form with a War of 1812 transfer, an unusual combination.

Frequency of Forms

It is important to note which forms the beginning collector will encounter in his collecting quest. The most common Liverpool form with an American Historical transfer are pitchers. Next in frequency are plates, then bowls, tankards and finally tureens. It is the same for Staffordshire pieces, with pitchers being the most common form. Plates with transfers of American interest are rarely encountered, as are tankards and tea services. Once again, this equation changes, when we study the underglaze blue transfer pieces of the 1820s. By then, tastes had changed, as had the subject matter of the transfers. Dark blue views of buildings and natural wonders had replaced the scenes of historical events and personages found on the earlier black-printed creamware and pearlware pieces, which seem to have been made for use at a tavern or inn. Full dinner services became available in the dark blue and the product was then acceptable in not only the tavern, but also the dining room.

The dates of production ran from 1760 - 1820 for Liverpool creamwares, with the Revolutionary War figures and events predominant. There are a few War of 1812 views which do occur on the Liverpool form, but these are considered rare. The historical pearlware production started in the early 1780's, but did not reach full flower until the War of 1812, and the 1824 visit of La Fayette to America. Pearlware with transfers normally found on Liverpool are quite rare. By 1820 through 1830, the underglaze blue printed ware had gained such popularity, that the older creamwares and plainly decorated pearlwares had fallen out of fashion and became the cheapest "china" one could purchase.

Transfer Colors and Applied Polychrome Enamels

Henry Ford once stated, when referring to the colors of the Model "T", that the public could have it in any color they wanted, as long as it was black. That is almost the case with the early creamware and pearlware. Normally all the transfers were done in black, with the exceptions of a very few pieces found with transfers in red, rust, carmine, sepia, lavender or green. The latter three are really quite rare. Certain Liverpool potters made it a practice to embellish the black transfers with a variety of hand applied enamels in red, blue, green, yellow and brown. The majority of these transfers have been attributed to the Shelton group, which will be discussed in detail in the next section of this

chapter. The Liverpool transfers that are *normally* found with polychrome decoration are (using the check-list numbers in chapter 5):

A.34.   AUT VINCERE AUT MORI BOSTON FUSILEER
H.12.   HOPE
J.8.   JEFFERSON ANNO DOMINI..ETC
M.15.   THE MEMORY OF WASHINGTON AND THE PROSCRIBED PATRIOTS
O.1.   O LIBERTY! THOU GODDESS
S.68a.   SUCCESS TO AMERICA WHOSE MILITIA...ETC.
S.81.   SUCCESS TO TRADE
U.6.   UNITED STATES FRIGATE GUERRIERE, COMMODORE MAC-DONNOUGH...ETC.
W.30a.   WASHINGTON CROWNED WITH LAURELS BY LIBERTY

Also, the majority of the various ship transfers are highlighted in color. Any other Liverpool transfer with a polychromed decoration is considered extremely rare.

The Staffordshire potters of the War of 1812 pieces rarely used enamels to highlight the transfers. There are a few portraits of naval captains that have been enhanced by the use of enamels, but they are few and far between and are considered great rarities.

Finally, we have a rather delicate subject which concerns those Liverpool pieces which are without a transfer and are wholly freehand art, such as W.49, WASHINGTON IN HIS GLORY and the green feather edge platter illustrated on the following page. We, *personally,* do not trust the authenticity of many of these pieces. In the period from 1890 to 1920 it was the vogue for women to form a group to decorate ceramics as a social pastime. Even the wife of President Benjamin Harrison (1889 - 1893), Caroline S. Harrison, painted ceramics, as is evidenced by the typically Victorian scalloped tray illustrated, which is signed "C. S. Harrison / Dec. '25 / 1891". These ladies were talented, as you can see from the pieces we have illustrated. So talented, that their groups were the basis of the hugely popular art pottery produced by the "Saturday Evening Girls" in Boston and the "Newcomb Pottery" of Louisiana. As a result

2.12 detail of figure 2.13.

13

2.13 Extremely rare, 17 1/2" creamware platter with a green feather edge and a hand-painted view taken from the dark blue "STATES" series by Clews. Central scene executed in shades of grey and black.

2.14 11 7/8" x 8 3/8" Limoges porcelain scalloped tray, decorated with ORCHIDS and signed by the artist, Mrs. Caroline Harrison and dated during the administration of her husband, President Benjamin Harrison (1889-1893). Ex- Collection of Paul C. and Gladys W. Richards.

of R. T. Haines Halsey's wonderful book, *Early New York on Dark Blue Staffordshire,* the collecting of transferware was entering its first phase of collecting popularity. So, this leads us to believe that the ladies of the day were easily capable of producing some of the pieces of enamel decorated creamware or pearlware which occasionally come to light. There are a few ship views which we have inspected in the collections of the Mariner's Museum and the Peabody-Essex Museum which are undoubtedly products of the early 19th century and should be considered as exceptional examples of maritime painting, but there are many other examples of freehand decoration, without transfers, that leave us extremely uncomfortable. We have noted that almost all of the legitimate examples of freehand decoration seem to have come from the Herculaneum Pottery. Therefore, if you obtain a painted masterpiece on a Liverpool pitcher, check to see if there are any other *transfers* on the piece which are attributed to Herculaneum. We have **NO** hard proof to substantiate our beliefs, but we remain suspicious of anything "too good to be true", since time after time, it has been proven that it *was* too good to be authentic. So a friendly warning to the beginning collector, if the enamel colors seem a bit too garish or if you entertain any doubts concerning the age of the decoration, beware.

Potters and Potteries

The Potters

All authors who have dealt with this subject have listed the makers of these pieces as being mostly "unknown." Unfortunately, this is still partially true. However, because of work done by both Ellouise Baker Larsen, published in her 1950 classic, *American Historical Views on Staffordshire China,* and more importantly the discoveries published by Alan Smith in his 1970 volume, *Liverpool Herculaneum Pottery,* we have a starting point in attempting to solve a bit more of the mystery. Throughout Chapter Five, you will note that we have listed pieces known to have been produced by a particular potter. Those potters include such familiar names as William Adams, Ralph and James Clews, Sadler and Green, Andrew Stevenson, Ralph Stevenson and Williams, Josiah Wedgwood and Ralph Wedg Wood.

The subject of the pottery produced in the city of Liverpool was thoroughly investigated by Alan Smith. He was able, after comparing, line by line, the various transfers found on marked Herculaneum pieces with unmarked pieces, to solidly attribute different transfers that had been previously unattributed. Taking these pieces and comparing them with those found in the collec-

tions we visited in conjunction with the preparation of this book, we have been able to attribute even more of the Liverpool transfers. We are now able to assign many of those views found on creamware for the American market, to the Herculaneum Pottery. Using this same technique, we have designated another group of transfers as the "Shelton" group, because they have all been found with the words "F. Morris Shelton" or "T. Fletcher Shelton" under the designs. Definite information concerning "T. Fletcher" remains a mystery to date, however it is known that Francis Morris was a free-lance engraver in the town of Shelton, Staffordshire, who is recorded as working during the period from 1800 through 1815. He was not a potter, but he apparently produced the engraved copper plates that some unknown potter used for these various views. Other views have also been attributed to Enoch Wood and Sons and to the Davenport pottery.

2.15 Black transfer "SEAL OF THE UNITED STATES" placed over a typical Herculaneum Pottery mark. This particular mark probably formed the basis of the generic term "Liverpool" to describe this ware.

However, of inestimable use were the multiple transfers found on three wonderful, gigantic Staffordshire pitchers (with transfers normally found on **both** Liverpool and Staffordshire items), that create the basis for three of the four distinct

2.16a/b Unique 15"h creamware barrel-shaped pitcher with four American historical transfers firmly attributed to the Herculaneum Pottery Company. Also a hand-painted enamel view of THE CUMBERLAND ENGINE No 8 SOCIETY in action fighting a fire.

groups of transfers that can now be attributed to Herculaneum, the Shelton group, Davenport and Enoch Wood. Eventually, we hope to be able to attribute the majority of transfers that the collector will encounter. Let us now explore each of these four manufacturers and their products, in detail.

The Herculaneum Group

The Herculaneum Pottery Company was opened in Liverpool at the end of the 18th century. The city of Liverpool had long been a center of both the manufacture of ceramics and shippers for the Staffordshire potters. It is a matter of record, well documented by Alan Smith in *The Illustrated Guide to Liverpool Herculaneum Pottery*, that this company not only shipped hundreds of thousands of pieces of their own wares to America, but that they also acted as agents for such potters as William Adams & Sons, Henshall & Williamson, Hicks & Meigh, J & W Ridgway, John & George Rogers and Wood & Caldwell. This huge volume of business with America continued until the embargoes and trade sanctions, occasioned by the War of 1812, interrupted the trade. The political upheavals resulting from the War of 1812 were one of the main causes for the loss of business for the Liverpool creamware manufacturers, and the gradual ascendancy of the Staffordshire potters. In the early 1820s, the blue printed wares of the Staffordshire potteries gained immense popularity, at the expense of the black printed Liverpool creamwares. As previously stated, Mr. Smith's attributions gave us a starting point, to enable us to compile a list of transfers firmly attributed to Herculaneum. This pottery must now be classified as the largest producers of

"Liverpool" for the American market, numbering over one hundred transfers, which we have listed in Addendum One, found on page 259. As more collections are examined, we feel sure that we will add to this list.

The Shelton Group - *"F. Morris" or "T Fletcher"*

Using the reference books that are currently available, plus inspecting many collections , one quickly notes a certain group of transfers bear the inscription "F. MORRIS SHELTON" or "T. FLETCHER SHELTON". As previously stated, Francis Morris is listed as an "engraver and printer of earthenware" in the business directories of the day. Located at Vale Pleasant, Shelton, he and Fletcher apparently supplied a series of stylistically related designs to an unidentified potter. We have been able to attribute over thirty transfers to this group. There are an equal number which can be strongly attributed on the basis of similarity in style. While we have omitted noting these in the individual listings in Chapter Five, we have noted them in the second Addendum on page 260. Once again, we believe time will see more discoveries to be listed under this group.

The Enoch Wood and Sons Group

The identification of this group was made possible because of the wonderful 20"h pitcher in the Collection of the Albany Institute of History and Art. This piece was listed in both the McCauley and Larsen books, but for some unknown reason, neither they nor

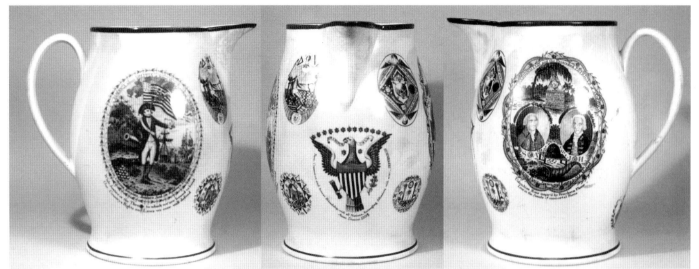

2.17a/b/c A large 15"h Liverpool pitcher with three transfers bearing the signature "F. Morris Shelton". In addition, there are four other smaller transfers of masonic views, and under the handle a small transfer of "fame". There is an 18"h Staffordshire pitcher, once in the Sussell Collection, that has five signed American View transfers by this engraver, plus several other smaller scenes. The American views on the Sussell pitcher are: By Virtue and Valour...etc (B.12); The Jefferson Quote (J.8); Washington and the Map of the United States (W.16) , Washington Crowned (W.30) and O Liberty! Thou Goddess (O.1).

anyone else bothered to illustrate this mammoth piece, which was made for Troy, New York merchant, Horace Jones, whose name is under the spout. Under the handle is the makers name, **Enoch Wood and Sons**. As you can see in the illustration, there are over a dozen different transfers that had heretofore been unattributed. Using the techniques already described, we can now state that there is an extremely high probability that the Wood firm was the potter responsible for *all* those pieces with the engraver's signature "***Bentley, Wear and Bourne, Engravers & Printers, Shelton, Staffordshire***", plus there is an equally high probability that this same firm made all the pieces with transfers of the portrait busts taken from Thomas Moses' "*Analectic Magazine*". Why? Because of the Albany pitcher, which ties both of these sources together with a potter. Another interesting fact we uncovered was that the Wood firm manufactured both Liverpool and Stafford-

shire forms for export to North America, and they seem to be responsible for *all* the pieces with artificial "grounds". We will discuss this in detail later.

Numbering over seventy five transfers, we have listed these in Addendum Three, found on page 261. There is no doubt, that as more research is accomplished, even more transfers will be added to this group. Thus we have determined the maker of another large group of views made for the American market. However, there is still one other group which merits our attention.

The Davenport Group

Perhaps you have noticed, while reading the section of Mrs.

2.18a/b *The* War of 1812 pitcher made by Enoch Wood and Sons, Burslem for Horace Jones, a Troy, New York merchant prior to the 1824 visit of General LaFayette. Over 20"h and 20"d, this monster contains no less than sixteen transfers. This is now in the Collection of the Albany Institute of History and Art, Albany, New York.

Comparisons of two portrait busts of Captain Hull. The transfer on the left **2.19** is from a pearlware plate with an impressed DAVENPORT mark. The transfer on the right **2.20** is from a pearlware pitcher which is attributed to Enoch Wood and Sons. Although both were taken from the same Gilbert Stuart portrait, you can readily observe the differences incorporated by the two different engravers of the copper plates. The Davenport bust is labeled simply CAPTAIN HULL, whereas the Wood bust bears the full inscription CAPT. HULL OF THE CONSTITUTION.

Larsen's book, titled "Portrait Plates in Various Colors by Staffordshire Potters", that she lists a small group as impressed DAVENPORT.[1] These transfers are a variant of those same portraits used by Enoch Wood and Sons. As a point of illustration, we are using side by side representations of two transfers of Captain HULL to illustrate these differences. Both transfers are from the same source, which is a painting by Gilbert Stuart, however there are significant differences in the two ceramic prints. This could have just been a stylistic difference between the two engravers of the copper plates, or it could be an added difference of taking the copper engraving from two separate source prints. There were several engravings published, including one by D. Edwin, which was used by Thomas Moses in *The Analectic Magazine*. Others, including those made by the Paris firm of Charles Bance, are illustrated later in this book. One telling difference, which we believe is quite significant, is the method of titling used by the two potters. Davenport strictly uses the rank and last name, while Wood uses the rank, last name and the ship or battle where the person achieved prominence. This is the first clue concerning the attribution of this grouping.

2.21 Extremely rare Staffordshire pitcher attributed to Davenport. Note how the title is stretched over the top of the transfer. This is the same technique used by this potter on the other pitchers noted in the text.

The next link occurs on the Staffordshire pitcher with a portrait bust of John Jay (check-list #J.7). On the reverse of one of these extremely rare JAY pitchers is the battle scene between two ships titled simply WASP AND FROLIC. This is the same titling technique used on several other variants, such as the CONSTITUTION AND GUERIERRE, CONSTITUTION AND JAVA and others. Also, this same WASP AND FROLIC appears on the reverse of two of the three known examples of THE ATTACK ON FORT OSWEGO, while the third Oswego contains a bust of John Jay. A common thread which ties these pieces together. One additional clue serves to strengthen our premise, the fact that the potter (Davenport) used a single print, *SPRIGS OF LAUREL* as the source for the majority of his maritime views. This single engraving contained nine different battle scenes drawn and engraved by William Strickland and published by John Kneas in Philadelphia. Of the five nautical titles we listed as Davenport's, four used this print as a source. Therefore, using our same methodology, we can attribute fourteen transfers to the Davenport firm. These are listed in Addendum Four on page 262.

As you use Chapter Five, you will note that all of the views we have attributed to the Davenport firm are considered "extremely rare". While we are quite certain that Davenport made ceramics for the American trade, almost all of these pieces (both blue and black transfer items) are rarities. This might indicate that while they did export to the American market during this period, the main thrust of their endeavors were aimed elsewhere.

There are undoubtedly many other potters who are responsible for the wealth of different transfers covering subjects that would appeal to the average American. Hopefully, as more research is completed concerning this field, more information will be uncovered that will eventually allow us to catalogue potters and views with the same thoroughness found in the field of dark blue transferwares. In many cases they will be the same potteries that produced both types of wares. In others, I'm sure we will learn more about the potters who are currently considered *minor* figures in the field of historical American transferware, such as Wilson, Moore, Fell or Burrows. These and other so-called minor figures may ultimately be proven as major exporters to the American market.

Sources of the Views and Portraits

As one starts to collect historical ceramics, it will quickly become apparent that the original sources for the majority of the views, were the finest artists and engravers of the late 18th and early 19th centuries. Collectors of these ceramics are actually collecting prints. Ceramic prints to be sure, but still prints. By examining the examples we have illustrated on this page, you can see just how faithfully the engravers of the copper plates copied the original sources. These sources were usually engravings, skillfully copied from paintings.

Legend has it that the process of transfer printing was discovered and commercialized by John Sadler and Guy Green of Liverpool. They attempted to keep the process a secret, so as to gain a commercial advantage over their competitors, but like most secrets, the trick to applying the images to uneven surfaces was eventually

2.22 On the left is a mezzo-tint "The Right Honourable William Pitt, Esq." by artist William Hoare engraved by J. Spilsbury. **2.23** On the right is an oval earthenware plaque taken from the same mezzo-tint, signed J. Sadler. Granted, the ceramic engraver has slightly changed some of the detail, but it is obviously an excellent copy of the original.

potters, most notably Josiah Wedgwood. David Drakard, in his work, *Printed English Pottery - History and Humor in the reign of George III 1760-1820*, listed the many print sellers and publishers who formed the backbone of the sources the potters used for their transfers. Anything was fair game, and any engraving that gained popularity with the English public, soon decorated a piece of ceramic. From political satire to courtship and matrimony. From the terrible

2.24 Above is the engraving by Abel Bowen, after a painting by Michele Corne, titled the "FIRST VIEW OF COM. PERRY'S VICTORY", which was published in Bowen's *Naval Monument*, in 1816 in Boston. Enoch Wood and Sons used the engravers Bentley, Wear and Bourne of Shelton to copy this print, which decorates the Staffordshire pitcher on the right **2.25**. Note the accuracy of the ceramic print, when closely compared to the original.

discovered by others, and the revolution in the production of ceramics spread across England and the rest of Europe. However, Sadler and Green were the first, and they not only decorated ceramics for their own products, but also for other

lives of soldiers and sailors, to the glamour of the Monarchy. Preachers and harlots. Napoleon and cossacks. The list is endless.

Usually, English social and historical subjects were reserved for the home market, but there are many instances of these subjects being used on Liverpool pitchers that had an American historical subject on the reverse. A favorite device used by the potter of Liverpool wares, would be to place an American historical scene on one side of the piece and a Masonic motif or the arms of a guild on the other. The arms of the guilds included most of the occupations of the day, such as bakers, blacksmiths, coopers, butchers, shipwrights and farmers. Landscapes and genre scenes were used extensively. The sources for these generic subjects are lost to us, but we do have a rather comprehensive list of artists, engravers and publishers, who provided the inspiration for the American historical subjects found on both Liverpool and Staffordshire wares. We will list these, both below, and in Chapter Three - Background and History of the Views.

Akin, James: (?) American satirical cartoonist responsible for the source drawing of the "Droll Scene in Newburyport" (check-list #D.12).

Ames, Ezra: (1768-1836) Portrait artist who worked in Albany, New York. Source for the medallion portrait of Governor DeWitt Clinton used on check-list #C.10.

Birch, Thomas: (1779-1851) Originally born in England, he immigrated to America and worked in Philadelphia painting landscapes, portraits and marine scenes. Source of paintings depicting THE CONSTITUTION AND GUERIERRE, THE CONSTITUTION TAKING THE CYANE AND THE LEVANT, and THE UNITED STATES AND THE MACEDONIAN.

Bowen, Abel: (1790-1850) Engraver and publisher working in Boston. Published *The Naval Monument* in 1816, in which he was the engraver of the following engravings used as the sources for the indicated views: THE CONSTITUTION TAKING THE CYANE AND LEVANT, CONSTITUTION IN CLOSE ACTION WITH THE GUERIERRE, ENTERPRISE AND BOXER, HORNET AND BON CITOYENNE, HORNET AND PEACOCK, MACDONNOUGH'S VICTORY ON LAKE CHAMPLAIN, FIRST & SECOND VIEWS OF COM. PERRY'S VICTORY, UNITED STATES AND MACEDONIAN, WASP BOARDING THE FROLIC and WASP AND THE REINDEER. Most of these views were after paintings by Michele Corne and were produced on ceramics by Enoch Wood and Sons.

Cochin, Charles N. : (1715-1790) Engraver and painter to the French court in Paris, he painted the famous portrait of Benjamin Franklin wearing a fur hat, found on Ralph Wedgwood's pitcher

2.26 George Delleker's engraving of Commodore William Bainbridge, published by J. Kneas in Philadelphia. This was used as the source print for the extremely rare Liverpool pitcher, check-list #B.2.

and bowl (check-list #F.10) and on other pieces of Liverpool (check-list #s F.5, F.6 and F.7).

Corne, Michele F. : (1752-1832) Originally from Italy, he worked in Newport, Rhode Island. Painted all of those naval scenes published by Abel Bowen in the *Naval Monument,* which were listed under Bowen.

Delleker, George: (?) Engraver who worked in Philadelphia and used the Gilbert Stuart portrait of William Bainbridge and the Samuel Waldo portrait of Oliver H. Perry as models for his prints. Used as the source for check-list #s B.2 and #P.22 - #P.25.

Du Simitiere, Pierre E. : (1735-1784) Originally from Switzerland, this portrait painter worked both in full-size and miniatures. Painted the famous portrait of Washington used on Liverpool. (check-list #s W.5 and W.6.)

Eights, James: (1798-1882) Albany, New York artist famous for his landscapes around the Albany area. He executed the ink drawing of the three views of the Erie Canal (check-list #s E.5, E.6, V.4 - V.6.)

Fulton, Robert: (1765-1815) American inventor and engineer who painted portraits in Philadelphia from 1782-1786, when he left for London. Studied (with Benjamin West) and painted portraits until 1793. Painted the portrait of Commodore Preble used on Liverpool (check-list #P.42) and Surrender of Cornwallis (check-list #S.84).

Geille, Amede F. : (1802-1843) French artist working in Paris who engraved the portrait of La Fayette used by Clews. (check-list #L.2).

Gimbrede, Thomas: (1781-1832) Originally French, he taught drawing at the Military Academy at West Point. Engraved the portrait of Jefferson used on Liverpool pitchers. (check-list #J.12).

Hoare, William: (?) Eighteenth century English portrait painter who executed the portrait of William Pitt used as the source for check-list #s P.31, P.32 and P.33.

Jarvis, John: (1780-1839) Philadelphia artist specializing in portraits. His portrait of Major-General Brown has been listed as the source for the Wood view (check-list #s B.7 and B.8).

Maverick, Samuel: (?) Engraver who worked in New York City and engraved the copper plate used for the circular engraving (used on snuff boxes) of "The Landing of Gen'l La Fayette at Castle Garden, August 14, 1824". He also engraved the small portrait of La Fayette used by Wood in the Washington-La Fayette portraits, check-list #L.13.

Peale, Rembrant: (1778-1860) Famous American portrait artist working both here and abroad. His portrait of Captain Jacob Jones was used on check-list #J.31.

Penniman, John R. : (1783-1838) Boston artist known to have decorated masterpieces of furniture, he also provided the painting for the "NAVAL MONUMENT" engraving, which was used by Abel Bowen in the *Naval Monument* as the frontispiece.

2.27 THE DEATH OF WOLFE, after the painting by American Benjamin West. The original mezzo-tint was engraved by William Woolet. This was used by Josiah Wedgwood as the source for his Liverpool pitcher, check-list #D.1.

Strictland, William: (1757-1854) American architect, engineer and artist. Leader of the Greek Revival movement in America and designer of many prominent buildings. Also known for his views of the War of 1812, especially those that appear on the multiple view print, SPRIGS OF LAUREL, used by Davenport as a source for his naval transfers.

Stuart, Gilbert: (1755-1828) Philadelphia, New York, Washington and Boston portrait painter who is responsible for most of the famous portraits of the Republic's early leaders such as: Washington, Ames, Bainbridge, Brown, Decatur, Hull, Jay, Jefferson, Lawrence and Winfield Scott, all of which served as sources for various Staffordshire and Liverpool pieces.

Sully, Thomas: (1782-1872) Originally English, he became a celebrated painter of portraits and various historical subjects, while working in Philadelphia. His paintings were the source of several important prints depicting naval battles during the War of 1812.

Thomas, Moses: (?) Publisher and engraver of *The Analectic Magazine,* which contained most of the portrait busts used on Staffordshire pitchers. Mrs. Larsen stated that this publication

M. Corne p.   A. Bowen, sc.

THE WASP BOARDING THE FROLIC.

2.28 Right: "THE WASP BOARDING THE FROLIC", a print from the *Naval Monument* by Abel Bowen. 2.29 Above: A Staffordshire pitcher with the same scene by Enoch Wood and Sons, who used the Bowen print as the source for the ceramic view.

was the source for those transfers, which we have now attributed to Enoch Wood and Sons.

Reynolds, Sir Joshua: (1723-1792) British artist who was first president of the Royal Academy, and painter to George III. His portrait of Tarleton was the source for the Liverpool pitcher (check-list #s T.1 and T.2).

Savage, Edward: (1761-1817) American painter and engraver who engraved the maritime scene of *L'Insurgent and Constellation* used as the source print for the Liverpool pitcher of the same title (check-list #L.31).

Waldo, Samuel: (1783-1861) American portrait painter trained in London and worked in New York. Painted the source used for Commodore Perry, published by Moses Thomas in the *Analectic Magazine* and used by the potters on Staffordshire/Liverpool pitchers (check-list #s P.19, P.20 and P.21).

West, Benjamin: (1738-1820) American artist who lived in London and taught Stuart, Sully and Morse. President of the Royal Academy (1792-1815). Painted the "DEATH OF WOLFE" used by Wedgwood on the Liverpool pitcher (check-list #s D.1 and D.2).

Wood, Joseph: (1778-1852) American miniaturist who worked in Philadelphia, New York and Washington. Painted the portrait of General Jackson used on the Staffordshire pitcher (check-list #s J.3 - J.6).

Notes - Chapter Two

[1] In our own collection we have two pieces marked by this potter. The first is a blue feather edge plate with a black transfer of HULL, (check-list #H.21) with an impressed DAVENPORT over an anchor (see Lockett and Godden, *DAVENPORT / China, Earthenware & Glass 1794 -1887,* Barrie & Jenkins. 1989. London. Page 73, #E 5). The other piece is a small cup plate with a polychromed SEAL OF THE UNITED STATES (fig. AI.33) with an impressed **Davenport** over an anchor (see above, page 72, #E 2)

Chapter Three
Background and History of
the Ceramic Views

Battle of Lake Erie - September 10, 1813

USS Constitution and HMS Guerriere - August 10, 1812

USS Chesapeake and HMS Shannon - June 1, 1813

Battle of the Thames - October 5, 1813

USS Wasp and HMS Frolic - October 18, 1812

USS Hornet and HMS Peacock - February 27, 1813

USS United States and HMS Macedonian - October 25, 1812

3.1 Map of the United States circa 1813 With Vignettes of Military Actions as Portrayed in Prints of the Period

The Battle of New Orleans - January 8, 1815

USS Constitution and HMS Java - December 29, 1812

3.2 "John Adams, President of the United States", stipple engraving by Edward Savage, circa 1800.

Adams, John: (1735-1826) Second President of the United States (1796-1800). Defeated for a second term by Thomas Jefferson. Subject of transfers on Liverpool pitchers and a child's mug (check-list #s A.2 - A.10). Also there is that exquisite French porcelain vase AIII.1.

3.3 Samuel Adams by John Singleton Copley reproduced from *The Dictionary of American Portraits* published by Dover Publications in 1967.

Adams, Samuel: (1722-1803) American revolutionary and politician from Massachusetts. Portrait bust found on PROSCRIBED PATRIOTS Liverpool pitcher (check-list #M.15).

Adair, John: (?) Brigadier General, commanding the Kentucky militia at the **Battle of New Orleans**. Name found on the ARMY HEROES Staffordshire pitcher (check-list #A.31).

AMERICAN ARMY HEROES: Found on a Staffordshire pitcher are the following names of army officers of distinction: Adair, Boyd, Brown, Gaines, Izard, Jackson, Lewis, McComb, Miller, Pike, Porter, Scott and Van Rensalaer. When possible, we have provided a biography of these men in this section (check-list #A.31).

AMERICAN NAVAL HEROES: Found on the reverse of the above Staffordshire pitcher are the following names of naval officers of

distinction: Bainbridge, Barney, Blakeley, Burrows, Decatur, Hull, Jones, Lawrence, MacDonnough, Perry, Porter, Rogers, Stuart and Warrington. Again, when possible we have provided a biography of these men in this section (check-list #N.1).

3.4 Fisher Ames after a painting by Gilbert Stuart, engraved for the *Analectic Magazine*, 1814. This is the source print for the portrait bust on china.

Ames, Fisher: (1758-1808) American politician from Massachusetts, active from 1789-1796. Portrait found on Liverpool and Staffordshire pitchers (check-list #A.20).

ATTACK ON FORT OSWEGO: On May 6, 1814, British ships under the command of Sir James Yeo landed a marine party and captured the American fort located on the southern shore of Lake Ontario. After they seized the stores and fired the buildings, they re-embarked and departed. The Americans then reoccupied the fort. View rarely found on Staffordshire pitchers (check-list #A.32).

3.5 Engraved medallion portrait of William Bainbridge after a painting by Gilbert Stuart, engraved by Charles Bance, Paris (1817-1825) for use on papier mache snuff boxes.

Bainbridge, William: (1774-1833) American naval officer. Imprisoned by Tripoli after loss of *USS Philadelphia* in Tripoli harbor on October 31, 1803. Commanded *USS Constitution* in the victory over *HMS Java* (1812). Portrait bust found on Staffordshire pitcher (check-list #B.1 and B.2) and listed on NAVAL HEROES Staffordshire pitcher (check-list #N.1) and NAVAL MONUMENT transfer (check-list #N.2). Also on a porcelain dessert service (AIII.2).

Barney, Joshua: (1759-1818) American naval officer. Served in American Revolution. Captured *HMS General Monk* (1782). Joined in the defense of Washington, DC (1814), where he was wounded and captured by the British (the third time in two wars). Name found on AMERICAN NAVAL HEROES Staffordshire pitcher (check-list #N.1).

3.7 James Biddle by Charles Wilson Peale, Courtesy Independence National Historical Park and reproduced from *The Dictionary of American Portraits* published by Dover Publications in 1967.

3.6 Portrait of Commodore John Barry by Gilbert Stuart. *The Barry-Hayes Collection* (Lot 64), American Art Association auction January 21, 1939.

Barry, John: (1745-1803) American revolutionary and naval officer who is considered the father of the American Navy. Held commission #1. Commanded several ships during the Revolution. Captured the *HMS Edward* (1776), was defeated while commanding the *USS Raleigh*, 32 guns by the *HMS Experiment*, 50 guns and *HMS Unicorn*, 20 guns (1778). Captain *USS Alliance*, 32 guns defeating *HMS Atalanta*, 16 guns and *HMS Trepassy*, 14 guns (1780). Fought last significant naval battle of Revolution, while returning from Havana in 1783, when he fought three British frigates, severely damaging one. Senior officer of the Navy 1794-1803. Name found on Naval Monument transfer (check-list #N.1).

Biddle, James: (1783-1848) American naval officer who was imprisoned with Bainbridge, when the *USS Philadelphia* ran aground in Tripoli harbor in late October, 1803. First Lieutenant under Jacob Jones, when the *USS Wasp* captured the *HMS Frolic*. Again imprisoned when both ships captured by the 74 gun *HMS Poictiers*. Assumed command of *USS Hornet* and defeated the *HMS Penguin* (1815). Name appears on Naval Monument transfer (check-list #N.2)

Blakeley, Johnston: (1781-1814) American naval officer who commanded the *USS Wasp* and defeated *HMS Reindeer* (June 28, 1814), *HMS Avon* (September 1, 1814) and *HMS Atalanta* (September 21, 1814). Disappeared with his ship and all hands sometime after October 9, 1814, at sea, south of Madeira. Name appears on the Naval Heroes pitcher (check-list #N.1) and the Naval Monument transfer (check-list #N.2).

3.8 Engraving of Johnston Blakely, probably after a painting by Gilbert Stuart. Published in the 1821 volume "*Life of Perry*" by John Niles.

Boyd, John: (?) General, (probably a Brigadier) who commanded at the losing **Battle of Chrysler's Farm** and who's name appears on the AMERICAN ARMY HEROES Staffordshire pitcher (check-list #A.31).

Brown, Jacob Jennings: (1775-1828) American army officer. Commanded invasion of Canada (1814) battles of **Lundy's Lane** and **Chippawa** (July, 1814). Commanding General, U. S. Army from 1821-1828. Name found on AMERICAN ARMY HEROES Staffordshire pitcher and portrait on two other Staffordshire pitchers (check-list #s A.31, B.7- B.9). Also on a porcelain dessert service (AIII.3).

25

3.9 Engraved medallion portrait of Jacob Brown after a painting by John Jarvis, engraved by Charles Bance, Paris (1817-1825) for use on papier mache snuff boxes.

Burrows, William: (? - 1813) American naval officer. Captain of the brig *USS Enterprise*, which defeated the brig *HMS Boxer* after a forty minute battle off the coast of New Hampshire on September 1, 1813. Both captains were killed in the battle. Name appears on the AMERICAN NAVAL HEROES Staffordshire pitcher (check-list #N.1).

Charlotte, Sophia: (1744-1818) Queen and wife of George III of England (m 1761). Niece of the Duke of Mecklenburg. Mother of fifteen children, including George IV. Last Queen of the American colonies. Portrait found on various types of Liverpool creamware (check-list #s C.3 - C.7).

Clay, Henry: (1777-1852) American politician. Leader of "War Hawks" advocating war with Britain in 1812. Leader of the economic policy labelled the "American System", which was a moderate attempt to protect American industry and trade that would benefit the "West". Portrait bust appears rarely on Staffordshire plates and platters (check-list #C.9).

Clinton, DeWitt: (1769-1828). American politician. Defeated by Madison in Presidential election of 1812. Governor of New York (1817-1823 and 1825-1828) and supporter of the Erie Canal (opened 1825). Portrait bust appears on heavy earthenware pitchers, now attributed to A. or R. Stevenson (check-list #C.10).

Cornwallis, Charles: (1738-1805) British Major General during American Revolution. Drove Washington out of New Jersey (1776); defeated Horatio Gates at **Camden** (1780); appointed commander of the Southern region (1780); defeated Nathanial Greene at **Guilford Court House** (1781); besieged and forced to surrender at **Yorktown** by combined American and French forces (October 19, 1781). Continued in the army with an illustrious career both in India and Ireland. Portrait appears on Liverpool wares (check-list #s C.27-C.28).

3.10 Gen. Charles Cornwallis by John Singleton Copley. Reproduced from *The Dictionary of American Portraits* published by Dover Publications in 1967.

THE CONSTITUTION AND THE GUERRIERE: Naval battle between the two frigates which occurred on August 19, 1812. Commanded by Captain Hull, the *USS Constitution* defeated the *HMS Guerriere*, commanded by Captain Dacres, in a thirty minute battle. The British suffered seventy-seven casualties, while the Americans had only fourteen killed or wounded. Two different scenes of the battle are found on Staffordshire pitchers, the first (check-list #C.22-C.23), titled THE CONSTITUTION IN CLOSE ACTION WITH THE GUERRIERE is taken from a painting by M. Corne, engraved by W. Hoogland, and published by Abel Bowen in the *Naval Monument* in 1816. The second view (check-list #C.19) is titled CONSTITUTION AND GUERRIERE, from the painting by Thomas Birch, which was engraved by Cornelius Tiebout. There is also a Paris porcelain plate (AIII.4) and a fine vase (AIII.5), which were decorated using the below circular print, taken from the Birch painting, as the source.

3.11 Engraved medallion of the *USS Constitution* capturing *HMS Guerriere* after a painting by Thomas Birch, engraved by Charles Bance, Paris (1817-1825) for use on papier mache snuff boxes.

THE CONSTITUTION AND THE JAVA: Naval battle between the two frigates off the coast of Brazil which took place on December 29, 1812. Commanded by Captain Bainbridge, the *USS Constitution* defeated the *HMS Java*, commanded by Captain Lambert (who later died of wounds received in the action), after a fierce battle that lasted almost two hours. American casualties were estimated at thirty, while the British incurred over one-hundred. Two different views of the battle are reported on Staffordshire pitchers, the first titled CONSTITUTION AND JAVA 1797, who's existence is doubtful (see check-list #C.21) and the second is titled CONSTITUTION AND JAVA, which used the print, SPRIGS OF LAUREL as the source (check-list #C.22).

3.12 CONSTITUTION AND JAVA, one of nine nautical scenes by William Strickland published on the single print SPRIGS OF LAUREL by John Kneas. This is the source print for the Davenport pitcher (check-list #C.22).

3.12a THE CONSTITUTION TAKING THE CYANE AND THE LEVANT from a painting by Corne and published by Abel Bowen in the *Naval Monument.* This is the source print for the ceramic view by Enoch Wood and Sons.

THE CONSTITUTION TAKING THE CYANE AND THE LEVANT: Naval battle which took place on February 20, 1815, between the *USS Constitution* (Captain Stewart) and *HMS Cyane* (a frigate) and *HMS Levant* (a sloop) off the coast of Madeira. This battle is found on a Staffordshire pitcher (check-list #C.25) titled as above.

THE DEATH OF WOLFE: This historical event ended the French and Indian Wars and culminated in the British takeover of Canada. On September 13, 1759, the British General Wolfe defeated the French General Montcalm on the Plains of Abraham, before the citadel of Quebec. Both Generals were killed in the action. The transfer is after a painting by American colonist Benjamin West, the original of which is in the Collection of the National Gallery of Canada in Ottawa (check-list #s D.1-D.2).

Decatur, Stephen: (1779-1820) American naval officer. Led the successful raid to burn the *USS Philadelphia* in Tripoli harbor (1804). Defeated the frigate *HMS Macedonian* (1812), while commanding the *USS United States,* and defeated the frigate *HMS*

Endymion while commanding the *USS President* (1815), which he was later forced to surrender to a British fleet. Killed in a duel. Author of the famous toast "Our Country! In her intercourse with foreign nations may she always be in the right, but our country, right or wrong!" (check-list #s D.3-D.9). Also on a porcelain dessert service (AIII.6).

3.13 Engraved medallion portrait of Stephan Decatur after a painting by Gilbert Stuart, engraved by Charles Bance, Paris (1817-1825) for use on papier mache snuff boxes.

Dickinson, John: (1732-1808) American Revolutionary politician who wrote *Letters from a Farmer in Pennsylvania, to the inhabitants of the British Colonies* and drafter of the Articles of Confederation. Member Continental Congress 1774-1776, 1779-1780. President of Delaware (1781 and delegate from Delaware to the Constitutional Convention). Portrait bust appears on a newly discovered Liverpool bowl (check-list #D.11).

3.14 John Dickinson by Charles Wilson Peale, Courtesy Independence National Historical Park and reproduced from *The Dictionary of American Portraits* published by Dover Publications in 1967.

(A) Droll Scene in Newburyport: A cartoon drawn and placed on ceramics by American cartoonist James Akin, which describes the end of a heated discussion between Akin and Edmund Blunt, a resident of Newburyport, Massachusetts. Apparently Blunt became so enraged by something Akin said, that he picked up an iron skillet and threw it at Akin, missed and hit a bystander. Using the cartoon that Akin sketched, the bystander placed the order with the potteries, and when the pieces arrived, the embarrassed Blunt quickly set about buying and destroying as many as he could. The cartoon appears on a very few Liverpool pitchers (check-list #D.12).

3.15 THE ENTERPRIZE AND BOXER after a painting by Michele Corne and an engraving by Abel Bowen, published in the *Naval Monument*, in 1816. This is the source print for the ceramic view by Enoch Wood and Sons (check-list #E.4).

THE ENTERPRISE AND THE BOXER: Naval battle fought on September 1, 1813. After a battle of forty minutes, the brig *HMS Boxer* surrendered to the brig *USS Enterprise*, commanded by Lt. William Burrows. Both captains were mortally wounded in the battle. They are buried side by side in Portland, Maine. One ceramic view is taken from a painting by Corne, engraved and published by Abel Bowen in the *Naval Monument* in 1816. The Davenport ceramic view is taken from the Kneas print, SPRIGS OF LAUREL, which used the William Strickland painting (check-list #s E.3 and E.4).

3.16 ENTERPRISE AND BOXER, one of nine nautical scenes by William Strickland published on the single print SPRIGS OF LAUREL by John Kneas. This is the source print for the Davenport pitcher (check-list #E.3).

Entrance of the Erie Canal into the Hudson at Albany: The Erie Canal, which was started on July 4, 1817, was formally opened by Governor DeWitt Clinton on October 26, 1825. The three-hundred sixty-two mile long canal quickly led to the emergence of New York City as the primary shipping port on the Atlantic seaboard. View found on pitchers by Stevenson differs from that view used by Enoch Wood on his series of dark blue Staffordshire china. This same Stevenson version of the view is found on an extremely rare (four known examples) group of blue cup plates with a Star and Flute border, also by an unknown maker (check-list #s E.5 and E.6).

3.17 FIRST VIEW OF COM. PERRY'S VICTORY: after a painting by Michele Corne and an engraving by Abel Bowen, published in the *Naval Monument*, in 1816. This is the source print for the ceramic view by Enoch Wood and Sons (check-list #F.3).

First/Second View of Com. Perry's Victory: Naval battle fought on Lake Erie on September 10, 1813, with the American fleet commanded by Oliver Hazard Perry supporting land operations commanded by General William Henry Harrison. The British fleet was commanded by Lt. Robert Barclay, who appeared to be winning during the initial phase of the battle. After his flagship, the *USS Lawrence* was battered, Perry shifted his command to the *USS Niagara* and the fortunes of battle turned to favor the Americans. After receiving Perry's famous message, "We have met the enemy and they are ours", Harrison attacked and captured **Amhurstburg** on the north side of the Lake, thus placing British Canada into jeopardy. Views are found usually on Staffordshire pitchers, although one instance of the "Second" view is known on a Liverpool pitcher. Source views are after a painting by Corne and engraved by Abel Bowen (check-list #s F.3 and S.42).

3.18 SECOND VIEW OF COM. PERRY'S VICTORY: after a painting by Michel Corne and an engraving by Abel Bowen, published in the *Naval Monument*, in 1816. This is the source print for the ceramic view by Enoch Wood and Sons (check-list #S.42).

Franklin, Benjamin: (1706-1790) American revolutionary, statesman, scientist, inventor, philosopher, printer and writer. Published *Pennsylvania Gazette* (1730-1748), *Poor Richards Almanac* (1732-1757). Formed the forerunner of the American Philosophical Society (1742) and the University of Pennsylvania (1751). Invented the Franklin stove, bifocal spectacles and the Lightning Rod. Retired in 1748, to become active in public life starting in 1754, when he was a Pennsylvania delegate to the Albany congress. Represented Pennsylvania, New Jersey and Massachusetts as "agent" in London (1764-1775). Member Second Continental Congress (1775), one of three chosen to draft treaty of alliance with France (1776), on committee to draft the Declaration of Independence and one of the signers of same (1776), appointed Plenipotentiary to France (1776-1785) and with Adams and Jay negotiated the peace with Great Britain which was signed September 3, 1783. Portrait busts appear on several Staffordshire, Liverpool and French porcelain pieces.

Gates, Horatio: (1728-1806) American army officer, once in British service. Forced Burgoyne to surrender at **Saratoga** (1777) and lost the **Battle of Camden** to General Cornwallis (1780). Relieved of command. Served at Washington's headquarters for remainder of the war (check-list #G.2).

Gaines, Edmund P: (1777-1849) American army officer who, as a captain, arrested Aaron Burr (1807). As a colonel, his regiment covered the retreat from the **Battle of Chryslers Field** during the **Montreal** campaign (1813). As Brigadier General he successfully commanded and defended **Fort Erie** against a British siege (1814). Name appears on ARMY HEROES Staffordshire pitcher (check-list #A.31).

George III: (1738-1820) George William Frederick (House of Hanover). King of Great Britain (1760-1820). Influenced the events, through the use of the patronage system, that led to the loss of the American Colonies. Suffered from severe mental illness and blindness. Because of the mental problems, his son became Regent in 1811. Married to Charlotte of Mecklenburg. Last King of the American colonies (check-list #'s G.4 - G.6).

3.20 "The Hon. John Hancock of Boston in New England, President of the American Congress" a mezzo-tint published by C. Shepherd, London 1775.

Hancock, John: (1737-1793) American Revolutionary politician, who was a member of the Continental Congress (1775-1780), President of Congress (1775-1777) and the first signer of the Declaration of Independence (1776). First Governor of Massachusetts (1780-1785) and again (1787-1793). Two different portraits found on Liverpool, one of which has been identified as a "stock" portrait also used for a "Phillip Crandall", James Monroe and an "I Baker". The other portrait does bear a resemblance and may be taken from a portrait of the period (check-list #'s H.1 and H.2).

Harrison, William Henry: (1773-1841) American army officer, politician and ninth President of the United States. Governor, Territory of Indiana (1800-1812). Led military forces against Indians which resulted in the **Battle of Tippecanoe** (1811). Appointed Brigadier General commanding armies of the Northwest (1812), took Detroit and won the **Battle of the Thames** (1813) against Indian and British forces. Member, U. S. House (1816-1819) and Senator (1825-1828) from Ohio. Unsuccessful Presidential candidate in 1836. Ran successfully for President in 1840.

3.21 William Henry Harrison from a photograph by Southworth and Hawes. Courtesy Metropolitan Museum of Art, Stokes-Hawes Collection and reproduced from *The Dictionary of American Portraits* published by Dover Publications in 1967. This is the source of several portrait busts on Staffordshire.

Died from pneumonia, after one month in office. Portrait busts found on several Staffordshire forms including porcelain, lustre pottery and earthenware plates and platters. Also rarely found on a pitcher made by the Jersey City Pottery Company.

Hopkins, Esek: (1718-1802) American Revolutionary War naval officer who was named Commodore of the Continental Navy. This fleet, under his command, raided the Bahamas capturing much needed military supplies (March, 1776). Congress removed him from command in 1777-78 for his failure to aggressively pursue the naval war. Portrait bust found on that extremely rare Colonial Revival bowl (check-list #H.13).

Hornet and the Peacock: Naval battle which took place on February 24, 1813. After being detached from the squadron commanded by Captain Bainbridge, the *USS Hornet*, a brig under the command of Master Commandant James Lawrence, blockaded

THE HORNET SINKING THE PEACOCK.

3.22 THE HORNET SINKING THE PEACOCK, after a painting by Michele Corne and engraved by Abel Bowen for the *Naval Monument*, published 1816. This is the source print for the Enoch Wood and Sons ceramic view.

the *HMS Bon Citoyenne* off San Salvador. Chased off the blockade by a superior force, the *USS Hornet* came upon the brig *HMS Peacock* and sank her after a battle of fifteen minutes. Upon his return to the United States, Lawrence was promoted and given command of the ill-fated *USS Chesapeake*. Two views of the battle are found on Staffordshire pitchers and plates. The first, THE HORNET SINKING THE PEACOCK, which is illustrated above, is by Corne and was published by Abel Bowen in the *Naval Monument* in 1816. (check-list #H.16). The second ceramic view is untitled and was taken from a print of James Lawrence, which has a vignette of the battle scene drawn and engraved by F. Kearny and is illustrated below (check-list #H.14). Also on French porcelain vases (AIII.11).

3.23 Vignette of a naval battle by Kearny illustrating James Lawrence's victory over the HMS Peacock. Mrs. Larsen was incorrect in her identification of 3.24 as the source for the untitled ceramic print of the HORNET AND PEACOCK (check-list #H.14). The above vignette was the source for this second Enoch Wood and Sons view of the battle. The Lawrence engraving is taken from a painting by Gilbert Stuart.

Hornet Blockading the Bon Citoyenne: This event took place in the harbor of San Salvador on December 29, 1813, until late February, 1814, when the *USS Hornet* was forced off station by the arrival of the British 74 gun ship of the line, *HMS Montagu*. The view found on Staffordshire pitchers was reported by Mrs. Larsen as being after a drawing by Michele Corne, engraved and published by Abel Bowen in the *Naval Monument* in 1816. This

is incorrect. Below we have illustrated the erroneous source print attributed by Larsen and the actual ceramic transfer below. As you can see, there is a bit of similarity, but the ships are going in the opposite directions. As an interesting aside, this view is not titled on the ceramics, but has the familiar BENTLEY, WEAR AND BOURNE, etc., where one would normally expect the title (check-list #H.15).

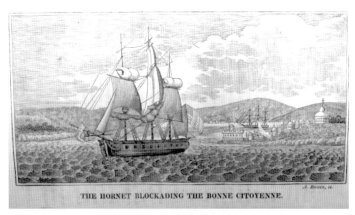

3.24 THE HORNET BLOCKADING THE BON CITOYENNE after a painting by Michel Corne, engraved by Abel Bowen for the *Naval Monument*, published 1816. As you can see, this is not the source for the ceramic transfer by Wood and Sons, as indicated by Mrs. Larsen.

3.25 Untitled - HORNET BLOCKADING THE BON CITOYENNE by Enoch Wood and Sons. Only the engraver's names are found beneath the transfer.

3.26 Engraved portrait medallion of Isaac Hull after a painting by Gilbert Stuart, engraved by Bance for use on papier mache snuff boxes.

Hull, Isaac: (1773-1843) American naval officer who commanded the *USS Constitution* in the victory over *HMS Guerierre* on August 19, 1812. Continued a long career in the Navy, culminating with the command of the Mediterranean squadron (1838-1841). Two portrait busts are found on Staffordshire plates and pitchers that are after a portrait by Gilbert Stuart (check-list #H.18-H.24).

Izard, George: (1776-1828) American army officer and public official, commissioned colonel of the 2nd artillery (1812), Brigadier General (1813) and took part in the unsuccessful **Montreal** operation in 1813, under General Wade Hampton. Heavily criticized for his actions, which left Plattsburg undefended, and his withdrawal in the face of the enemy at **Niagara**. Resigned commission in 1815. Name found on ARMY HEROES Staffordshire pitcher (check-list #A.31).

3.28 John Jay, 1st Chief Justice of the United States. An engraving after the portrait by Gilbert Stuart. This is the source print for the ceramic transfer by Davenport.

3.27 Major General Andrew Jackson by John Wesley Jarvis. Courtesy Metropolitan Museum of Art and reproduced from *The Dictionary of American Portraits* published by Dover Publications in1967.

Jefferson, Thomas: (1743-1826) American revolutionary politician, scholar and third President of the United States. Author of the Declaration of Independence (1776), while a member of the Continental Congress (1775-1783). Governor of Virginia (1779-1781), U. S. Secretary of State (1790-1793), U. S. Vice President

3.29 Thomas Jefferson, President of the United States by Rembrant Peale. Courtesy Princeton University and reproduced from *The Dictionary of American Portraits* published by Dover Publications in1967.

Jackson, Andrew: (1767-1845) American politician, army officer and seventh President of the United States. Member U.S House and Senate (1796-1798) and (1823-1825). Major General of Militia (1802), defeated Creek Indians at **Horseshoe Bend** (1814), captured **Pensacola, Florida** (1814). Commissioned Major General U.S. Army (1814) and successfully defended **New Orleans** (1815). President of the United States for two terms (1828-1836). Three different portraits are found on Staffordshire plates, pitchers and cup plates. The most common is after a portrait by Joseph Wood, which was engraved by C. G. Childs in Philadelphia in 1828. The origins of the others are unknown, although one is probably the Geille portrait of La Fayette (check-lists #s J.1 - J.6).

Jay, John: (1749-1829) American revolutionary statesmen and judge, who was a member of the Continental Congress (1774-1779), President of that Congress (1778-1779), drafted first constitution (1777), chief justice of New York Supreme Court (1777-1778), Minister to Spain (1779), joined peace commission drafting treaty with England (1782) and U. S secretary for foreign affairs (1784-1789). First Chief Justice, U. S. Supreme Court (1789-1795). Governor of New York (1795-1801). Portrait found on a Staffordshire pitcher (check-list #J.7).

(1797-1801) and President of the United States (1801-1809). Purchased territory of Louisiana from France and prohibited further importation of slaves. One of the founders of the University of Virginia. Several different portraits appear on both Liverpool and Staffordshire pitchers that are attributed to various artists such as Peale and Stuart (check-list #s J.12-J.30). Also on French porcelain vases (AIII.12) and a dessert service (AIII.13).

Jones, Jacob: (1768-1850) American naval officer. Captain of the *USS Wasp*, who sighted a British convoy escorted by a brig, the *HMS Frolic*. After a battle lasting forty-three minutes, the *Frolic* was captured and a prize crew placed aboard. Unfortunately for Captain Jones, the two ships were overhauled by a British 74 gun ship of the line and both captured. Jones later commanded the *USS Macedonian* in Decatur's squadrons' action against Tripoli (1815). Two similar portraits are found on Staffordshire pitchers, taken from a painting by Rembrant Peale, which was engraved by Edwin and published in the *Analectic Magazine* in 1813 (check-list #s J.31-J.32). Also on a porcelain dessert service (AIII.14).

3.30 Engraved medallion portrait of Jacob Jones after a painting by Rembrant Peale, engraved by Charles Bance, Paris (1817-1825) for use on papier mache snuff boxes.

Jones, John Paul: (1747-1792) American Revolutionary War naval officer who as captain of the *Alfred* captured or destroyed sixteen British vessels in a six week period. In 1778 he raided the British coast aboard the *Ranger* and captured the first British warship, the *HMS Drake*, to surrender to an American vessel. As captain of the *Bonne Homme Richard*, accompanied by the frigate *Alliance* and two French vessels, captured the British Baltic trading fleet, after capturing the fifty gun ship, *HMS Serapis*. Portrait bust found on the extremely rare Colonial Revival bowl (check-list #J.33).

Knox, Henry: (1750-1806) American Revolutionary War officer, who was Washington's trusted advisor and chief of artillery. Youngest major general in the Continental Army. Upon Washington's resignation from the army, he became the senior general officer, until he became Secretary of War (1785-1794). Portrait bust found on the extremely rare Colonial Revival bowl (check-list #K.1).

LaFayette, Marie-Joesph-Paul-Yves-Roch-Gilbert du Motier de: (1757-1834) French statesman and army officer, who entered American service in the Revolutionary War (1777). Commissioned Major General (1777) and instrumental in the defeat of Cornwallis at **Yorktown**, Virginia (1781). An intimate of George Washington. Returned in a triumphant visit to the United States in August, 1824. Much beloved by the American people, he was given a hero's welcome during his extended tour of this country. Several different portraits by Amede Geille, Samuel Maverick and others are used on ceramics (check-list #s F.2, L.1 - L.15). Also on French porcelains (AIII.15 - AIII.17).

3.31 Marie-Joesph-Paul-Yves-Roch-Gilbert du Motier de LaFayette from an engraving published by Charles Bance in Paris, after the American Revolution.

Landing of La Fayette: The arrival of LaFayette was one of the most momentous occasions in the city of New York. The Marquis landed at Castle Garden on August 16, 1824 aboard the ship *Chancellor Livingston*. After a celebration the next day, which included thousands of people, LaFayette toured the country, receiving the adoration of the majority of the American public. Innumerable ceramics were produced to commemorate this visit.

3.32 Papier Mache snuff box "Landing of General LaFayette" from a drawing and engraving by Samuel Maverick.

3.33 Engraved medallion portrait of James Lawrence after a painting by Gilbert Stuart, engraved by Charles Bance, Paris (1817-1825) for use on papier mache snuff boxes.

3.34 Rare aquatint showing "Action between the *USS Constellation* and *L'Insurgent* - On the 9th February 1799" after a painting by Edward Savage. One of the earliest aquatints showing a naval action produced in the United States, printed by Savage in 1799. Used as the source for check-list #L.31.

Lawrence, James: (1781-1813) American naval officer, who was second in command of Decatur's successful raid on Tripoli (1804) and commanded the *USS Hornet* in the victory over *HMS Peacock* (1813). Assumed command of the *USS Chesapeake*, where he suffered a mortal wound during the unsuccessful battle with the *HMS Shannon*. Uttered the famous motto "Don't Give Up the Ship", as he was dying. Two similar portraits are found on Staffordshire pitchers, after a painting by Gilbert Stuart, which was published in the *Analectic Magazine* in 1813 (check-list #s L.17-L.18). Also on a porcelain dessert service (AIII.18).

Lewis, Morgan: (1754-1844) American army officer and public official, who declined President Madison's appointment as Secretary of War (1812) in favor of a commission as Quartermaster General. Promoted to Major General (1813) and assumed command of the Niagara frontier. Used large sums of his own fortune to ransom American prisoners of war held in Canada. President of the Society of the Cincinnati (1839-1844). Name found on ARMY HEROES Staffordshire pitcher (check-list #A.31).

Little, George: (1754-1809) American Revolutionary War naval officer, who took part in Commodore Saltonstall's unsuccessful expedition to Penobscot Bay (1779). Captured by the British in 1781, he escaped from Plymouth prison and fled to France. In 1782, as captain of the sloop *Winthrop*, he captured the entire British force at Penobscot Bay. Commissioned captain of the frigate *USS Boston* in 1799, he captured the French privateer *Deux Anges* (October, 1800) and the French National corvette *Berceau* (October, 1800) during the quasi-war with France. Name appears on the NAVAL MONUMENT transfer (check-list #N.2).

L'Insurgent and Constellation: Naval battle fought February 10, 1799 between the frigate *USS Constellation,* under the command of Thomas Truxton, and the Directory Government of France ship, *L'Insurgent*, under Captain Barreault. The French ship was defeated after a ninety-minute fight off the coast of Nevis and taken as a prize to the port of St. Kitts (check-list #s L.30-L.31).

3.45 James Madison, President of the United States by Gilbert Stuart. Reproduced from *The Dictionary of American Portraits* published by Dover Publications in 1967.

Madison, James: (1751-1836) American revolutionary politician, scholar and fourth President of the United States. Member of the Virginia Legislature (1776-1780 and 1784-1786), Continental Congress (1780-1783), U. S. House of Representatives (1789-1797), U. S. Secretary of State (1801-1809) and President of the United States (1809-1817). Commander in chief during the War of 1812. The same portrait bust is used for both Jefferson (check-list #s J.16 - J.18) and Madison (check-list #M.7) on Liverpool pitchers. Another pitcher with a different portrait is also found on Liverpool, while the name only is found on a Staffordshire mug (check-lists #s M.4 - M.8).

MacDonnough, Thomas: (1783-1825) American naval officer, who accompanied Decatur in the successful raid on **Tripoli** (1804) and commanded the American fleet on Lake Champlain (1812-1814), which defeated and captured the British squadron at the **Battle of Plattsburgh** on September 11, 1814. Scenic view of this battle is found on Staffordshire pitchers (check-list # C.16), which are after a painting by Michel Corne. His name is found on

3.36 Master Commandant Thomas MacDonnough from a print by Reed and Stiles, published in the 1821 volume "*Life of Perry*" by John Niles.

the Staffordshire pitchers containing the names of Naval Heroes and on another with The Naval Monument (check-list #s N.1 and N.2).

Manley, John: (1734-1793) Revolutionary War naval officer, who commanded "Washington's Fleet" (1776), which consisted of six schooners and a brigantine. Captured *HMS Nancy* and other stores vessels, giving the army much needed artillery and other supplies. Commissioned Captain (commission #2) in the Continental Navy and given command of the frigate *Hancock*, 32 guns, which he lost to *HMS Rainbow*, 44 guns, after defeating and capturing *HMS Fox*, 28 guns (1777). Imprisoned in New York and exchanged (1778), he became a privateer and was captured and again imprisoned in Plymouth (1779). Upon his release he assumed command of the frigate *USS Hague* and successfully engaged and escaped from four British vessels (including a 74 gun ship of the line). In 1783, he captured the *Baille*, the last valuable prize taken by a Continental vessel. Name found on the Naval Monument transfer (check-list #N.2).

3.37 Papier mache snuff box with an engraving of Alexander McComb after a painting by Thomas Sully.

McComb, Alexander: (1782-1841) American army officer who was colonel in command of the 3rd artillery at **Sackett's Harbor, New York** (1812). Promoted to Brigadier General (1813) under Izard, he and 4500 men repulsed the invasion of New York by Sir George Prevost. Promoted to Major General for this success, he was named commanding general of the army (following Brown's death on May 29, 1828). Took the field against the Seminoles in Florida (1835) and remained commanding general until his death in 1841. Name found on Army Heroes Staffordshire pitcher (check-list #A.31).

Miller, James: (1776-1851) American army officer, who as a major in the 4th infantry was victorious in the **Battle of Maguaga** (Michigan) against British regulars and the Indian Tecumseh. Present at the capture of **Fort George** by General Dearborn (1813) and distinguished himself at **Chippewa** (July, 1814). Became a National hero, when, at the **Battle of Lundy's Lane**, he was asked by General Winfield Scott if he could capture a British battery, answering simply "I'll try, sir." He did, and the tide of battle turned to favor the Americans. Breveted Brigadier General for his bravery. Name found on Army Heroes Staffordshire pitcher (check-list #A.31).

3.38 James Monroe. Engraved bust rarely found on Paris Porcelain plates (#AIII.19) mugs and cups, which was taken from an engraved medallion portrait of James Monroe, published and engraved by Charles Bance, Paris (1817-1825).

Monroe, James: (1758-1831) American revolutionary politician and fifth President of the United States. Member Continental Congress (1783-1786), U. S. Senator (1790-1794), U. S. Minister to France (1794-1796), governor of Virginia (1799-1802 & 1811), U. S. Minister to England (1803-1807) U. S. Secretary of State (1811-1817), U. S. Secretary of War (1814-1815), President of the United States (1817-1825). Author of "Monroe Doctrine" (1823). Unfortunately, there is no true likeness on either Staffordshire or Liverpool china, but there are two Paris Porcelain likenesses recorded, one on plates, mugs and cups of the period, with a true likeness, recorded (check-list #AIII.19). The other is on a fine urn (check-list #AIII.20). The one portrait bust recorded on a Liverpool pitcher is a "stock" transfer that has been titled "I Baker", "Phillip Crandall" and "Hancock." There are children's mugs with the name recorded (check-list #s M.17, M.20, M.21).

3.39 "The Naval Monument" after a painting by Boston artist J. R. Penniman and engraved by W. B. Annin for the *Naval Monument*. Used by Abel Bowen as the frontispiece for the book, which was published in Boston in 1816. This is the source print for the ceramic view.

Naval Monument: A patriotic engraving after a sketch by J. R. Penniman, which was published as the frontispiece for Abel Bowen's 1816 volume titled *Naval Monument*. The transfer shows "Columbia" driving a pair of horses, carrying the American flag in the foreground, in the background is the monument bearing oval plaques of some named heroes, while the names of others are inscribed on the stone itself. Beneath all this is a wide ribbon containing Perry's message, "We Have Met the Enemy and They Are Ours." Names are Washington, Independence, Manly, Truxton, Jones, Preble, Barron, Little, Barry, Hull, Jones, Decatur, Bainbridge, Stewart, Lawrence, Perry, MacDonnough, Porter, Blakely and Biddle. When possible, biographies of these men are included in this section. This is rarely used as an under the spout decoration on Staffordshire pitchers (check-list #N.2).

3.40 Thomas Paine by Charles Wilson Peale formerly in the Collection of John Lane, London. Present location unknown

Paine, Thomas: (1737-1809) American political philosopher and author of *Common Sense* (1776), which espoused the Revolutionary cause and greatly influenced members of the Continental Congress. Served in Continental Army (1776), published a pamphlet entitled *Crisis* (1776-1783), which upheld the American Cause. Secretary to Congress' Committee of Foreign Affairs (1777-1779) and Clerk of the Pennsylvania Assembly (1779-1781). Wrote *The Rights of Man* (1791-1792) while in England, which urged the overthrow of the monarchy and supported the French Revolution. Expelled from England (1792), arrested and imprisoned in France (1792-1793) and returned to America (1802), after writing *The Age of Reason* in Paris (1794-1796). Last ten years were spent in poverty and ridicule. Likeness and anti-Paine sentiment found on Liverpool pitchers (check-list #s P.1 - P.5).

3.41 Engraved medallion portrait of Oliver Hazard Perry after a painting by Samuel Waldo, engraved by Charles Bance, Paris (1817-1825) for use on papier mache snuff boxes.

Perry, Oliver Hazard: (1785-1819) American naval officer who was ordered to Lake Erie (1813) to construct and man a fleet to control the Lake. Victor of the **Battle of Lake Erie** (September 10, 1813) and in cooperation with General Harrison gained control of the area after the **Battle of the Thames**. Sent the message to Harrison "We have met the enemy and they are ours." Continued on active duty and died of yellow fever while in command of a squadron operating off the coast of Venezuela (1819). Likeness found on Staffordshire pitchers and plates and rarely on Liverpool pitchers (check-list #s P.19-P.26). Also on a porcelain dessert service (AIII.21).

A Picturesque View of the State of the Nation for February, 1778: An anti-embargo satirical print published in the *Westminster Magazine* (1778) depicting the commerce of Britain as a cow having an American (represented by an Indian) shearing her horns, a Dutchman milking her (stealing trade) and sharing the milk with a Spaniard and a Frenchman. In the background is a city labeled Philadelphia with the grounded *HMS Eagle*, the flagship of Admiral Lord Howe, who is represented, along with his brother, drunk and asleep amid a clutter of empty wine bottles. Transfer found on Liverpool pitchers (check-list #P.27).

3.42 "A Picturesque View of the State of the Nation for February, 1778." One of the versions of the anti-Long Embargo satirical cartoons used by the Liverpool potters. This is the source print for P.27.

3.44 Engraving of Zebulon Pike, possibly after a painting by Samuel Waldo and engraved by the artist. Published in the 1821 volume *Life of Perry* by John Niles. Possible source print for check-list #P.28.

3.43 Engraved medallion portrait of Zebulon Pike after a painting by Thomas Gimbrede, engraved by Charles Bance, Paris (1817-1825). This engraving is usually used on papier mache snuff boxes.

Pitt, William, 1st Earl of Chatham: (1708-1778) British politician, often called "the Elder" (Pitt). He provided the leadership which vigorously opposed French expansion and brought about the defeat of France in Canada, India and Africa. His support of naval operations defeated the French navy, which had been contesting British seapower. These policies ultimately laid the foundation for the creation of the British Empire. Collapsed on the floor of Parliament while protesting pacifist policies which led to the military withdrawal from America. He did oppose taxes on the American colonists, which were one of the causes of the Revolution. Portrait found on Liverpool pitchers and plaques (check-list #P.31-P.34).

Pike, Zebulon Montgomery: (1779-1813) American army officer and explorer, who led the expedition to the headwaters of the Mississippi (1805-1806) and to the headwaters of the Arkansas and Red Rivers (1806-1807). Discovered Pike's Peak (1806). As a Brigadier General, he led the assault against **York** (Toronto), Canada. He was killed in this assault (April 27, 1813). Portrait bust found on Staffordshire pitchers and plates (check-list #s P.28-P.30). Also on a porcelain dessert service (AIII.24).

3.45 The Right Honourable William Pitt Esq. a mezzo-tint by J. Spilsbury after a painting by William Hoare. This is the source for the plaque (check-list #s P.31-P.34).

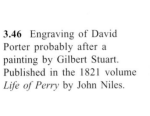

3.46 Engraving of David Porter probably after a painting by Gilbert Stuart. Published in the 1821 volume *Life of Perry* by John Niles.

Porter, David: (1780-1843) American naval officer who, as a midshipman, was with Commodore Truxton when he defeated the French National Frigate *L'Insurgent* (1799) and was later captured with Bainbridge in Tripoli, when the *USS Philadelphia* ran aground (1803). Imprisoned until 1805. Captain of the *USS Essex* in 1812, when on a cruise off New York, he captured nine prizes, including the *HMS Alert* (16 guns). Sailed into the Pacific and ravaged the British whaling fleets for over a year (1813-1814). Entering Valpariso Harbor, he encountered two British ships, which captured him after a storm dismasted the *USS Essex*. After the war, he served as commander-in-chief of the Mexican navy and later as consul-general to Algiers, and minister to Turkey. His son, David Dixon Porter and David Glasgow Porter (his adopted son) were both distinguished naval officers. His name appears on the NAVAL HEROES Staffordshire pitcher and in the NAVAL MONUMENTS transfer (check-list #sN.1 and N.2). There is also a newly discovered porcelain plate and mug with a transfer taken from the Bance engravings (AIII.25)[1].

Porter, Peter: American army officer who was a Major General at the **Battles of Erie** (September 17, 1814), **Chippewa** (July 5, 1814) and **Niagara** (July 25, 1814). Name appears on the American Army Heroes Staffordshire pitcher (check-list #A.31).

3.47 Edward Preble, after a painting by Robert Fulton and engraved by Thomas Kelly. This is the source print used for check-list #P.42.

Preble, Edward: (1761-1807) American naval officer who was commissioned as a midshipman in the Massachusetts navy and served aboard the frigate *Protector,* which was captured by the British. Upon his release from the prison ship *Jersey*, he served under Captain Little aboard the *Winthrop.* Commissioned in the United States Navy as captain in 1799, serving in convoy and anti-pirate duty in the East Indies. In May 1803, as captain of the *USS Constitution* and commander of the U. S. Squadron before Tripoli, he learned of the capture of Captain Bainbridge and the *USS Philadelphia.* He blockaded the city and ultimately burned the *Philadelphia* (raid led by Lt. Stephen Decatur) and bombarded the city. On September 11, 1804, Commodore Barron arrived with reinforcements and assumed command. Preble returned to the United States, where his health declined and he died on August 25, 1807. Portrait bust and battle scene found on Liverpool pitchers (check-list #C.17 and P.40-P.43) and on the NAVAL MONUMENT transfer (check-list #N.2).

Ripley, Eleazer: (1782-1839) American army officer who as colonel commanding the 21st Infantry took part in Pike's assault on **York** (April, 1813) and in General Dearborn's capture of **Fort George** (May 27, 1813). In April, 1814, as a Brigadier General under Jacob Brown, he saw action at **Fort Erie** (July 3, 1813), **Chippewa** (July 5th) and **Lundy's Lane** (July 25th), where Generals Brown and Scott were wounded. He assumed command and withdrew to Fort Erie and was blamed by Brown for not continuing the battle. Name appears on the ARMY HEROES Staffordshire pitcher (check-list #A.31).

Rogers, John: (1773-1838) American naval officer who served under Truxton during the *USS Constellation - L'Insurgent* (1799) battle and commanded the *USS President* when she defeated the *HMS Little Belt* (1811) prior to the actual War of 1812. As ranking officer of the Navy, he commanded squadron patrols in the Atlantic from the Indies to the Cape Verdes islands. In 1815, he was chosen by the President to form the Board of Naval Commissioners, along with Isaac Hull and David Porter. Served briefly as Secretary of the Navy in 1823 and commanded the Mediterranean Squadron (1824-1827). Name found on the NAVAL HEROES Staffordshire pitcher (check-list #N.1).

Scott, Winfield: (1786-1866) American army officer and Presidential Candidate. Brilliant officer who served at **Battle of Queenstown**, Ontario (October 13, 1812), capture of **Fort George** (1813), **Montreal** campaign (1813), **Chippewa** (1813), severely wounded at **Lundy's Lane** (July 25, 1813). After the War of 1812, he took part in the **Black Hawk Wars** (1832), **Second Seminole War** (1836) **Aroostock War** (1838) and the movement of the Indians from the South to the Indian Territory (1838). As Commanding General of the Armies he sent Taylor to Mexico in 1846 and personally planned and commanded the first amphibious invasion of the U.S. Army at **Vera Cruz** (March 9, 1847). Won the **Battle of Cerro Gordo** (April 18th) due to a brilliant flanking movement commanded by Captain Robert E. Lee. Captured **Puebla** (May 15), **Churubusco** (August 20) and **Mexico City** (September 14). Military Governor of Mexico until 1848, when he returned to the United States. Whig Presidential Candidate in 1852, which he lost to Franklin Pierce. In 1855 promoted to Lt. General (a rank last held in 1799). In 1860, just before the Civil War, he attempted to reinforce Southern posts and armories and directed the recruitment and training of the new troops pouring into the Union army.

He retired in November, 1861, having served his nation for over fifty years. Name found on ARMY HEROES Staffordshire pitcher (check-list #A.31) and portrait found on rare Paris Porcelain items (check-list #AIII.26 - AIII.27).

3.48 Engraved medallion portrait of Winfield Scott after a painting by Joseph Wood, engraved by Charles Bance, Paris (1817-1825) for use on papier mache snuff boxes.

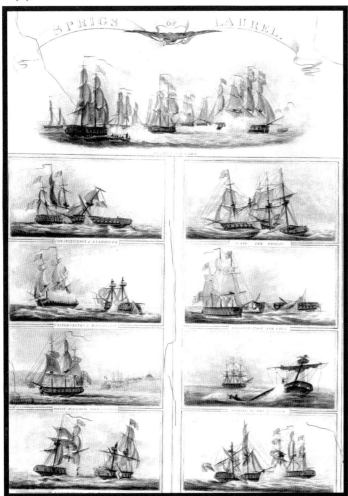

3.49 SPRIGS OF LAUREL an aquatint with nine views of naval engagements drawn and engraved by Strickland and published by Kneas.

Sprigs of Laurel: an aquatint containing nine scenes of various naval battles drawn and engraved by William Strickland and published by John Kneas of Philadelphia. Across the top of the print is PERRY'S VICTORY. Down the left side are CONSTITUTION AND GUERRIERE, UNITED STATES & MACEDONIAN, HORNET BLOCKADING THE BON CITOYENNE and ENTERPRISE AND BOXER. Down the right side are WASP AND FROLIC, CONSTITUTION AND JAVA, SINKING OF THE PEACOCK and PEACOCK AND LEPERVIER. This is the source print used by Davenport for four of the five nautical scenes used on ceramics.

Strong, Caleb: (1745-1819) American revolutionary politician who was a member of the Continental Congress (1787), one of the first two senators from Massachusetts (1789-1796) and Governor of Massachusetts (1800-1807 and 1812-1816). One of the New England politicians who opposed the War of 1812. The following slogan appears on a Liverpool pitcher, THE GRATITUDE OF THE PEOPLE OF MASSACHUSETTS FOLLOWS CALEB STRONG TO NORTH-AMPTON (check-list #S.66), which was probably ordered in 1816, when he left the Governor's office.

3.50 Charles Stewart from a portrait by Gilbert Stuart and engraved by D. Edwin.

Stuart (sic)/Stewart, Charles: (1778-1869) American naval officer who served under Barry and Preble prior to the War of 1812. At the outbreak of the War, he commanded both the *USS Argus* and *USS Hornet*. As captain, in 1813, of the *USS Constitution,* he destroyed several British ships in a year long sweep of the Atlantic. On February 20, 1815, he defeated the *HMS Cyane* (34 guns) and *HMS Levant* (20 guns). After the War, he commanded the European Squadron (1816-1820), the Pacific Squadron (1820-1824) and became a member of the Examining Board (1830-1832). Commanded the Philadelphia Naval Yard (1838-1841, 1846, and again in 1854-1861). Commanded the Home Squadron (1842-1843). Congress promoted him to senior flag officer in 1859. As a side-note, his grandson was Charles Stewart Parnell, the Irish nationalist. Misspelled name appears on the NAVAL HEROES Staffordshire Pitcher (check-list #N.1) and on the NAVAL MONU-MENT Transfer (check-list #N.2).

Success to Our New Governor General Brooks: (?) American Revolutionary army officer and politician who commanded a regiment at the **Battle of Saratoga** (1777), and was a staff officer at the **Battle of Monmouth** (1778). Governor of Massachusetts (1816-1823). Appears on a Liverpool pitcher, the reverse of which concerns outgoing Governor Caleb Strong (check-list #S.70).

Surrender of Cornwallis: Occurred when the combined forces of the Continental Army under Washington-Rochambeau and the French Fleet under DeGrasse, beseiged the British army of the Southern Region under Charles Cornwallis, October 6 through October 19, 1781, at **Yorktown**, Virginia. The scene, which is found on Staffordshire pitchers and rarely on tea services, (check-list #S.84), is taken from a sketch by Robert Fulton, later painted by William Smirke and engraved by James Heath.

3.51 Lt. Colonel Banastre Tarleton in the uniform of the British Legion painted by Sir Joshua Reynolds and engraved by John R Smith, London, 1782. This print was the source of check-list #T.1and T.2. The painting was executed within a year of the Colonel's return from America.

Tarleton, Sir Banastre: (1754-1833) British army officer who accompanied Lord Cornwallis to America (1776), assisted in Clinton's capture of **Charleston** (May, 1780), victorious at the **Battle of Waxhaw Creek** (May, 1780), victorious over Gates at **Camden, S. C.** (August, 1780), victorious at **Catawba Ford** (Fishing Creek) (August, 1780) was defeated by Morgan at **Cowpens** (Jan, 1781). With Cornwallis at **Yorktown** (October, 1781). Commander of the British Legion active in the extremely

cruel war in the South during the Revolution. Portrait appears on Liverpool pitchers (check-list #T.1 - T.3).

3.52 Papier mache snuff box titled OLD ENGLAND RECEIVES PEACE FROM THE VICTORIOUS AMERICA DECEMBER 25TH, 1814. Probably French, this box was made to celebrate the Treaty of Ghent

Treaty of Ghent: Treaty between England and the United States signed December 25, 1814, which ended the War of 1812. Due to the slow communications of the day, **The Battle of New Orleans** (January 8, 1815), the capture of the *USS President* after her defeat of the *HMS Endymion* (January 14, 1815), the defeat of the *HMS Cyane* and *HMS Levant* by the *USS Constitution* (February 20, 1815), and the *USS Hornet*'s defeat of the *HMS Penguin* (March 28, 1815) all took place after the Treaty was signed.

3.53 Captain Thomas Truxton after a painting by Archibald Robinson. Reproduced from *The Dictionary of American Portraits* published by Dover Publications in1967.

Truxton, Thomas: (1755-1822) American Revolutionary naval officer who served as a privateer, then as a Lieutenant on the *Congress, Independence, Mars* and *St. James*, capturing many prizes. Appointed captain in the U. S. Navy in 1794, he assumed the task of constructing and then command of the *USS Constellation* and was Commodore of a squadron based in the Leeward Islands at the outbreak of the quasi-war with France (1799). On February 9, 1799, he defeated the National French Frigate *L'Insurgent* and a year later he outfought the superiorly gunned

French frigate *La Vengeance*, breaking off action when his main mast was sheared. Authored several books on seamanship and tactics. Name appears in the verse of the transfer *L'Insurgent* and *Constellation* (check-list #s L.30-L.31) and on the Naval Monument transfer (check-list #N.2).

3.54 THE U. S. FRIGATE UNITED STATES STEPHEN DECATUR ESQ COMMANDER CAPTURING HIS B. M'S FRIGATE MACEDONIAN OCTOBER 25, 1812. Painted by Thomas Birch engraved by Charles Bance, Paris (1817-1825) for use on papier mache snuff boxes.

United States and Macedonian: Naval battle which took place between the *USS United States* (44 guns), commanded by Captain Stephen Decatur, defeating the *HMS Macedonian* (49 guns) on October 25, 1812. View found on the Staffordshire pitcher is taken from a drawing by Abel Bowen and published in the *Naval Monument* in 1816 (check-list #s M.1-M.2, U.5 and U.9).

Warrington, Lewis: (1782-1851) American naval officer who as Master Commandant was the Captain of the sloop *USS Peacock* when she defeated smaller brig *HMS Lepervier* (April 29, 1814). Later he raided the Grand Banks, Ireland and the Shetland Islands, returning to New York with fourteen prizes (October, 1814). Sailed into the Indian Ocean and captured more prizes, including an East Indiaman, all after the Treaty of Ghent had been signed. Held several ship commands from 1816-1821, the Norfolk Naval yard (1821-1824), commanded the squadron operating against pirates (1824-26). Name appears on the NAVAL HEROES Staffordshire pitcher (check-list #N.1).

Washington, George: (1732-1799) Revolutionary army officer and first President of the United States. Colonel in the Virginia militia during the French and Indian War. Years later, when tensions were developing between the Colonies and England, he was appointed commander of several Virginia militia units and on June 15, 1775, was chosen as Commander in Chief of the Continental Army, a command which he held until the successful conclusion of the Revolution. Once one of the richest men in Virginia, he had taken no pay for the eight years he served as Commander, and his holdings suffered due to his absence. Left the army and proceeded to rebuild his fortune. Selected as presiding officer of the

Federal Constitutional Convention (May, 1787) and later (1789) became the first President of the United States. Built his cabinet adhering to sectional and political balance, and carefully avoided

3.55 Papier mache snuff box with General George Washington from the engraving after a painting by John Trumbull.

setting any potentially harmful precedents or causing any internal strife in his new government. During his second term, division did break out between Jefferson (Democrats) and Hamilton (Federalists) with Washington leaning toward the Federalist views. In March, 1797, he returned to Mount Vernon, but was later appointed as General in Command of the Army by President Adams (see check-list #A.5), when war threatened with France in 1798. A national hero, both during his life and after his death, he remains one of the most monumental figures in the history of the United States. Portraits and name found on enumerable Liverpool and Staffordshire pitchers, tankards, plates and plaques. Also on French porcelain vases and earthenware pieces.

Washington, Martha: (1732-1802) Wife of George Washington. (She had married Daniel Parke Custis in 1749 and he died in 1757.) Through a son from her first marriage (John Parke Custis), she had four grandchildren, two of which were adopted by George Washington, after the death of their father. Portrait appears on Colonial Revival teapots and bowls (check-list #W.62).

Washington, William: (1752-1810) American Revolutionary War army officer, cousin of George Washington. Served during the Long Island campaign (1776) and distinguished himself at **Trenton** (1778). Defeated by Tarleton at **Monk's Corner, S.C.** (1780) and personally fought and wounded Tarleton himself at **Cowpens** (January, 1781), receiving his own wound during the fight. Fought at **Guilford Court House** (March 15, 1781), **Hobkirk's Hill** (April 25, 1781) and **Eutaw Springs** (September 8, 1781), where he was captured. Portrait bust found on that extremely rare Colonial Revival bowl (check-list #W.63).

THE WASP BOARDING THE FROLIC/WASP AND FROLIC: Naval battle which took place on October 18, 1812, when the *USS Wasp,* under Captain Jacob Jones defeated the *HMS Frolic* off Cape Hatteras. There are two views found on Staffordshire pitchers. One, by Enoch Wood and Sons, is after a painting by Michele Corne, engraved and published by Abel Bowen in the *Naval Monument*. (check-list #W.65). The other is by the Davenport firm, which used an unknown source print for it's ceramic view (check-list #W.64).

THE WASP BOARDING THE FROLIC.

3.56 The WASP BOARDING THE FROLIC after a painting by Michele Corne and an engraving by Abel Bowen for the *Naval Monument* published in 1816. This print is the source of the ceramic view by Enoch Wood and Sons.

WASP AND THE REINDEER: Naval battle which took place on June 28, 1814, when the *USS Wasp,* under command of Master Commandant Johnston Blakely, defeated the *HMS Reindeer* off the coast of England. The view, which is found on Staffordshire pitchers, is after a painting by Michele Corne and engraved and published by Abel Bowen in the *Naval Monument* (check-lists #W.66).

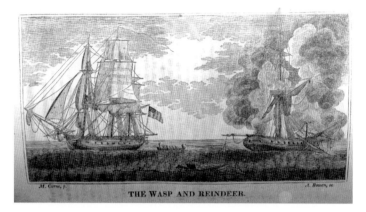

THE WASP AND REINDEER.

3.57 THE WASP AND REINDEER after a painting by Michele Corne and an engraving by Abel Bowen published in the *Naval Monument* in 1816. This is the source print for the ceramic view by Enoch Wood and Sons.

Notes - Chapter Three

[1] Irving S. Olds, on page 427 of *Bits and Pieces of American History,* states that the Bance engraving "as originally published, contained fifteen such medallion portraits as well as the two views of the naval engagements." He illustrated a partial print containing fourteen subjects and listed the following portraits and views, which appeared on the illustration: 1. James Lawrence; 2. Jacob Jones; 3. Robert Fulton; 4. Andrew Jackson 5. Isaac Hull; 6. General Pike; 7. James Monroe; 8. William Bainbridge; 9. Oliver H. Perry; 10. Jonathan Russell *(one of the American negotiators of the Treaty of Ghent)*; 11. Major Gen'l. Brown; 12. Winfield Scott; 13. Constitution and Guerierre and 14. United States and Macedonian. The illustration consisted of three rows of four subjects each and one row containing the two naval battles centered in the sheet. To the casual observer, it seems there should be one more **complete** row of either two or four additional subjects, for a total of either sixteen or eighteen subjects.

In our own collection, we have thirteen of the Bance engravings, including all of those mentioned, with the exception of: 4. Andrew Jackson; 7. James Monroe and 10. Jonathan Russell. We do have two that Olds does not list, which are Isaac Chauncey and Stephen Decatur. This would bring the total number of subjects to sixteen.

While examining the magnificent collection at Winterthur, we discovered that Juliet Chase, an assistant curator in the Decorative Arts Department, had discovered two heretofore unknown portraits, which came from this same Bance engraving. They are David Porter and George Washington. This brings the total to sixteen portrait busts and two naval engagements. Originally used to decorate the covers of paper mache snuff boxes, this group of prints also served as the source for the decorations on a lovely French porcelain dessert service and fine vases, manufactured for the American market.

Chapter Four
Valuation

Elements Contributing to Value

There are several elements one must evaluate when attempting to arrive at a monetary value for any piece of historical ceramics. We do not expect you to agree with us on all the following points (because we don't even agree upon them between ourselves). The relative value of a piece of Liverpool or Staffordshire lies strictly in the minds of the seller and more importantly, the buyer. No matter which side of the fence you are on, you should consider the following factors when attempting to determine the value of a piece.

    1. transfer or subject - this <u>IS</u> the most important element in the whole equation.

    2. damage - some damage is more damaging than others.

    3. ground - this can raise the value considerably, depending on type of ground and type of ware.

    4. form - this can increase the value if it is not the norm.

    5. transfer color - once again, this can increase the value, if it is not the norm.

    6. polychrome decoration - a massive increase in value, if it is not the norm.

    7. size - overly large or extremely small, increases the value.

As you can see from this listing, anything outside the norm can change the value of a piece. To arrive at the *approximate* value of an item, one should take into account everything listed above. In order to simplify this a bit, we have reduced the thought process to a simple arithmetic model, which looks like this:

$$
\begin{array}{rl}
 & \mathbf{T}\text{(transfer value)} \\
- & \mathbf{D}\text{(damage)} \\
\hline
\times & \mathbf{G}\text{(ground)} \\
\hline
+ & \mathbf{F}\text{(form)} \\
+ & \mathbf{T}\text{(transfer color)} \\
+ & \mathbf{P}\text{(polychrome transfer)} \\
\hline
= & \mathbf{Value}
\end{array}
$$

If math isn't your strong suite, don't panic, we are only using this "addition-subtraction" model as a rough guide. After reading this

Chapter, you can use whatever framework you desire, to systematically examine each of these factors and arrive at some sort of "ball-park" value. We hope this will help the beginning collector, and those of you who are now buying or selling, to determine a rough value for any given piece. Let us now examine each of these criterion in detail, so you can see how we use them in arriving at a monetary value.

4.1 "THE FARMER'S ARMS" black transfer on a Liverpool creamware body. These Guild transfers add little value to American view pitchers

Transfers - Value

While no piece of Liverpool or Historical Staffordshire one may encounter is considered common, some will be found more frequently than others. Also, for our purposes, some transfers have little value. Those include the following:

    1. Genre scenes
    2. Classical scenes
    3. Masonic decorations
    4. Arms of the various Guilds
    5. Generic ship transfers
    6. Sentimental subjects
    7. Religious subjects

Basically, anything which does not touch upon the political or historical happenings of the period from 1760 - 1830. While we are mostly concerned with those events pertaining to America, the military and political transfers which concern England's ongoing battle with the rest of Europe, often impacted upon events in the Americas. Thus, we have included transfers of English military and political figures who influenced events in the American colonies. England was at war during much of the period, from the

French and Indian War to the final defeat of Napoleon at Water-loo, (our War of 1812 was considered to have given aid and comfort to Napoleon during this struggle). Some familiarity with the history of the period is important, so you will be able to identify those Europeans who had an impact on American history.

In the matter of American historical subjects, we have assigned an arbitrary value "factor" to each of the recorded views listed in Chapter Five. This is strictly our opinion as to the relative value of a transfer *vis a vis* the other listed pieces. Before you are able to use these factors, you should have enough experience in the field to determine the **current** pricing for a cross-section of the views.

In our experience, the transfers to which we have assigned a value factor of 1.0, are those that are considered common or plentiful within the field. By attending a few auctions or pricing a few pieces at antiques shows and shops, one should be able to determine the current valuation for these items. For example: if a 1.0 transfer is being quoted and/or sold for $1,000.00, then a piece with a factor of 1.5 should be valued at $1,500.00 and a piece with a factor of 2.0 should be valued at $2,000.00. However, just like the New York Stock Exchange, the value of antiques fluctuates. It does not remain constant.

But wait! These pitchers have more than one transfer....they have two or three or sometimes four or more. How does one determine the value of this? It isn't easy. For the next step, let's assume the piece has two transfers and once again, 1.0 equals $1,000.00.

Transfer #1 is listed in Chapter Five with a value factor of 5.0 and transfer #2 is listed with a value factor of 1.2. **In Our opinion,** the piece is worth $5,000.00 to $6,000.00, with the true value towards the lower number. Why? Because the collector will usually only be interested in the more rare of the two transfers and will totally discount the second. Usually this maxim will hold true in the majority of cases when the value of one transfer is high and the other is low. When both transfers are rated from 1.0 to 2.0, the highest value of the two, will equal the value for both. A combination of a 1.0 and a 1.0 is valued at 1.0. Sorry, but that is the way the real world operates in the field of historical transferware. If you have three transfers on a piece that list at 1.0, 1.5 and 2.0, the value lies around the 2.0 range.

Let's venture into a different category, that of TWO definite rarities. The **DEFENSE OF STONINGTON** (check-list #G.1) is considered quite rare and very desirable. It is sometimes found with a transfer of a ship titled **UNITED STATES FRIGATE GUERRIERE, COMMODORE MACDONNOUGH, BOUND TO RUSSIA, JULY 1818** (check-list #U.6) on the reverse. As you can see by checking in

4.2 The rare "GUERRIERE" and "DEFENSE OF STONINGTON" pitcher, which we rate as having a value of $25,500.00. The "GUERRIERE" transfer is polychromed, but that is normal, therefore there is no added value. (See Chapter Two).

Chapter Five, the **STONINGTON** is rated at a whopping 18.0 and the **GUERRIERE** at a strong 15.0. Once again, using 1.0 as a value of $1,000.00, the immediate value of this piece is at least $18,000.00. In our opinion, in cases like these, you take the highest value and add it to one-half the value of the second transfer (only if that transfer has a value factor of over 2.0). So in our mind, this particular combination on a <u>perfect</u> piece is worth approximately $25,500.00.

Rarity Scale

It is really impossible to determine just how many of these pieces of historical china have survived. We use the rarity scale below to reflect over twenty-five years of experience within the field and do not attest to it's complete accuracy. It is our hope that this book will lead to the listing of examples which we have not encountered in our references and personal experiences. In Chapter Five, we have listed **our opinion** of the relative rarity of each transfer according to this scale:

> *plentiful/common* - over fifty examples probably exist
> *scarce* - thirty to fifty examples probably exist
> *rare* - twenty to thirty examples probably exist
> *very rare* - ten to twenty examples probably exist
> *extremely rare* - one to ten examples probably exist
> *unique* - **one to three examples actually recorded by the authors**. This is a transitory rarity classification and will change as more examples are recorded by the authors and others interested in this field.

We have already taken into account the effect of rarity **and** desirability of a particular transfer in those value factors which we assigned the individual transfers in Chapter Five. One must keep in mind, that a transfer that is listed as *unique*, while so very, very rare, may have a very low desirability quotient, which means no one particularly wants an example in their collection. This lack of interest most certainly affects the value. So, using the values we have assigned in Chapter Five, you can ascertain the "**T**" value in our model.

Damage - Value

Damage, no matter how you look at it, is a minus. There is NO way a piece with damage can have the same value as a perfect piece (all other factors being equal), unless the buyer desires the piece so much, they must have it at an inflated price, in spite of the damage. The following are the figures we use when determining the value of a damaged item:

an unseen chip	-5% - 10%
a visible spout, rim or base chip	-10% - 20%
a faint hairline	-10% - 20%
a crack	-15% - 25%
stain/mellowing (with gold enamel on the body, which will be lost when cleaned)	-5% - 20%
stain/mellowing (w/o gold)	-5%
a crack which affects the **major transfer**	-30% - 50%
a crack which affects the **lesser transfer**	-20% - 40%
multiple scratches through the **transfer**	-40% - 60%
transfer mutilated by scratches	-50% - 80%
missing handle or spout	-30% - 50%
missing bottom (exterior sides not effected)	-30% - 50%
a faded transfer (depending on severity)	-20% - 80%
restoration that includes **painting in the transfer** or the **transfer title** of the view	-50% - 80%

When addressing the subject of condition, it is obvious we feel the condition of the transfer itself is the single most important item. These pieces were used in a sometimes raucous environment, which made the possibility of damage almost a certainty.

Repairs and restorations are often found on these fragile pieces. We have listed below our definition of the terms and the effect each has on value:

repair - this is an amateurish attempt to camouflage the damage and is obvious. It adds nothing to the value of a piece and may even detract from the value.

restoration - same as a repair, but done by someone with some training. The damage is usually only partially hidden. Once again little or no added value.

professional restoration - should be almost totally invisible with a great color match. Can add between 10% to 25% of what you subtracted for the original damage, depending on expertise.

invisible professional restoration - totally invisible, so that one absolutely can not tell, what, if anything has been done to the piece. This quality of restoration is as rare as a perfect rarity. Can add up to 50% of what you subtracted for the original damage.

One modifier to the subject of restoration. In our opinion, we have never seen a totally invisible professional restoration to the transfer itself. If the transfer is damaged, the value of the piece, no matter how rare it is, suffers. This mythical rarity can be minus handle and spout with the bottom broken out and have decent value as long as the transfer is strong, black and unaffected. Once the transfer is damaged, the piece suffers. This is the "**D**" which we use in our model.

Grounds - Value

Grounds are the color of the body of a piece, *__as artificially modified by the potter__*. We have already determined in Chapter Two, that creamware has a cream-colored body with a clear glaze. Pearlware has been defined as having a pure white body, with a slight blue tint to the glaze. **Liverpool** items have so far only been found with three artificial grounds. They are:

1. Applied yellow-glaze (canary). Extremely rare, this will increase the value of a common transfer by a factor of 500%. It will effect a rare transfer by a factor of 700%. For example, if you have a Liverpool pitcher with two transfers rated at a 1.0, your value would normally be $1,000.00 (once again assuming that is your market's current rate). However, if it has a yellow-glazed body, this common piece suddenly becomes something very special and the value shoots from $1,000.00 to between $5,000.00 and $10,000.00.

2. The second ground (we know of four examples in Liverpool) is a robin's egg blue enamel. Usually found with a black transfer and applied gilding, this ground, while not particularly attractive, would raise the value of a common piece by a factor of 700% to 1000%.

3. The final Liverpool ground is an overall Sunderland pink splash lustre, recorded on only a very few pitchers. This attractive coloration would also raise the the value by 700% to 1000%.

4.3 One of only three recorded Liverpool pitchers with the rare robins egg blue enamel ground.

The subject of grounds on the **Staffordshire** pitchers is far more complex and varied. There are two types of these grounds, "all-over" and "partial", leaving the area where the transfers are placed the original white of the body. These grounds are, in order of rarity:

4.4 "PIKE BE ALWAYS READY TO DIE FOR YOUR COUNTRY" black transfer on a **LIVERPOOL** pitcher. Extremely rare ground and a rare instance of a War of 1812 subject on a Liverpool form.

1. Applied, somewhat unattractive, red/maroon enamel around white ovals, containing a black transfer over a white body, and having a collar of pink splash Sunderland lustre. (one recorded).

2. Buff-color body with a medium blue band around the collar, and a black transfer applied on the buff body. An extremely rare and attractive combination that is often seen on pitchers with genre scenes. We only have three examples recorded in historical ceramics, but there are

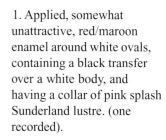

4.5 "THE WASP BOARDING THE FROLIC" Staffordshire pitcher with a buff ground and a blue band around the collar.

probably more. We believe this ground would raise the value by 600%.

3. Pale yellow-cream body usually with a rust-red,

4.6 "JAMES LAWRENCE, ESQ *LATE OF THE UNITED STATES NAVY*" on a Staffordshire pitcher with a pale yellow ground and a wide purple lustre band. Maroon transfer.

maroon or black transfer. Occurs occasionally with a transfer of either Lawrence or Jay. An unknown number exists. Not especially attractive. This ground would probably not influence the value of the piece.

4. Applied Sunderland "pink splash lustre" around white ovals. This is one ground you either think is gorgeous or garish. There are less than fifteen known examples.

However, we expect more to be recorded with the publication of this book. In **our** opinion, this ground would raise the value of a piece by a factor of 600%.

5. Applied yellow enamel around white ovals containing black transfers and having a collar of pink Sunderland splash lustre. Mrs. Larsen records less than a dozen, but we are aware of several others that have been "discovered" recently. This ground would raise the value of a pitcher by a factor of 500%.

6. Canary yellow enamel around white ovals containing black transfers and **without** the pink lustre collar. This ground would raise the value by a factor of 500%.

7. Overall yellow-glazed (canary) body with a black transfer. However, there are several transfers normally found with this ground that are not considered unusual, and the value does not change. They are (using the numbering system from Chapter Five):

4.7 "CAPT. JONES OF THE MACEDONIAN" with a black transfer and canary yellow enamel ground with pink splash lustre collar.

A.14   AMERICA
M.14   MAY THE TREE OF LIBERTY EVER FLOURISH
P.9   PEACE AND PROSPERITY TO AMERICA
S.4   SEAL OF THE UNITED STATES
S.8   SEAL OF THE UNITED STATES
S.80   SUCCESS TO THE UNITED STATES OF AMERICA

Any view other than those listed above with this overall yellow-glaze ground is extremely rare and would raise the value of the piece by a factor of 500%.

8. Applied "apple-green" enamel around white ovals containing black transfers and having a collar of pink splash Sunderland lustre. This is the most common of these uncommon applied enamel grounds, but is still extremely difficult to obtain. In

our opinion, it is also the most attractive and pleasing of the color combinations. This ground would raise the value of a pitcher by a factor of 400%.

9. Applied green enamel ground surrounding white ovals containing black transfers. No pink lustre band on the collar. This would raise the value of a pitcher by a factor of 400%.

4.8 "THE ESCAPE OF THE CONSTITUTION...ETC", a black transfer with a white oval surrounded by an apple-green ground. The collar has a pink splash Sunderland lustre band.

10. Overall buff colored (light tan) body with a black

4.9 "ARMY HEROES", a maroon transfer on an overall buff ground. Pink lustre band around the lip. This transfer color and ground are the norm for this transfer.

transfer. May have pink or copper lustre highlights. This is the most common artificial ground that the collector will encounter. It would raise the value of a piece by a factor of 150%.

11. No ground. White pearlware or creamware body with a black transfer with black enamel or lustre highlights.

As you can see, the "**G**" factor can have a pronounced effect on the value of a transfer.

Forms - Value

Liverpool usually contains one distinctive group of transfers and Staffordshire another. When one of these transfers appears on an unusual form, this increases the value of the piece. As we stated in Chapter Two, the subject matter of Liverpool usually deals with the period from 1760 to 1820, with the emphasis on the people and events of the Revolution and the early Republic. One would therefore expect to find such subjects as Washington, Adams, Jefferson, Monroe and

4.10 "PERRY   WE HAVE MET THE ENEMY AND THEY ARE OURS", black **War of 1812 subject** on a classic **Liverpool** pitcher.

Madison on these forms. The presidential term of Madison marked the end of the creamware period. The War of 1812 marked the rise of Staffordshire pearlware, and this ware dominated the industry throughout the 1830's to 1850's. A few of the events of the War of 1812 are normally found on Liverpool and do not merit any adjustment in value due to the form. They are:

4.11 "AMERICA WHO'S MILITIA...ETC", usually found on Liverpool with a black transfer, shown here with a lavender transfer on a **Staffordshire** pitcher.

B.2. WILLIAM BAINBRIDGE
D.4 - D.6. COMMODORE DECATUR FREE TRADE..ETC.
G.1. THE GALLENT DEFENSE OF STONINGTON
P.22. O. H. PERRY, ESQ.
P.23. COMMODORE PERRY
P.24. PERRY
P.25. O. H. PERRY
M.1. UNITED STATES AND MACEDONIAN
M.2. UNITED STATES AND MACEDONIAN
U.6. UNITED STATES FRIGATE GUERRIERE, COMMODORE MACDONNOUGH BOUND TO RUSSIA JULY 1818

In our opinion any other transfer relating to the War of 1812 found on a Liverpool form would be considered an extreme rarity. This would raise the value by a factor of 200% to 300%, depending on the desirability of the transfer. The converse is also true. Any transfer normally found on a Liverpool pitcher, that is discovered on a Staffordshire form, rates the same raise in value of 200% to 300%.

On Staffordshire War of 1812 pitchers, only rarely is there a transfer under the spout. These are normally found with only two side transfers. Add an additional 25%, plus the value of the third transfer (in accordance with the rules set forth on the second page of this Chapter, describing the procedures for dealing with more than one transfer on a piece), for one of these rare combinations. Also, in Staffordshire pitchers which relate to the portrait busts of the commodores and the sea battles, the combination usually found is sea battle / sea battle and commodore / commodore. Only rarely are the two mixed with a commodore on one side and a sea battle on the other. In our opinion, this really doesn't affect value, but we think it is an interesting observation.

Transfer Colors - Value

The normal transfer color for both Liverpool and Staffordshire forms is black. There are exceptions to this statement, such as the cup plates with LAFAYETTE AND WASHINGTON (check-list #L.13) or the JACKSON, HERO OF NEW ORLEANS (check-list #J.6) cup plates, which are found in red as often as black. For the advanced collector, who has one color and not the other, this might increase the desirability of a piece as much as 10% to 20%, but for most, it is of little consequence.

Applied Polychromed Decoration - Value

The application of polychrome enamels to the transfer was discussed in Chapter Two, where we listed the Liverpool views

4.12 A War of 1812 subject highly polychromed in red, green, grey, yellow, blue and ochre, "ARMS OF THE UNITED STATES". This IS the norm for this particular transfer.

which are normally found with color. Any Liverpool view not found on this list, that has color decoration, is considered extremely rare. This would affect the value by 300% to 400%. There are a very small group of War of 1812 pitchers with portrait busts, that have a yellow or green ground with the portrait transfer highlighted in flesh, blue, yellow, green and brown. These are rare, rare, rare! They would command a premium, using a factor of 300% to 700% over the base value of an undecorated transfer of the same bust. The value of the ground would not bear on this scenario, since all recorded examples have an enamel ground.

Under this category of applied decoration, there is a special instance related to plates. Liverpool and Staffordshire plates with American historical views are quite rare. The Liverpool variety normally has only a black transfer with some type of floral transfer on the shoulder. The vast majority of these plates do not have enamel decoration, except for "ship" transfers (where this is the norm), and those that do, should be considered very rare and their value raised by a factor of 250%. As to the Staffordshire plates, they are normally pearlware with a blue enamel feather edge. However, there are two examples of "Pike" (check-list #P.29) that are not the norm. One is a *creamware* plate with a border of green leaves and red berries. The other Pike plate has a pink Sunderlund splash lustre band enclosing a more narrow canary yellow band. Both of these are very rare and their value should be raised by 250%. Should these or other unusual border decorations be found on a Staffordshire War of 1812 plate, the value would raise by 300%+. We have never seen a polychromed bust on a War of 1812 plate.

4.13 "HULL" (untitled) black transfer within a white oval surrounded by a canary yellow ground, with the transfer highlighted in blue, yellow, flesh, green and brown enamels. Plain white body around the collar.

To summarize, the color used on the transfer would normally not affect the value "**T**" of our model, all that much, while a polychromed highlight applied to the transfer, "**P**" would give a significant rise in value.

Size - Value

Liverpool creamware pitchers normally are found in a size range of 6"h to 13"h, with 13"h considered quite large. Staffordshire pitchers are usually smaller, with the sizes ranging between 4"h to 10"h, with a 10"h considered very big. Anything smaller or larger than the above heights should be regarded as a rarity, subject to a value adjustment. How much of an adjustment is rather complex, with a Liverpool piece considerably smaller than 6"commanding a raise in value of over 150%. The same would hold true if it is considerably larger than 13"h. Of course, if it also contains multiple historical transfers, the value would be a great deal higher. Should a Staffordshire pitcher of less than 3"h be discovered, it would also rise in value by a factor of 150%+. A Staffordshire pitcher of 13"h or more would increase in the same amount. There are Liverpool pitchers known in the 15"h to 20"h size. Several of these giants are recorded and three are illustrated in this volume (see 2.16a/b, 2.17a/b/c, and 2.18a/b). All three are considered "unique".

4.14

The Equation of Value

Now to attempt to make sense of all these modifiers of value, so that you can quickly come to a range of value for the piece you are contemplating purchasing. Let's walk through a complex example: illustrated above is a common Liverpool pitcher with the common "glebe" transfer (check-list #L.23). In creamware with a black transfer it is worth $1,000.00 (we're using 1.0 = $1,000.00 for simplicity). For the purposes of our example, the reverse has a simple "ship" print, which adds nothing to the value of the piece. So in this case **T** is $1,000.00.

Let's assume it has a star-crack in the bottom, which will have us subtract 15% or $150.00, leaving us a value of $850.00 ($1,000.00 - $150.00 = $850.00).

However, it seems this crack has been invisibly restored, so we should add approximately 75% of the $150.00 we subtracted. So in this case, **D** is only minus $50.00.

Next we note that it has a yellow-glaze ground. Wow! Take that $950.00 and multiply it by the minimum factor of 500%. So in this example, **G** is a 5.

Then we check to see if this transfer is commonly found on the Liverpool shape. Yes, this is normal, so the **F** is zero.

Finally, we remember to check out whether there is a presence of polychrome decoration (there isn't, so **P** is zero), or a transfer in a really weird color (no, it's black, so **T** is also zero). So our model looks like this

$1,000.00	T
- $50.00	D
$950.00	
x 5	G
$4,750.00	V

So, our little yellow-glaze Liverpool pitcher with a minimal transfer value of a 1.0 and a restored base crack, is not so common after all. The value is approximately $4,500.00 to $5,000.00. Please note, this example is purely hypothetical, since we do not record a "Glebe" transfer with a canary ground.

A Final Word Concerning Valuation

We could write many more pages on the subject of value, but after all is said and done, it really comes down to a simple axiom - the only value of ***anything*** is what the market is willing to pay. If you are attempting to sell an extremely rare piece of historical ceramics and you only have one customer interested, the value is dramatically lower than if you have many buyers, all convinced they *must* have the piece. The antiques market is one of the last truly "free markets" in the Capitalistic system, which is totally free of any controls and interference. Only "the market" knows the true value of any given item. The deeper the pool of collectors, the higher the demand and thus the higher the price. A shallow pool of collectors means a dead or dying market. A sobering fact, but unfortunately so very true.

Grounds - Liverpool

4.15

4.15 Left: Extremely rare blue enamel ground on a Liverpool pitcher.

4.16 Right: Extremely rare yellow-glaze (canary) ground on a Liverpool pitcher.

4.16

Grounds - Staffordshire

4.17

4.17 Left: The most common ground is plain **Buff**, which is the color of this rare and massive pitcher with an unusual shell-form handle under the spout. This was placed there to assist in pouring, since the weight, when full of liquid, would place an undue strain on both the handle and the person pouring. **4.18 Right:** This is the **Pale Yellow** ground, which, while rather rare, is not especially attractive and does not really add to the value of the piece.

4.18

4.19 Below Left: This is the extremely rare and lovely **Buff** body with medium **Blue Band** around the collar. It rarely occurs on Historical ceramics and in the three cases we have recorded, it is highlighted with pink lustre bands. **4.20 Below Right:** The applied **Pink Splash Lustre** ground is another rarity, with only a few examples on Liverpool and only two recorded on Staffordshire. Some think this is garish and unattractive (one of the authors) and others think it is gorgeous (the male of the two authors). This is the third Liverpool ground. It has been recorded on pitchers with a Liverpool shape, barrel shape and Staffordshire shape. Also, one tankard is known. All the recorded pieces have a black transfer within an oval or round medallion as is found on the barrel-shaped pearlware pitcher illustrated here.

4.19

4.20

49

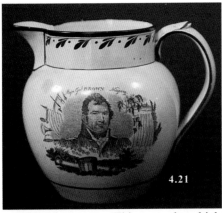

4.21 Left: This typical Staffordshire pitcher has an overall **Yellow-glazed (canary)** ground over the entire body, with a black transfer. While there are several views that are usually found with this ground, (and thus the value is not affected), this pitcher with MAJOR GEN'L BROWN is quite unusual and worth 500% more than the same transfer on a white body. **4.22** Right: A very unusual **Apple-green** ground which normally occurs with either a pink splash lustre collar (see below) or a plain white collar, and has the transfer within a white oval/circular reserve. This example, which has the rare transfer of "THE HORNET BLOCKADING THE BON CITOYENNE", has an *octagonal* white reserve and a *green ground collar*. This is the only recorded example with these eccentricities.

4.23 Left: Here is the very rare **Canary yellow** enamel ground with the normal oval reserve and plain white collar. **4.24** Right: One of the loveliest of the different ground combinations is this **Apple-green** with **Pink Sunderland splash lustre** collar. Considered the most common of the applied ground combinations, it is still highly desirable and will bring a premium of 300% over a typical Staffordshire pearlware pitcher with a common white body. The transfer on this particular example is "THE ENTERPRISE AND BOXER."

4.25 Left: An extremely rare **Canary yellow** enamel ground with **Pink Sunderland splash lustre** collar. This is a prime rarity and very few are recorded. However, when placed next to the piece on the right, it somewhat pales in comparison. **4.26** Right: An extremely rare **Canary yellow** enamel ground Staffordshire pitcher with an even more rare *polychromed* portrait bust of "CAPTAIN HULL OF THE CONSTITUTION." A top of the line rarity, the only thing one could wish for, would be the attractive pink Sunderland lustre collar. The black enamel highlights do add to the beauty of the piece, as they serve to really set-off the various colored enamels. This combination would raise the value 5 to 10 times that of a typical white bodied Staffordshire pitcher, with the identical transfer.

The three rounded copper lustre pitchers to the right, all have the "CORNWALLIS SURRENDERING HIS SWORD" transfer, but two have the typical canary enamel band around the center, while the third has a rust colored band. These are the normal colors found on copper lustre pitchers with this transfer in either the rounded or the "slant-sided" shape illustrated below.

4.27 4.28 4.29

4.30

Those pitchers, with the transfer of "ANDREW JACKSON HERO OF NEW ORLEANS" are sometimes found in the rounded shape, but usually in the slant-sided form illustrated. The "JACKSONS" normally have either a blue band **4.30** or a canary band **4.31**. Any other colored band on these copper lustre pitchers, with these transfers, would be considered unusual and therefore more valuable.

4.31

4.32

4.32 Left: One of the many varieties of form found with the "HARRISON" and "TO LET IN 1840" transfers. The enamel bands on this group include not only the tan example illustrated, but also canary, blue and plain white. The transfers are usually black, magenta or rarely, green. **4.33** Right: This untitled transfer of HIS EXCELLENCY GEORGE WASHINGTON ESQ. is normally found on Liverpool. This is the only example we have recorded on a copper lustre Staffordshire pitcher. It is untitled. It is quite large, being over 8"h.

4.33

4.34

4.34 Left: The Enoch Wood version of the GENERAL PIKE plate is normally found with a typical blue feather edge. The pearlware example on the left has a mixed ground of **Pink Sunderland splash lustre** encircling another ground of **Canary yellow** enamel. **4.35** Right: This is a creamware plate with a "PIKE" transfer enclosed by a green and brown decoration of leaves with bright red berries. Reminiscent of the earlier Wedgwood creamware plates, this is a most attactive variation.

4.35

51

Transfer Colors - Liverpool

4.36

4.37

While black is the normal color of the Liverpool and Staffordshire transfers, there are some exceptions. **4.36** Left: This very rare tankard bears a common transfer that is usually only found on pitchers and sometimes on bowls. In **Rust-red** on a *tankard* makes it very special...to the tune of two to three times the value of the same transfer on a pitcher. **4.37** Right: Here we have illustrated a **Red** transfer on a Liverpool pitcher. The verse is previously unrecorded and is the only known example, however, the red transfer, in this particular case, would not add to its already considerable value.

4.38 Below Left: A wonderful Liverpool creamware tankard with a War of 1812 transfer in bright **Orange**. **4.39** Below Center: An unusual combination of a "silver resist" collar, with orange highlights and a **Mulberry** transfer. **4.40** Below Right: Another very unusual *Liverpool* Transfer on a *Staffordshire* pitcher in a **Lavender** transfer. The medium blue enamel highlights are lovely. There are only two recorded examples of this piece.

4.38

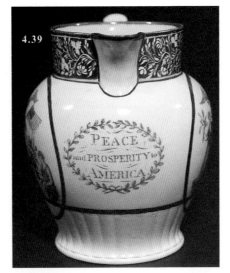

4.39

4.40

Transfer Colors - Staffordshire

4.41

Once again, black is the normal color of the transfers found on Staffordshire historical ceramics, with the few exceptions mentioned in the text. However, other than the fact that the example on the right is a recent marked *reproduction*, these pitchers are identical in form, size, transfer and transfer color. Note how the color of the ground affects the transfer (which really is the same **brick-red**). On the left it indeed looks **brick-red** (**4.41**), while the ground of the repro on the right (**4.42**) has changed the color to a **Bright red.**

4.42

52

4.43 Left: To find this **Brownish-red** transfer of a portrait bust of CAPT. HULL OF THE CONSTITUTION on a Staffordshire pitcher, especially one with a rare **Green ground,** is extremely rare. This is definitely one of those pieces mentioned in the text, that an advanced collector would consider an invaluable addition to his/her collection. **4.44** Right: The **Orange** "LAFAYETTE CROWNED" transfer on a tiny bowl, is unusual because of transfer color *and* the **Blue** and **Yellow polychrome** highlights found <u>on</u> the transfer. The enameled embossed animals around the rim are also a value enhancer.

4.45 Left: On this very unusual example, the potter used the same lustre enamel used for the "free hand" decoration for the transfer, resulting in an extremely rare **Pink lustre** transfer. **4.46** Right: Although this transfer color may appear to be the same as that on the left, it does not contain the metallic additives to the enamel which produce the lustre. In this case, it is termed **Carmine** and is a fired enamel paint. When examined side by side, one has a metallic sheen and the other an enamel sheen.

Polychrome Decoration - Liverpool

Three examples of Liverpool creamware with a typical black transfer, highlighted by the application of various colored enamels. In Chapter Two, we listed several transfers, where polychrome decoration is the norm and thus does not effect the value. All three of these transfers, two of which are quite desirable, fall into this catagory. **4.47** The UNITED STATES FRIGATE GUERRIERE, COMMODORE MACDONNOUGH BOUND FOR RUSSIA, 1816, on the far left and **4.49** the BOSTON FUSILEER on the far right are both quite valuable. **4.48** The HOPE plate in the center, while quite attractive, does not receive the same amount of attention from the collector. Therefore it is considerably less valuable.

4.50

Polychrome Decoration - Liverpool (continued)

On the other hand, here we have two examples where common transfers have been poly-chromed, thus adding a factor of 300% to 700% to the value. **4.50** Left: Occasionally this BY VALOR AND VIRTUE transfer is found with a bit of green or red enamel splashed on it. This particular example has wonderful shades of pale blue, brown, light green , ochre, red and yellow that bring it to the realm of "art". **4.51** Right: Transfers don't get much more common than the GLEBE transfer shown here. However, this has red, green, brown and yellow enamel highlights, which make it a prime rarity. It is the only example we have recorded.

4.51

4.52

4.52 Left: Dated "1784" this polychromed transfer of BAN. TARLETON ESQ^R is another example of the striking use of color employed by the British potters. Since this is the only recorded example of this piece, we don't know if all such transfers were decorated with color. **4.53** Right: This transfer has been identified by Drakard as THE IRISH VOLUNTEERS, who were pressed into service in Ireland during the American Revolution, to replace troops bound for the rebellious colonies. However, the other examples we have seen, have the soldiers in either green or red, which are British uniform colors. These are in Blue Continental colors, and are on the reverse of a BY VIRTUE AND VALOR transfer obviously made for the American market. From this we assume the potter intended to show Americans, using a stock transfer.

4.53

Polychromed Decoration - Staffordshire

4.54

The Staffordshire potters did not apply polychrome decoration very often, except on the example on the left **4.54**. This particular transfer, ARMS OF THE UNITED STATES, is normally enamel decorated. **4.55** Right: This beautifully decorated Staffordshire pitcher is another transfer normally found on Liverpool pitchers, that is also titled ARMS OF THE UNITED STATES. The biggest difference in this rarity is the lovely application of the multitude of vivid enamels, resulting in a rare and beautiful pitcher.

4.55

4.56

4.56 Left: This very rare plate has the typical blue feather edge, but the potter has applied a varied palette of delicate polychrome colors to the black transfer INDEPEN-DENCE, JULY 4TH 1776. **4.57** Right: This great rarity, THE LANDING OF LAFAYETTE is always found with this exemplary polychromed decoration, which appears to have been executed by a very talented artist. That is probably the reason for it's rarity, since it would have been quite time consuming to complete, and therefore very expensive to purchase.

4.57

4.58   4.59   4.60   4.61

Above (**4.58, 4.59, 4.60, 4.61**) and Right (**4.62, 4.63, 4.64**): All of the Staffordshire plates illustrated here are shown as they would *normally* be found. The various colored transfers of blue, orange, red and black are normal, and as such, their color would not increase the value. The applied enamel decorations that highlight the embossing on the borders are also normal, and should not be considered, when determining value.

4.62   4.63   4.64

4.65   4.66   4.67

4.68   4.69

Left and above: This group of Staffordshire plates illustrate the variety of colors found in the various SEALS OF THE UNITED STATES. **4.65** The red transfer in the upper left, has a blue feather edge and is impressed ADAMS. **4.66** The "buzzard"-type eagle next to it is considered quite rare, as is the "long-winged" eagle above (**4.67**) . **4.68** The "yellow" eagle on the far left is rated as "scarce", while **4.69** the green feather edge variety next to it is the version most commonly found. On these plates, the Staffordshire potters normally made liberal use of the entire spectrum of enamel colors.

4.70

4.71

4.72

The three Paris Porcelain vases above are exceptional examples executed with a great amount of skill and talent. Above left: **4.70** This rarity has a portrait bust of President John Adams. Above center: **4.71** This urn is the reverse of a portrait bust of a young Winfield Scott. The lavender and green combination is especially attractive. Above right: **4.72** Undoubtedly made to commemorate his visit in 1824, this fine portrait bust of Lafayette also exhibits a high degree of skill and artistry. This is in marked contrast to the pair of vases

4.74

shown on the right: **4.73** This pair of matching vases have portrait busts of Martha and George Washington. As you can see, these were not painted by a skilled artist and are far less desirable and far less valuable than those three vases illustrated above. They are also only worth approximately 10% of the value of 4.70, 4.71 and 4.72. Left: **4.74** This small plate has an excellent quality bust of President Martin Van Buren. This is highly valued, not only because of the high quality of the decoration, but also the fact that period ceramics with likenesses of this President are practically nonexistent

4.73

4.75

Left: **4.75** This English porcelain handled basket has a wide border in deep cobalt blue, highlighted with a green and gold rim. The central view is of the Capitol, Washington. Executed with a great amount of skill, as one would expect of a piece of this quality. The building is early, since it does not have the two massive attached wings evident. Below: **4.77** This fine pair of English knobs have a polychromed transfer of Commodore Thomas Truxton, commander of the victorious U.S.S. Constellation in the battle with the French National Frigate L'Insurgent in 1799.

4.76

Chapter Five
An Illustrated Check-list

W elcome to the heart of this book, which, as the title of the Chapter indicates, is an illustrated check-list of those views found on Liverpool and Staffordshire wares of the period between 1760 and 1860. However, before we explain the layout of this check-list, we believe we should discuss the criteria we used when determining the difference between known views, and those views which we list as "previously unknown."

Prior to this publication, the only references that dealt with this

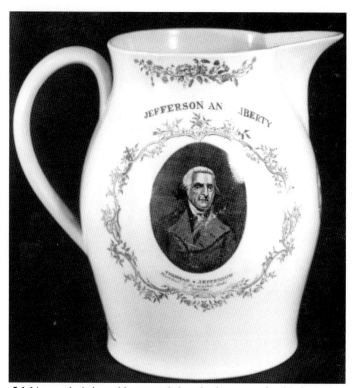

5.1 Liverpool pitcher with a portrait bust having a transfer title beneath the portrait THOMAS JEFFERSON PRESIDENT OF THE UNITED STATES

subject in depth were Ellouise Baker Larsen's *American Historical Views On Staffordshire China* and Robert H. McCauley's *Liverpool Transfer Designs on Anglo-American Pottery*. Mrs. Larsen, as the title of the book denotes, dealt strictly with Staffordshire wares and Mr. McCauley, likewise, limited his work to Liverpool. There were a few instances of cross-overs by the authors between the two different wares, but not much. Mrs. Larsen listed approximately seventy-five different views and Mr. McCauley listed approximately one-hundred seventy-five views, some of which they duplicated, as mentioned earlier. Using these two references as our data base, we began listing the items we have recorded over the last thirty years. We discovered some surprising facts.

First, as Laidacker-trained china dealers/collectors, we always assumed that the potters did not poach the designs of their competitors. This had been dogma for all those who collected Historical dark blue Staffordshire, where views and borders, *in most cases*, were linked to a single manufacturer. This proved to be wrong. As our investigation delved further and further into private and public collections, we found many cases where two or more *similar* transfers had been used by as many different

5.2 Liverpool pitcher with the same portrait bust as figure 5.1, but in this instance titled in a ribbon over the portrait JAMES MADDISON (sic) PRESIDENT OF THE UNITED STATES OF AMERICA

potters. This will undoubtedly cause some major changes in information when we begin the second volume in this trilogy, which deals with Historical Blue.

Second, it became rather clear that the majority of these pieces were manufactured by three potteries; Herculaneum, Davenport and Wood. Although the vast majority of the pieces are unmarked, careful comparisons, such as those explained by Alan Smith in his 1970 volume, *Herculaneum Liverpool Pottery*, left no room for doubt in this area. Hopefully, the remaining unattributed pieces will someday be traced to their origin as more research is done in this field.

Third, we were amazed at the amount of different transfers we discovered that had been previously unrecorded. Mrs. Larsen and Mr. McCauley's combined totals of known views numbered approximately two-hundred twenty-five to two-hundred fifty transfers. We have more than doubled that amount. Does that mean this book contains a comprehensive listing of all known views that were produced by the potteries? Absolutely not! There is no doubt in our minds that there are probably several hundred more transfers, which will ultimately be listed in the future.

5.3 Liverpool pitcher titled PATTEY CRANDELL

5.4 Liverpool pitcher titled PHILLIP CRANDALL

previous page are perfect examples of this practice. Does this mean that although the transfers are the same, but the names different, we are dealing with two separate transfers? Yes.

On this page we illustrate a transfer of (left) PHILLIP CRANDALL and his wife PATTEY. These may have been actual likenesses of this couple or a "stock transfer" the potter used when he received an order for this presentation jug. However, whatever the case, through-out the ages, this pair will be known as the Crandalls. Being a rather keen businessman, the potter decided to use the very same

5.5 Liverpool pitcher titled HANCOCK

The criteria for declaring a view as "previously unrecorded" was basically simple. We used Mrs. Larsen's definition, as stated at the beginning of her chapter titled VARIOUS COLORED DESIGNS ON JUGS, PITCHERS, TEAPOTS, ETC., which stated "A previously recorded view may be sur-rounded by a different border *and produced in colors not hereto used*. It then becomes a new item." We disregarded that portion of her statement which dealt with colors, since we are only concerned with the transfer, no matter what color the potter used. Taking this a bit further, if the transfer was markedly different, this constituted a new view. If the **transfer** title was different, this was a new view. There were many items that had simply not been listed in any reference in the past. These, of course, are a new view.

Fourth, during the course of our studies, we also confirmed what most collectors already knew, that the potters often used the same portrait bust to portray more than one historical figure. By simply changing the name associated with a given bust, the potter saved the expense of a totally new copper plate. The MADDISON (sic) and JEFFERSON transfers illustrated on the

5.6 Liverpool pitcher titled JAMES MONROE / PRESIDENT OF THE UNITED STATES

likeness to depict JOHN HANCOCK (left), a rising star in Revolutionary America. When Hancock died in 1793, the potter probably shelved the copper plate, only to update it in 1817, when JAMES MONROE (right) became the fifth Presi-dent of the United States. Same transfer, three names. All three are relevant for our purposes, so the transfer is listed as both HANCOCK AND MONROE

5.7 Detail of the poem on the three pitchers illustrated on the next page. The word "JEFFERSON" was changed to MADDISON or WASHINGTON

5.8a/b/c Liverpool pitchers with the same poem, but the Presidential name changed. From left to right: MADDISON, WASHINGTON and JEFFERSON

(Crandall is not listed, because we don't know for sure if he had anything to do with America).

Above we have illustrated three Liverpool pitchers with what seems to be the same transfer. Close examination reveals the fact that our thrifty potter used the same transfer and substituted the name of the appropriate President in the fifth line from the bottom. So, we end up with three different transfers with the names (left to right) of MADDISON, WASHINGTON and JEFFERSON. Odds are there is probably an unrecorded example of ADAMS laying around somewhere. It is known that all the pieces shown in illustrations 5.1 through 5.8 are products of The Herculaneum Pottery Company, which shows that even the very largest of the potteries made a practice of this frugal deception.

5.9 Lustre Staffordshire pitcher with the scalloped shell spout and the notched handle used by Enoch Wood on the majority of pitchers with a buff ground. This is the side view of S.82.

Fifth and finally, we discovered that almost 100% of the colored grounds found on the various pieces were manufactured by Enoch Wood and Sons. Not only does that include the various Staffordshire-shaped pitchers with the blue band, the pink Sunderland, the green, the canary and the buff grounds, but it also includes those few extremely rare yellow-glaze Liverpool examples. They're all Enoch Wood. The few examples we cannot attribute to this factory are the buff and yellow-glazed Staffordshire pitchers with specific transfers such as ARMS OF THE UNITED STATES check-list #A.23 - A.25) and JAMES LAWRENCE ESQ. LATE OF THE UNITED STATES NAVY (check-list#L.18). However, we truly believe that time will prove these to also be products of the immense Wood operation.

In summary, it has become clear to us that ALL the yellow-glaze Liverpool pitchers were made by the Wood factory. It has also become clear that all the Staffordshire-shaped pitchers with

5.10 Extremely rare yellow-glaze Liverpool pitcher with a portrait bust of JACOB JONES by Enoch Wood and Sons.

colored grounds and/or polychromed transfers, were also manufactured by this factory. The only exceptions to this sweeping statement are those pitchers, both with polychromed transfers and with yellow-glazed grounds, with the ARMS OF THE UNITED STATES (check-list #A.23 - A.25). Think about this for a second, this means that Wood, a Staffordshire potter, also made a Liverpool shaped pitcher after the War of 1812. Is it possible that he made the same form prior to that war and that this factory could be another major manufacturer of the Liverpool form? Or could Wood have been the potter who used the Shelton Group as engravers and manufactured the pieces we list under that heading in Chapter Two? Possible, if not probable. Time will tell, as additional research and discoveries are published.

A Sample Listing of The Check - list

Dra - David Drakard, *Printed English Pottery*

L - E. B. Larsen, *American Historical Views On Staffordshire China*

Mc - R. H. McCauley, *Liverpool Designs on Anglo-American Pottery*

Smith - Alan Smith, *Liverpool Herculaneum Pottery*

¹   ²   ³   ⁴

A.1 JOHN ADAMS, PRESIDENT OF THE UNITED STATES (Mc #1) Very Rare. Wood. L. —— ⁶

⁵   ⁷   ⁸

pitchers............12.5

1. This is the alpha-numeric designation given to the transfer for reference purposes. As we feel certain that additional transfers will be recorded in the future, we did not want to restrict ourselves by numbering the transfers in this book sequentially. Therefore we have transfers designated alphabetically and by a number indicating where the transfer is listed under that letter. Thus, the sample designation refers to transfer number **1**, in the **A** section.

2. This is the title, as it appears on the transfer. If the subject of the transfer is a person, we have listed it under that person's last name.

3. This indicates where the transfer is listed or illustrated, using abbreviations for the author's last name. If there is an asterisk (*) after the reference, this means the referencing author had not personally observed the transfer. The author code is as follows:

4. *Our opinion* of the rarity of the transfer as discussed in Chapter Four - **Rarity Scale**.

5. When known, the pottery/factory that is believed to have used this particular transfer.

6. The type of ware where the transfer is normally found with "L" indicating a Liverpool form and "S" a Staffordshire form.

7. This is a listing of the functional forms that have been recorded with a particular transfer. They should be self-explanatory.

8. This is a value factor as discussed in detail in Chapter Four for that particular *transfer*. This is used to determine the *approximate* value of an <u>individual</u> <u>transfer</u>, <u>NOT</u> the value of the *ceramic article illustrated*. In order to find the approximate value of the ceramic article, one should use the formula discussed in Chapter Four.

An Illustrated Check-list

A.1 THE ABIGAIL SHUBAEL PINKHAM (previously unrecorded) Unique. Probably Wilson. L.

      soup plates (two recorded).....3.0

A.1 THE ABIGAIL SHUBAEL PINKHAM polychromed black transfer on an early creamware bowl. Border highlighted with green leaves and purple fruits. This bowl is an exact match in form to A.33, which is impressed WILSON.

A.2 ADAMS (previously unrecorded) Extremely rare. Probably Enoch Wood and Sons. S.

      child's mug......7.5+

A.2 Badly stained childs mug with a blue transfer on pearlware titled ADAMS.

A.3 ADAMS Seal of the United States (previously unrecorded) Unique. Possibly Enoch Wood and Sons. S.

  child's mug (one recorded).....6.5

A.3 ADAMS   Seal of the United States blue transfer on a pearlware child's mug.

A.4 JOHN ADAMS, PRESIDENT OF THE UNITED STATES (Mc #1) Very rare. L.

  pitchers.....12.5
  bowls.........15.0

A.4 JOHN ADAMS   PRESIDENT OF THE UNITED STATES black transfer on a creamware pitcher.

A.5 ADAMS AND LIBERTY (Poem) (Mc #5) Extremely rare. L.

  pitchers.....10.0
  tankards.....10.0

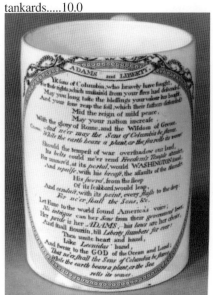

A.5   The poem ADAMS AND LIBERTY with a black transfer on a creamware tankard. Below: detail.

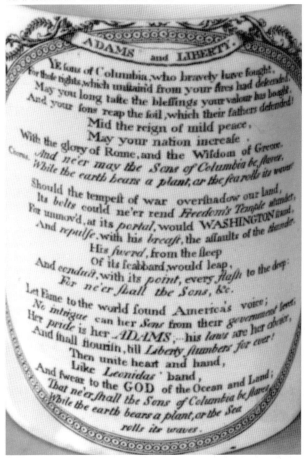

A.6 ADAMS (Mc #4) Extremely rare. L

  pitchers.....20.0+

Listed by McCauley as a full face portrait bust with ADAMS turned to the right with the portrait flanked by a Seal of the United States. All this is placed above a cartouche containing the name. This is the only record of this particular transfer. We have never seen it.

61

A.7 JOHN ADAMS. PRESIDENT. GENERAL GEORGE WASHINGTON. JAMES BRYDEN, FOUNTAIN INN (Previously unrecorded) Unique. Herculaneum Pottery. L.
jelly mold (one recorded).....15.0+

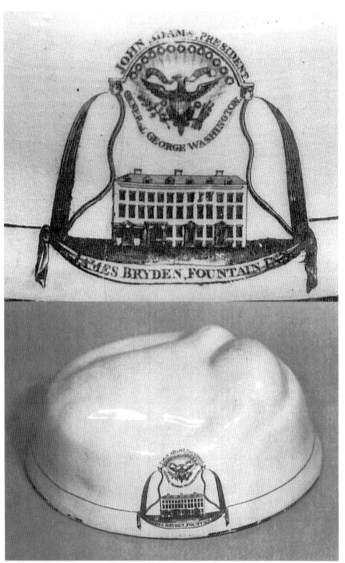

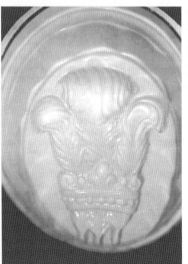

A.7 JOHN ADAMS. PRESIDENT. GENERAL GEORGE WASHINGTON. JAMES BRYDEN, FOUNTAIN INN black transfer on a unique **(Center)** creamware jelly mold. This transfer can be dated to that brief moment in time, when President John Adams appointed Washington as senior general to oversee the defense of the Country from both the French and/or British in 1798-1799. **(Left)** The interior of the mold, which is a heavily embossed symbol for the Prince of Wales. **(Top)** A detail of this important transfer showing the Fountain Inn of Baltimore, Maryland, which was owned and operated by James Bryden. The Seal of the United States is supported by a device which encloses the building and flanks the eagle with two tiny heads, which are spewing liquid from their mouths. This exact device, with the heads and liquid, was also used by Herculaneum in W.69.

A.8 JOHN ADAMS, PRESIDENT OF THE UNITED STATES (Mc #2, *Mc #3*[(1)]) Very rare. Shelton Group. L.
pitchers.....15.0

A.8 JOHN ADAMS PRESIDENT OF THE UNITED STATES black transfer on a creamware pitcher highlighted in blue, flesh, red and green enamel.

A.9 JOHN ADAMS PRESIDENT OF THE UNITED STATES (previously unrecorded) Unique. L.
pitcher (one recorded).....20.0

A.9 JOHN ADAMS PRESIDENT OF THE UNITED STATES gold highlighted black transfer on a blue enamel ground Liverpool creamware pitcher. This is the only recorded example of this transfer and the value factor listed above, does not take into account the blue ground.

A.10 ADAMS Map of the United States (Mc #58c) Extremely rare. Probably Shelton Group. L.

      pitchers.....3.5

A.10 ADAMS Map of the United States black transfer on a creamware pitcher. The name within a ribbon over his head. The detail shows the name. The only difference between this transfer and the more common WASHINGTON Map of the U.S. (W.15) is this name.

A.11 AGRICULTURE COMMERCE and the **FREEDOM** of the **SEAS** (previously unrecorded) Extremely rare. L.

      pitchers.....1.5

A.11 AGRICULTURE COMMERCE and the FREEDOM of the SEAS black transfer on a creamware pitcher.

A.12 ALBANY THEATRE 1824 (previously unrecorded) Unique. Attributed to R. Stevenson and Williams. L.

      small pitcher (one recorded).....6.5
      washbowl (one recorded).....8.0

A.12 ALBANY THEATRE 1824 black transfer on a small creamware pitcher which we attribute to R. Stevenson and Williams, since the transfer appears to have been made using the same copper plate as that unique vegetable dish base in the American Antiquarian Society, Worcester, Massachusetts.[2]

A.13 The United States Frigate **ALLIANCE** (Previously unrecorded) Unique. Herculaneum Pottery. L.

      pitcher (one recorded).....3.5

A.13 The U. S. Frigate U.S.S. ALLIANCE with the initials P. H. under the spout for Patrick Hayes, the nephew of Commodore John Barry. John Barry was Captain of this vessel in 1780 when she defeated two British vessels.

A.14 ᴀᴍᴇʀɪᴄᴀ (Previously unrecorded) Very rare. Probably Enoch Wood and Sons. S.
     pitchers.....2.5

A.16 AMERICA (previously unreported) Unique. L.
     pitcher (one recorded).....1.5

A.14 Staffordshire pearlware pitcher with a yellow-glaze ground and a black transfer of an Indian above the title "ᴀᴍᴇʀɪᴄᴀ". This is normally found in yellow-glaze with either a black or lustre line border.

A.16 AMERICA black transfer on a creamware pitcher. Black enamel lettering.

A.15 AMERICA E PLURIBUS UNUM (previously unrecorded) Possibly unique as a "side" transfer. Enoch Wood. S.
     pitcher (one recorded - side transfer).....3.5
     pitchers (underspout).....+0.4

A.17 Aᴍᴇʀɪᴄᴀɴ Mᴀɴᴜғᴀᴄᴛᴜʀᴇs Cᴀʙʟᴇs & Cᴏʀᴅᴀɢᴇ ᴍᴀɴᴜғᴀᴄ-ᴛᴜʀᴇᴅ ʙʏ Gᴇᴏ. & Pᴇᴛᴇʀ Cᴀᴅᴇ ᴀᴛ ᴛʜᴇɪʀ ROPE WALK ɴᴇᴀʀ Bᴇᴀᴄᴏɴ Hɪʟʟ BOSTON N.B. Sʜɪᴘᴘɪɴɢ sᴜᴘᴘʟɪᴇᴅ ᴡɪᴛʜ ʟᴀʀɢᴇ ᴏʀ sᴍᴀʟʟ Qᴜᴀɴᴛɪᴛɪᴇs (previously unrecorded) Unique. Herculaneum Pottery. L.
     pitcher (one recorded).....15.0+

A.15 ᴀᴍᴇʀɪᴄᴀ E Pʟᴜʀɪʙᴜs Uɴᴜᴍ black transfer on a buff ground pearlware pitcher by Enoch Wood and Sons. This is the only recorded example of this transfer used as a side view. The transfer normally found (see S.18) is much smaller and placed under the spout.

A.17 Aᴍᴇʀɪᴄᴀɴ Mᴀɴᴜғᴀᴄᴛᴜʀᴇs Cᴀʙʟᴇs & Cᴏʀᴅᴀɢᴇ ᴍᴀɴᴜ-ғᴀᴄᴛᴜʀᴇᴅ ʙʏ Gᴇᴏ. & Pᴇᴛᴇʀ Cᴀᴅᴇ ᴀᴛ ᴛʜᴇɪʀ ROPE WALK ɴᴇᴀʀ Bᴇᴀᴄᴏɴ Hɪʟʟ BOSTON N.B. Sʜɪᴘᴘɪɴɢ sᴜᴘᴘʟɪᴇᴅ ᴡɪᴛʜ ʟᴀʀɢᴇ ᴏʀ sᴍᴀʟʟ Qᴜᴀɴᴛɪᴛɪᴇs enamel decoration on a cream-ware pitcher sold by auctioneers F. O. Bailey, Port-land, Maine.

A.18 AMERICA DECLARED INDEPENDENT JULY 4TH
1776 (Mc #183) Very rare. Shelton Group or Stevenson. L.

      pitchers.....3.0
      tankards.....3.25

A.18 AMERICA DECLARED INDEPENDENT JULY 4TH 1776 black transfer on a creamware tankard.

A.19b The source print for A.19, as discovered by J. Jefferson Miller II, is taken from Isaac Weld's 1799 travel book titled, *Travels Through the States of North America and the Provinces of Upper and Lower Canada, during 1795, 1796 and 1797.* Weld was not only the author of the book, but he was also the artist. The scene refers to that portion of Weld's journey between Philadelphia and Baltimore in November of 1795.

A.19 AMERICAN STAGE WAGGON (previously unrecorded)
Unique. L.

      pitcher (one recorded).....12.5+

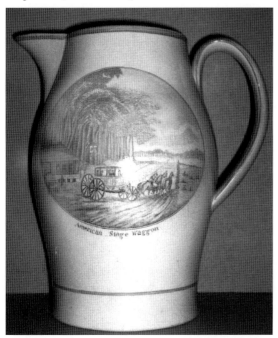

A.19a AMERICAN STAGE WAGGON black transfer on an early creamware pitcher which has green enamel highlights.

A.20 FISHER AMES (Mc #6) Rare. Some marked Wood and Caldwell. S.

      Staffordshire pitchers.....1.75
      Liverpool pitcher (one recorded).....3.5+

A.20a FISHER AMES black transfer on a pale yellow ground with a broad dark pink lustre band around the neck. Recorded with a "Wood and Caldwell" transfer under the spout.

A.20b FISHER AMES black transfer on a Liverpool creamware pitcher. This is the only recorded example of this transfer on this form.

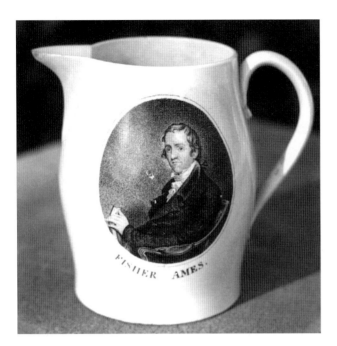

A.22 UNTITLED - AN EMBLEM OF AMERICA (Mc #170) Rare. L. pitchers.....2.75

A.22 Untitled transfer of AN EMBLEM OF AMERICA. Black transfer on a creamware pitcher with vignettes of COLUMBUS, RALEIGH, WASHINGTON, FRANKLIN, ADAMS and an unknown.

A.21 AN EMBLEM OF AMERICA (Mc #170) Scarce. Herculaneum Pottery. L.
pitchers.....2.5

A.23 ARMS OF THE UNITED STATES E PLURIBUS UNUM (Mc #161, L #722) Scarce. Probably Enoch Wood and Sons. S. pitchers.....1.85

A.21 AN EMBLEM OF AMERICA black transfer on a creamware pitcher with multiple portrait busts titled COLUMBUS, RALEIGH, WASHINGTON, FRANKLIN, ADAMS and an unknown.

A.23 ARMS OF THE UNITED STATES E PLURIBUS UNUM black polychromed transfer on a pearlware pitcher. Pink lustre bands. Eagle highlighted in green, red, brown, black and yellow. This transfer is normally found polychromed and is the most common version of this transfer.

A.24 ARMS OF THE UNITED STATES E PLURIBUS UNUM
(previously unrecorded) Probably Very rare. Probably Enoch Wood and Sons. S.

pitchers.....2.0

A.24 ARMS OF THE UNITED STATES E PLURIBUS UNUM black polychromed transfer on a pearlware pitcher. Pink lustre bands. Eagle highlighted in green, red, brown, black and yellow.

A.25 ARMS OF THE UNITED STATES E PLURIBUS UNUM
(previously unrecorded). Probably very rare. Probably Enoch Wood and Sons. S.

pitchers.....2.0

A.25 ARMS OF THE UNITED STATES E PLURIBUS UNUM lightly polychromed black transfer on a pearlware pitcher.

A.26 ARMS OF THE UNITED STATES E PLURIBUS UNUM
(Mc #150A) Very rare. L.

pitchers.....1.5

A.26 ARMS OF THE UNITED STATES. E PLURIBUS UNUM black transfer on a creamware pitcher.

A.27 ARMS OF THE UNITED STATES E PLURIBUS UNUM
MAY SUCCESS ATTEND OUR AGRICULTURE (Mc #150B) Extremely rare. S.

pitchers.....2.5

A.27 ARMS OF THE UNITED STATES E PLURIBUS UNUM MAY SUCCESS ATTEND OUR AGRICULTURE polychromed black transfer on a pearlware pitcher. Transfer highlighted with tan, red and black enamels. Possibly a product of Enoch Wood and Sons.

A.28 ARMS OF THE UNITED STATES. E PLURIBUS UNUM MAY SUCCESS ATTEND OUR AGRICULTURE (Mc #150B) Very rare. L.

pitchers.....1.5

A.28 ARMS OF THE UNITED STATES. E PLURIBUS UNUM MAY SUCCESS ATTEND OUR AGRICULTURE black transfer on a creamware pitcher.

A.29 ARMS OF THE UNITED STATES. E PLURIBUS UNUM MAY SUCCESS ATTEND OUR AGRICULTURE TRADE AND MANUFACTURES (Mc #150C) Rare. L.

pitchers.....1.5

A.29 ARMS OF THE UNITED STATES. E PLURIBUS UNUM MAY SUCCESS ATTEND OUR AGRICULTURE TRADE AND MANUFACTURES black transfer on a creamware pitcher.

A.30 ARMS OF THE UNITED STATES E PLURIBUS UNUM MAY SUCCESS ATTEND OUR AGRICULTURE TRADE AND MANUFACTURES (Mc #150C, L #655) Very Rare. Probably Enoch Wood and Sons. S.

pitchers.....2.25
plates.....2.75

A.30 ARMS OF THE UNITED STATES...etc. greyish-black transfer on a pearlware plate which has a blue feather edge.

A.31 ARMY HEROES - BROWN JACKSON SCOTT GAINES ADAIR BOYD IZARD LEWIS McCOMB MILLER PIKE PORTER VAN RENSALAER(Mc #159, Mc #160, L #723) Scarce. Enoch Wood and Sons. S.

pitchers.....2.5

A.31 ARMY HEROES - BROWN JACKSON SCOTT GAINES ADAIR BOYD IZARD LEWIS McCOMB MILLER PIKE PORTER VAN RENSALAER magenta transfer on a buff ground pearlware pitcher. Pink Lustre bands.

A.32 ATTACK ON FORT OSWEGO (Mc #127, L #741) Unique. Davenport. S.

       pitchers (3 known).....6.5+

A.34 AUT VINCERE AUT MORI SUCCESS TO THE INDEPENDENT BOSTON FUSILIERS. INCORPORATED JULY 4, 1787, AMERICA FOR EVER. (Mc #251) Very rare. Herculaneum Pottery. L.

       pitchers.....18.0

A.32 ATTACK ON FORT OSWEGO black transfer on a pearlware pitcher. One of three recorded.

A.34 AUT VINCERE AUT MORI - BOSTON FUSILIERS polychromed black transfer on a creamware pitcher. One of the most desirable Liverpool transfers.

A.33 AURORA OF NEWPORT, JOHN CALHOONE (previously unrecorded) Extremely rare. Some impressed WILSON. L.

       plates.....3.0

A.33 AURORA OF NEWPORT, JOHN CALHOONE polychromed black transfer on a creamware plate impressed WILSON.

B.1 COMMODORE BAINBRIDGE (Mc #8, L #606, L #725) Common. Enoch Wood and Sons. S.

        pitchers.....1.1
        plates.....2.5

B.1 COMMODORE BAINBRIDGE black transfer on a pearlware pitcher with a black enamel band highlighted with black enamel "leaves".

B.2 COMMODORE BAINBRIDGE AVAST BOYS SHE'S STRUCK CAPTUR'D AND DESTROYED THE JAVA (Mc #7). Extremely rare. L.

        pitchers.....5.0
        tankards.....5.0

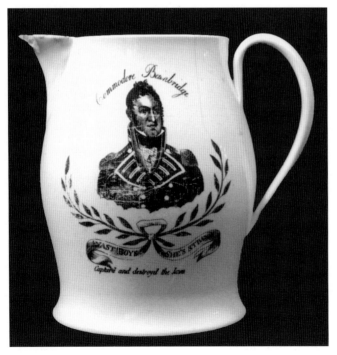

B.2 COMMODORE BAINBRIDGE AVAST BOYS..ETC. black transfer on a creamware pitcher.

B.3 BATTLE LOG OF THE U.S.S. CONSTITUTION (Mc #108) Unknown rarity. S? L?

Existence Doubtful - McCauley lists this view as a "printed design" which lists five events in the life of this famous vessel. We have never seen an example or an illustration of the view, except for that reproduction illustrated in Chapter Six (illustration 6.16)

B.4 BALTIMORE MARGARET DELANY (Under spout) GREEN FLAG W/GOLDEN HARP (previously unrecorded). Probably unique. Herculaneum Pottery. L. Illustrated to show type and value range for presentation pitchers w/American cities named......1.2

B.4 MARGARET DELANY BALTIMORE WITH IRISH FLAG black transfer on a creamware pitcher. Flag polychromed in green and gold.

70

B.5 Untitled - THE BENEFIT OF NEUTRALITY (Drakard #411)
Extremely rare. Wedgwood. L.
> pitchers.....2.75

B.5 Untitled - THE BENEFIT OF NEUTRALITY black transfer on a creamware pitcher. One of the many versions of that print, circa 1745, illustrated on page 36. Due to the "WEDGWOOD" mark, this pitcher can be dated 1780s and therefore relating to the American Revolution.

BON HOMME RICHARD AND THE SERAPIS (Mc #103)
> **Cancelled. View mentioned by McCauley is actually an untitled MACEDONIAN AND UNITED STATES**

B.6 THE BRIG ELIZABETH WRECKED 1ST DECEMBER 1821.
(previously unrecorded) Unique. L.
> pitcher (one recorded).....2.0

B.6 THE BRIG ELIZABETH WRECKED 1ST DECEMBER 1821. black transfer on a creamware pitcher. THE ELIZABETH was reportedly an American vessel.

B.7 MAJ GEN'L BROWN NIAGARA (Mc #10A, L #607, L #727)
Common. Enoch Wood and Sons. S.
> pitchers.....1.1
> plates.....2.5
> tankards.....2.5

B.7 MAJ GEN'L BROWN NIAGARA black transfer on an extremely rare Sunderland Splash lustre ground. Two known examples in this form and this ground. This rare ground raises the value from the above 1.1 to 5.5+.

B.8 BROWN The Hero of Niagara (beneath portrait) (Mc 10B)
Extremely rare. Davenport. S.
> pitchers.....3.5

B.8 BROWN THE HERO OF NIAGARA (beneath portrait) black transfer on a pearlware pitcher. Pink lustre bands.

71

B.9 GENERAL BROWN (Previously unrecorded) Unique. S.
pitcher (one recorded).....3.5

B.9 GENERAL BROWN pink lustre enamel decoration with scenic views on the sides and the title and name in script under the spout.

B.10 BY VIRTUE AND VALOUR WE HAVE FREED OUR COUNTRY, EXTENDED OUR COMMERCE, AND LAID THE FOUNDATION OF A GREAT EMPIRE. (Mc #199, L #784) Scarce. Herculaneum Pottery. L.
pitchers.....1.8
bowls.....2.5
tankards.....3.0

B.10 BY VIRTUE AND VALOUR WE HAVE FREED OUR COUNTRY, EXTENDED OUR COMMERCE, AND LAID THE FOUNDATION OF A GREAT EMPIRE black transfer on a creamware pitcher.

B.11 BY VIRTUE AND VALOUR WE HAVE FREED OUR COUNTRY, EXTENDED OUR COMMERCE, AND LAID THE FOUNDATION OF A GREAT EMPIRE. (L #784) Unique.
Herculaneum Pottery. S.
pitchers (one recorded).....5.0

B.11 BY VIRTUE AND VALOUR WE HAVE FREED OUR COUNTRY, EXTENDED OUR COMMERCE, AND LAID THE FOUNDATION OF A GREAT EMPIRE black transfer on a Staffordshire shaped pitcher. This transfer on this form is extremely rare.

B.12 Untitled - BY VIRTUE AND VALOUR (Mc#200a) Extremely rare.
Shelton Group. L.
pitchers.....2.25
bowls.....3.0

B.12 Untitled - BY VIRTUE AND VALOUR black transfer on a creamware bowl.

B.13 BY VIRTUE AND VALOUR.....ETC. (L #700) Unique. L.
   plate (one recorded).....4.5

B.13 BY VIRTUE AND VALOUR.....Etc. black transfer on a pearlware
plate.

C.1 CAPITAL, ALBANY with medallions of **KENT, COKE, PRESIDENT WASHINGTON, GOVERNOR CLINTON, JEFFERSON, LAFAYETTE THE NATION's GUEST** (previously unrecorded) Extremely rare. Probably Ralph or Andrew Stevenson. S.

> washbowls.....8.0

C.1 CAPITAL, ALBANY with medallions of KENT, COKE, PRESIDENT WASHINGTON, GOVERNOR CLINTON, JEFFERSON, LAFAYETTE THE NATION's GUEST black transfers on a white creamware washbowl.

C.2 Census - **PROSPERITY TO THE UNITED STATES of AMERICA** (Mc #166) Extremely rare. L.

> pitchers.....5.5
> tankards.....6.5

C.2 CENSUS - PROSPERITY TO THE UNITED STATES of AMERICA black transfer on a creamware tankard.

C.3 CHARLOTTE QUEEN OF GREAT BRITAIN (variant of Dra #399) Extremely rare. Sadler - Wedgwood. L.

> teapots.....1.5
> tankards.....1.5

C.3 CHARLOTTE QUEEN OF GREAT BRITAIN black transfer on a creamware tankard.

C.4 CHARLOTTE QUEEN OF GREAT BRITAIN (Dra #399) Extremely rare. Sadler - Wedgwood. L.

> teapots.....1.75

C.4 CHARLOTTE QUEEN OF GREAT BRITAIN.

C.5 CHARLOTTE QUEEN OF GREAT BRITAIN (Dra #392)
Extremely rare. Wedgwood. L.
  pitchers.....1.5
  teapots.....1.5

C.5 CHARLOTTE QUEEN OF GREAT BRITAIN

C.7 Untitled - CHARLOTTE QUEEN OF GREAT BRITAIN
(similar to Dra #395) Extremely rare. Worcester. Porcelain.
  tankards.....2.0

C.7 Untitled - CHARLOTTE QUEEN OF GREAT
BRITAIN black transfer on a porcelain tankard.

C.6 CHARLOTTE QUEEN OF GREAT BRITAIN (Dra #395)
Extremely rare. Wedgwood. L.
  teapots.....1.5
  pitchers.....1.75

C.6 CHARLOTTE QUEEN OF GREAT
BRITAIN black transfer on a creamware
pitcher impressed WEDGWOOD.

C.8 CONN. CHARTER OAK Type reversed on the transfer
(Previously unrecorded) Unique. Andrew or Ralph Stevenson. L.
& S.
  pitcher (one Liverpool-type recorded).....4.5
  plate (one pearlware example recorded).....2.5

C.8a CONN. CHARTER OAK (title reversed on transfer) black transfer
on a creamware pitcher.

C.8 (cont.) CHARTER OAK, CONNECTICUT Type reversed on the transfer.

C.9 HENRY CLAY STAR OF THE WEST (L #609) Unique. Probably John Wedg Wood. S.

    platter (one recorded).....12.0

    plates (three recorded).....4.5

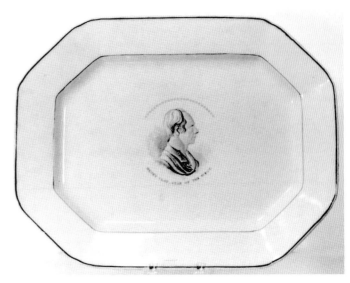

C.9a HENRY CLAY, STAR OF THE WEST light blue transfer and a thin blue line border on a pearlware platter. Only recorded example.

C.8b CHARTER OAK CONNECTICUT (reversed on the transfer) blue transfer on an embossed pearlware plate. Detail shows the typeface horizontally reversed.

Chesapeake and Shannon (Mc #122).

Cancelled - both Larsen and McCauley list this title when discussing that large "War of 1812 pitcher" in the Collection of the Albany Institute of History and Art. The transfer which they both reference is illustrated below. As you can see, this is an untitled view of THE CONSTITUTION IN CLOSE ACTION WITH THE GUERRIERE (check-list #C.21)

C.9b HENRY CLAY, STAR OF THE WEST, black transfer with the "chick-weed" border.. One of three recorded.

C.10 GOVERNOR CLINTON (Arman II, #862) Extremely rare. Probably A. or R. Stevenson. Staffordshire-type shape.
pitchers.....2.25

C.10 GOVERNOR CLINTON black transfer on a thick, heavy, pale cream-colored pitcher.

C.11 Untitled - COLUMBIA (previously unrecorded) Unique. L.
pitcher (one recorded).....1.5

C.11 Untitled - COLUMBIA black transfer on a creamware pitcher.

C.12 Untitled - COLUMBIA (Mc # 167) Rare. Herculaneum Pottery. L.
pitchers.....1.5
plates.....2.0
soup tureen (one recorded).....17.5
undertray (one recorded).....7.5

C.12 COLUMBIA black transfer on a **(a)** Right: creamware plate (note the "pickle" border), **(b)** Above: on a creamware pitcher as an "under-spout" decoration and **(c)** Below: on a "unique" soup tureen.

C.13 Come Freedom's sons & join the choir Let patriot pride your hearts inspire....etc (Poem) (Previously unrecorded) Unique. L.

          pitcher (one recorded)......5.0

C.13 Come Freedom's Sons..etc red transfer on a creamware pitcher.

C.14 COMMERCE TRADE and **PEACE ALL NATIONS JOYS INCREASE** (Mc #168) Rare. L

          pitchers.....1.0

C.14 COMMERCE TRADE AND PEACE ALL NATIONS JOYS INCREASE black transfer on a creamware pitcher.

C.15 COMMERCE REVIVED (Mc 169) Rare. L.

          pitchers.....1.0

McCauley describes this transfer as an oval containing a seated Britannia with a crouched lion in the foreground. A woman, an Indian and a Black kneeling in front. All this under the title COMMERCE REVIVED.

C.13 Detail - Come Freedom's sons and join the choir...etc red transfer on a Liverpool creamware pitcher.

C.16 COMMODORE MacDONNOUGH'S VICTORY ON LAKE CHAMPLAIN (Mc #130, L #772) Very rare. Enoch Wood and Sons. S.

pitchers.....3.5

C.16 COMMODORE MACDONNOUGH'S VICTORY ON LAKE CHAMPLAIN black transfer on a large pearlware pitcher with a pink lustre design around the neck and an applied shell handle under the spout.

C.17 COMMODORE PREBLES SQUADRON ATTACKING THE CITY OF TRIPOLI, AUG. 3 1804. THE AMERICAN SQUADRON UNDER COMMODORE PREBLE, CONSISTING OF THE CONSTITUTION OF 44 GUNS 2 BRIGS 3 SCHOONERS, 2 BOMBS AND 6 GUN BOATS ATTACKING THE CITY AND HARBOUR OF TRIPOLI AUG. 3 1804 THE CITY WAS DEFENDED BY BATTERIES MOUNTING 15 PIECES OF HEAVY CANNON AND THE HARBOUR BY 19 GUN BOATS 2 BRIGS, 2 SCHOONERS 2 GALLIES AND A ZEBECK THE CITY RECEIVED GREAT DAMAGE SEVERAL OF THE TRIPOLITAN VESSELS WERE SUNK 3 OF THEIR GUN BOATS TAKEN AND A GREAT NUMBER OF MEN KILLED (Mc #107) Scarce. Herculaneum Pottery. L.

pitchers.....2.5

C.17 COMMODORE PREBLES SQUADRON...ETC black transfer on a creamware pitcher

C.18 CONSTITUTION (previously unrecorded) Unique. L. pitcher (one recorded).....1.5

C.18 CONSTITUTION black transfer on a creamware pitcher. Faded name CONSTITUTION beneath the transfer in gold.

C.19 CONSTITUTION AND GUERRIERE (Mc #112, L #729) Unique. Davenport. S

pitcher (one recorded).....3.5

C.19 CONSTITUTION AND GUERRIERE black transfer on a pearlware wash pitcher. One recorded example of this unusual form. One recorded example of this "unique" transfer.

C.20 Constitution's escape from the British Squadron after a chase of sixty hours (ships names) Africa Constitution Shannon Eolus Guerriere Belvidera (Mc #109, L #733) Rare. Enoch Wood and Sons. S.

　　　pitchers.....2.5

C.20 Constitution's escape from the British Squadron after a chase of sixty hours (ships names) Africa Constitution Shannon Eolus Guerriere Belvidera black transfer on a buff ground pearlware pitcher with pink lustre bands. The ships are identified under the scene.

C.21 Constitution and Java 1797 (Mc #119) S.

Existence questionable - McCauley lists this as two ships in combat with the above title. He further states that the date probably refers to the date the ship was launched.

C.22 CONSTITUTION AND JAVA (Mc #118, L#730) Extremely rare. Davenport. S.

　　　pitchers.....3.5

C.22　CONSTITUTION AND JAVA black transfer on a creamware pitcher.

C.23 Untitled - The CONSTITUTION In Close Action With the GUERRIERE (previously unrecorded) Unique. Enoch Wood and Sons. S.

　　　pitcher (if discovered on another piece).....1.75

C.23 Untitled - THE CONSTITUTION IN CLOSE ACTION WITH THE GUERRIERE black transfer on that large pitcher in the Collection of the Albany Institute of History and Art illustrated on page 16.

C.24 CONSTITUTION IN CLOSE ACTION WITH THE **GUERRIERE**
(Mc #111, L #734) Scarce. Enoch Wood and Sons. S.
    pitchers.....1.5

C.24 CONSTITUTION IN CLOSE ACTION WITH THE GUERRIERE black
transfer on a creamware pitcher highlighted with pink lustre bands.

Constitution Leaving Boston Harbor (Mc #110, L #732) S.
    Existence questionable[3]

C.25 CONSTITUTION TAKING THE CYANE AND LEVANT (Mc #131, L
#731) Very rare. Enoch Wood and Sons. S.
    pitchers.....2.0

C.25 CONSTITUTION TAKING THE CYANE AND LEVANT black transfer surrounded by
a green ground and a pink splash lustre band around the mouth.

C.26 THE DEATH of Captain **COOK** by the natives of O
Whyhee (previously unrecorded) Unique. L.
    pitcher (one known).........10.0+

C.26 THE DEATH OF CAPTAIN COOK BY THE NATIVES OF O WHYHEE black
transfer on a creamware pitcher.

C.26 Detail - **THE DEATH** OF CAPTAIN **COOK** BY THE NATIVES OF **O
WHYHEE**

C.27 LORD CORNWALLIS (Drakard #423 and #424) Scarce. William Greatbach. L.

>   teapots.....2.0
>   tankards.....2.0

C.27 LORD CORNWALLIS polychromed black transfer on a creamware teapot by William Greatbach, circa 1781 - 1791.

C.29 CORNWALLIS RESIGNING HIS SWORD AT YORKTOWN OCT. 19, 1781 (Mc #104, L #736) Common. Enoch Wood and Sons. L.

>   Liverpool pitchers (extremely rare).....2.5
>   Staffordshire pitchers.....0.75
>   child's mug.....1.2
>   teapot (one recorded).....2.25
>   tea cups.....0.25
>   loving cups (extremely rare).....2.25

C.29 Untitled - SURRENDER OF CORNWALLIS black transfer on a pearlware teapot. Pink lustre highlights. LAFAYETTE CROWNED on the cover (L.1).

C.28 MARQUIS CORNWALLIS JUSTICE MERCY To whose Clemancy (sic) & Bravery Ireland owes her Preservation (previously unrecorded) Rare. Herculaneum Pottery. L.

>   pitchers.....1.25

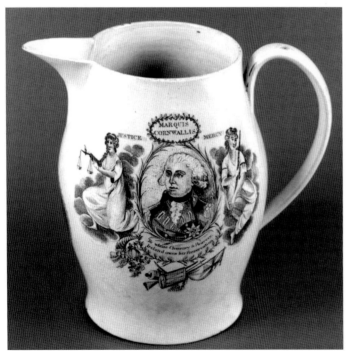

C.28 MARQUIS CORNWALLIS JUSTICE MERCY To whose Clemancy (sic) & Bravery Ireland owes her Preservation black transfer on a creamware pitcher. This portrays Cornwallis in the 1790's, long after his adventures in America, however we include it in this listing due to his earlier American connection.

C.30 CUMBERLAND, ENGINE, NO 8, SOCIETY (Smith #49 and #52) Unique. Herculaneum. L.

>   15 1/2"h pitcher (one recorded).....35.0+

C.30 CUMBERLAND, ENGINE No. 8, SOCIETY multiple black transfers on a large 15 1/2"h creamware pitcher. These large multiple transfer pitchers are usually one-of-a-kind and therefore any attempt to place a value on them is futile.

C.31 Untitled - CHANCELLOR LIVINGSTON (previously unrecorded)
Extremely rare. Enoch Wood and Sons. S.
      soup plates.....1.25

C.31 Untitled - CHANCELLOR LIVINGSTON black transfer on a pearlware plate highlighted with a blue enamel edge. This rarity was recorded by the authors for the first time when it appeared in an Ohio auction just prior to the printing of this book, which is the reason for it being out of alphabetical order. The CHANCELLOR LIVINGSTON was the name given by Robert Fulton to his second steam vessel, which sailed from New York to Albany and New York to Providence. Wood also made a tea service in dark blue using the same transfer. In the blue tea service there is an American flag on the vessel, while in this transfer, the flag consists of a swallow-tailed pennant with an asterisk-like device in the field. According to Mrs. Larsen, the source print for this transfer is an "old print" reproduced in Samuel Wards 1895 volume titled, *American Steam Vessels.*

D.1 Untitled - Death of Wolfe (Mc #100, L #13) Very rare. Wedgwood. L.

        pitchers.....3.5
        teapots.....3.5
        bowls.....3.75

D.1 Untitled - DEATH OF WOLFE - black transfer on a creamware pitcher.

D.2 Untitled - Death of Wolfe (previously unrecorded) Extremely rare. L.

        pitchers.....4.0

D.2 Untitled - DEATH OF WOLFE black transfer on a creamware pitcher. This is an extremely rare reversal of the previous transfer, which was probably pirated from Wedgwood.

Death of Montgomery (Mc #102) L.
    Existence questionable[4]

Death of Warren (Mc #101) L.
    Existence questionable[4]

D.3 STEPHEN DECATUR ESQ. *OF THE UNITED STATES NAVY* (Mc #13, Dra #699) Extremely rare. Enoch Wood and Sons. L. & S.

        pitchers.....4.0
        tankards.....4.0

D.3a & b STEPHEN DECATUR ESQ. *OF THE UNITED STATES NAVY* black transfers on a **(a)** creamware tankard and on **(b)** a pitcher with an unusual form and a pale yellow ground.

D.4 COMMODORE DECATUR FREE TRADE AND SAILORS RIGHTS (Mc #14A) Extremely rare. L.

        pitchers.....5.0
        tankards.....5.0

D.4 COMMODORE DECATUR FREE TRADE AND SAILORS RIGHTS black transfer on a creamware tankard.

D.5 COMMODORE DECATUR FREE TRADE AND SAILORS RIGHTS DESTROYED THE FRIGATE PHILADELPHIA AND BROUGHT IN THE MACEDONIAN (Mc #14C) Extremely rare. L.

      pitchers.....4.5

D.5 COMMODORE DECATUR FREE TRADE AND SAILORS RIGHTS DESTROYED THE FRIGATE PHILADELPHIA AND BROUGHT IN THE MACEDONIAN black transfer on a creamware pitcher.

D.6 COMMODORE DECATUR FREE TRADE & SAILORS RIGHTS DESTROYED THE FRIGATE PHILADELPHIA 1804. CAPTURED AND BROUGHT IN THE BRITISH FRIGATE MACEDONIAN 1812. (Mc #14D) Extremely rare. L.

      pitchers.....5.0

D.6 COMMODORE DECATUR FREE TRADE & SAILORS RIGHTS DESTROYED THE FRIGATE PHILADELPHIA 1804. CAPTURED AND BROUGHT IN THE BRITISH FRIGATE MACEDONIAN 1812 black transfer on a creamware pitcher.

D.7 DECATOR (Mc #12, L #608, L #738) Common. Enoch Wood and Sons. S.

      pitchers.....1.1
      plates.....2.5
      tankard (reported by Larsen).....2.5

D.7 DECATOR black transfer on a Sunderland pink splash lustre ground on a Staffordshire form pitcher. Extremely rare form for a pink lustre ground. This rare ground, coupled with the rare form for the ground, would raise the value of this particular *pitcher* from the 1.1 quoted above for the DECATOR transfer to 6.5+.

D.8 DECATOR (previously unrecorded) Unique. Davenport. L.

      pitcher (one recorded)....5.0

D.8 DECATOR black transfer on a pearlware pitcher.

85

D.9 COMMODORE DECATURE (previously unrecorded) Unique. Enoch Wood and Sons. S.

      pitcher (one recorded).....3.5

D.9 COMMODORE DECATURE pink lustre enamel name in script under the spout. Both sides have an extremely rare UNITED STATES & MACIDONIAN (sic)(U.9a) transfer.

D.11 J. DICKINSON ESQR. MEMBER OF CONGRESS *AND AUTHOR OF LETTERS OF A FARMER OF PENNSYLVANIA* (Previously unrecorded) Unique. Probably Herculaneum Pottery. L.

      7"d bowl (one recorded).....5.0

D.11 DETAIL J. DICKINSON ESQR. MEMBER OF CONGRESS *AND AUTHOR OF LETTERS OF A FARMER OF PENNSYLVANIA* black transfer on a creamware bowl. One recorded example.

D.10 DEUS NOBIS HAEC OTIA FECIT (*God has given us this era of peace*) Chain of the thirteen States. (Mc #182) Extremely rare. Herculaneum Pottery. L.

      pitchers.....4.5
      bowls.....4.75

D.10 DEUS NOBIS HAEC OTIA FECIT black transfer on a cream-ware pitcher. The chain bears the names of the original thirteen States. This is the only transfer that has only thirteen States listed, all others have fifteen or sixteen.

D.12 A DROLL SCENE IN NEWBURYPORT (Mc #257) Unique. Herculaneum Pottery. L.

      pitchers (three recorded).....7.5

D.12 A DROLL SCENE IN NEWBURYPORT black transfer on a creamware body. One of three known examples. *Collection of Mrs. Miles White, Jr.* sold at Anderson Galleries, New York, December, 1936.

E.1 Untitled - EASTON POINT (SHIP AND HOMESTEAD AT EASTON POINT OF CAPTAIN GRAHAM)[5] (previously unrecorded) Unique. Herculaneum Pottery. L.

pitchers (one recorded, another reported).....12.5

E.1 Untitled - EASTON POINT (SHIP AND HOMESTEAD AT EASTON POINT OF CAPTAIN GRAHAM) polychromed black transfer on a creamware pitcher.

E.2 THE ENTERPRISE (previously unrecorded) Unique. L.
pitcher (one recorded).....3.0

E.2 The United States warship THE ENTERPRISE green transfer on a creamware pitcher. This is a very rare color for a creamware transfer.

E.3b ENTERPRISE AND BOXER black transfer on a creamware mug by Davenport. This is the same transfer used on E.3a. One example recorded.

E.3 ENTERPRISE AND BOXER (Mc # 124, L #739) Extremely
rare. Davenport. S.
pitchers.....5.0
mug (one recorded).....5.0

E.4 THE ENTERPRISE AND BOXER (Mc #123) Common.
Enoch Wood and Sons. S.
pitchers.....1.5

E.3a ENTERPRISE AND BOXER black transfer on a creamware wash pitcher. One example recorded on this extremely rare form.

E.4 THE ENTERPRISE AND BOXER black transfer on a buff ground pitcher. Note the distinctive form used by Wood for this <u>ground</u>.

E.5 ENTRANCE OF THE ERIE CANAL INTO THE HUDSON AT ALBANY (Mc #253) Unique. Andrew or Ralph Stevenson. L.

pitcher (one recorded).....2.5

E.5 ENTRANCE OF THE ERIE CANAL INTO THE HUDSON AT ALBANY black transfer on a creamware footed pitcher. Besides the arrangement of the title, there are several other differences between this transfer and E.6.

E.6 ENTRANCE OF THE ERIE CANAL INTO THE HUDSON AT ALBANY (Mc #253) Unique. Andrew or Ralph Stevenson. S-type & L.

footed pitcher (one recorded).....2.75
thick pitchers (see E.6b).....2.0

E.6a ENTRANCE OF THE ERIE CANAL INTO THE HUDSON AT ALBANY black transfer on a creamware footed pitcher. This piece is finely potted and reflects the fine quality of English workmanship of this period.

E.6b ENTRANCE OF THE ERIE CANAL INTO THE HUDSON AT ALBANY black transfer identical to E.6a. This is placed on one of those thick, crude, heavy pitchers having a creamy pale yellow ground and a "screw" device "attaching" the handle. The origin of this pottery is unknown, but the transfer is Stevenson's.

E.7 E PLURIBUS UNUM (previously unrecorded) Very rare. S.

pitchers.....2.5

E.7 E PLURIBUS UNUM black transfer on a pearlware pitcher.

E.8 E PLURIBUS UNUM (previously unrecorded) Extremely rare. Signed within transfer **T. Hadley, Hanley, Staffordshire.** L. pitcher (one recorded).....2.5

E.10 E PLURIBUS UNUM (previously unrecorded) Unique. S. child's mug (one recorded).....0.35

E.10 E PLURIBUS UNUM greyish-green transfer on a pearlware child's mug. This is probably circa 1850 or later.

E.8 E PLURIBUS UNUM black transfer on a creamware pitcher.

E.9 E PLURIBUS UNUM (previously unrecorded) Unique. S.

child's mug 1.0

E.11 E PLURIBUS UNUM (previously unrecorded). Unique. S. very large pitcher (one recorded).....2.5

E.9 E PLURIBUS UNUM blue transfer on a pearlware child's mug.

E.11 E PLURIBUS UNUM polychromed black transfer on a huge pearlware pitcher with a spectacular enamel decorated spout and collar. This enameling, plus the size of this example, place its value far above the value factor of 2.5, quoted for just the transfer.

For additional Eagles see P.36 - P.37 and S.4 - S.41.

E.12 EXCELSIOR (THE ARMS OF THE STATE OF NEW YORK) (previously unrecorded) Extremely rare, possibly unique. Barrow and Company. S.

pitcher (one recorded).....4.0

E.12 EXCELSIOR polychromed black transfer on an earthenware pitcher. Arms of New York State on one side and a family crest on the reverse. Marked Barrow and Company. *Cuthbertson Collection* sold at Anderson Galleries, April, 3, 1927.

E.13 EXCELSIOR THE PEOPLE OF THE WESTERN PART OF THE STATE OF NEW YORK, WEALTHY, POPULOUS, AND INDEPENDENT, READY AT THE CALL OF THEIR COUNTRY TO CONVERT THEIR PEACEABLE PLOUGHSHARES INTO INSTRUMENTS OF WAR (previously unrecorded) Extremely rare. L.

pitchers.....4.0

E.13 EXCELSIOR THE PEOPLE OF THE WESTERN PART OF THE STATE OF NEW YORK, WEALTHY, POPULOUS, AND INDEPENDENT, READY AT THE CALL OF THEIR COUNTRY TO CONVERT THEIR PEACEABLE PLOUGHSHARES INTO INSTRUMENTS OF WAR black transfer on a creamware pitcher.

E.14 EXCELSIOR NEW YORK STATE ARMS THE PEOPLE OF THE WESTERN PART OF THE STATE OF NEW YORK, WEALTHY, POPULOUS, AND INDEPENDENT, READY AT THE CALL OF THEIR COUNTRY TO CONVERT THEIR PEACEABLE PLOUGHSHARES INTO INSTRUMENTS OF WAR (Mc #258) Extremely rare. L.

pitchers.....4.0

E.14 EXCELSIOR NEW YORK STATE ARMS THE PEOPLE OF THE WESTERN PART OF THE STATE OF NEW YORK, WEALTHY, POPULOUS, AND INDEPENDENT, READY AT THE CALL OF THEIR COUNTRY TO CONVERT THEIR PEACEABLE PLOUGHSHARES INTO INSTRUMENTS OF WAR black transfer on a creamware pitcher.

F.1 Untitled - Farewell with American flag ship (previously unrecorded) Extremely rare. L.

beakers.....0.75
bowls.....1.0

F.1 Farewell with American flag ship black transfer on a small creamware beaker. Very unusual form.

F.3 FIRST VIEW OF COM. PERRY's VICTORY (M#125, L #780) Rare. Enoch Wood and Sons. S.

pitchers.....2.5

F.3 FIRST VIEW OF COM. PERRY's VICTORY black transfer on a buff ground Staffordshire pearlware pitcher.

F.2 FAYETTE THE NATIONS GUEST In Commemoration of the visit of Genᴸ La Fayette, to the U.S, of America in the year 1824 (L #740) Very rare in black, extremely rare in blue. R. Hall & Son. S.

pitchers.....3.5
mugs.....2.5

F.2 FAYETTE THE NATIONS GUEST In Commemoration of the visit of Genᴸ La Fayette, to the U.S, of America in the year 1824 dark blue transfer on a pearlware pitcher. Extremely rare in this color.

F.4 THE FOEDERAL (sic) **UNION** (previously unrecorded) Unique. Shelton Group or Stevenson. L.

pitcher (one recorded).....7.5
bowl (one recorded).....8.0

F.4 THE FOEDERAL (sic) UNION black transfer on a creamware pitcher.

F.5 BENJAMIN FRANKLIN Born at Boston in New England the 17th Jan. 1706 (Mc #16) Extremely rare. Herculaneum Pottery. L.

pitchers.....4.5

F.5   BENJAMIN FRANKLIN   Born at Boston in New England the 17th Jan. 1706 black transfer on a creamware pitcher.

F.6 BENJ. FRANKLIN L.L.D.F.R.S. BORN AT BOSTON IN NEW ENGLAND 17 JAN. 1706 (Previously unrecorded) Unique. Probably Herculaneum Pottery or Wedgwood. L.

tankard (one recorded).....4.0
canary beaker (one recorded).....4.5

F.6   BENJ. FRANKLIN L.L.D.F.R.S.   BORN AT BOSTON IN NEW ENGLAND 17 JAN. 1706 black transfer on a creamware tankard.

F.7 BENJ. FRANKLIN L.L.D.F.R.S. BORN AT BOSTON IN NEW ENGLAND 17 JAN. 1706 (Mc #15) Scarce. Herculaneum Pottery or Wedgwood. L.

pitchers.....3.5
bowls.....2.5

F.7   BENJAMIN FRANKLIN L.L.D.F.R.S. Born at BOSTON IN NEW ENGLAND 17 JAN. 1706 black transfer on a creamware bowl.

F.8 DR. FRANKLIN. (Mc #19) Unique. Herculaneum Pottery. L.

plaque (one recorded).....10.0+

F.8 DR. FRANKLIN. a black transfer on an oval creamware plaque. Illustration from Barber, *ANGLO-AMERICAN POTTERY*, 1899 edition. Only recorded example.

F.9 Benjᴺ. Franklin ESQ. L.L.D. & F.R.S. The brave
defender of His Country..etc (Mc #17) Extremely rare.
Herculaneum Pottery. L.
pitchers.....5.0

F.10 Dr. FRANKLIN (Mc #18, L #507) Extremely rare. R.
Wedgwood. S.
pitchers (three recorded).....5.0+
footed bowl (one recorded).....10.0+

F.10 Dr. FRANKLIN greenish-grey transfer on a creamware
Staffordshire pitcher. One of three recorded in this form.

F.9 Benjᴺ. Franklin ESQ L.L.D. & F.R.S The brave defender of His
Country..etc black transfer on a creamware pitcher.

F.11 Untitled - Benjamin Franklin (previously unrecorded)
Scarce. Unknown. S.
child's mug......0.50

F.11 Untitled - Benjamin Franklin child's
mug with red transfer. Staffordshire, circa
1840-80

F.9 detail.

F.12 BENJAMIN FRANKLIN (previously unrecorded) Scarce. S.
    child's toy saucer.....0.20
    other pieces probably exist

F.12 BENJAMIN FRANKLIN red transfer on a pearlware toy saucer. Staffordshire district circa 1840-1880.

F.14 BENJAMIN FRANKLIN (previously unrecorded) Unique. Fell and Company. L-type.
    large teapot (one recorded).....1.5

LATE, PROBABLY COLONIAL REVIVAL, CIRCA 1876

F.14 BENJAMIN FRANKLIN black transfer on a late earthenware teapot.

F.13 BENJAMIN FRANKLIN (previously unrecorded) Rare. S.
    child's mug.....0.50

F.13 BENJAMIN FRANKLIN lavender transfer on a pearlware child's mug. Blue enamel line around the inner lip.

F.15 As FRANKLIN ROBINSON AND CO....ETC (previously unrecorded) Unique. L.
    pitcher (one recorded).....5.0

As Franklin, Robinson and Co.
Imported in the Ship Ontario;
Twelve hundred Chests of Bohea Tea,
The best that e'er was in America.

The next thing if you must know,
Who could dislike the Ship Ontario;
For every Chest, two Cents and half,
Makes Heyer, King and Hodge to laugh.

The Ship Ontario from India came,
Wish ev'ry day we had one of the same;
With the Captain bold as any horned deer,
And Hodge the B----r in his easy Chair.

Now let us drink success unto the Ontario,
In spite of Hodge, who is our daily foe;
Likewise unto the foreign India Trade,
And to these wealthy Merchants it has ...

1797-8.

F.15a As FRANKLIN ROBINSON AND CO....ETC[6] black transfer on a creamware pitcher. See detail next page.

97

Below: **F.15b** detail. See the footnote[6] for further information regarding this unusual poem.

Its Franklin, Robinson and Co.
Imported in the Ship Ontario,
Twelve hundred Chests of Bohea Tea,
The best that e'er was in America.

The next thing if you must know,
Who could dislike the Ship Ontario;
For every Chest, two Cents and half,
Makes Heyer, King and Hodge to laugh.

The Ship Ontario from India came,
Wish ev'ry day we had one of the same;
With the Captain bold as any horned deer,
And Hodge the B***r in his easy Chair.

Now let us drink success unto the Ontario,
In spite of Hodge, who is our daily foe;
Likewise unto the foreign India Trade,
And to these wealthy Merchants it has ma

1797-8.

F.17 FREE TRADE AND SAILORS THEIR - RIGHTS (previously unrecorded) Scarce. Enoch Wood and Sons. S.

under spout decoration.....1.0
side decoration.....1.5

F.17 FREE TRADE AND SAILORS THEIR - RIGHTS black transfer on a pearlware pitcher. Note the difference in the implements below the motto in this transfer as compared with F.16 and F.18.

F.16 FREE TRADE AND SAILORS THEIR RIGHTS (previously unrecorded) Scarce. Enoch Wood and Sons. S.

under spout decoration.....1.0
side decoration.....1.5

F.16 FREE TRADE AND SAILORS THEIR RIGHTS black transfer on a pearlware pitcher.

F.18 FREE TRADE AND SAILORS RIGHTS (previously unrecorded) Scarce. Enoch Wood and Sons. S.

under spout decoration.....1.0
side decoration.....1.5

F.18 FREE TRADE AND SAILORS RIGHTS black polychromed transfer on a pearlware pitcher.

F.19 FREEPORT ARTILLERY (previously unrecorded) Rare.
Herculaneum Pottery. L.
      pitchers (under spout/handle).....+0.3

F.19 FREEPORT ARTILLERY black transfer on a creamware pitcher. Presentation piece for a Thos MEAINS.

G.1 The Gallant Defense of Stonington Aug. 9th 1814
Stonington is free whilst her heroes have one gun left
(Mc #129, L #785) Rare. Herculaneum Pottery. S. & L.
Liverpool pitchers.....18.0
Staffordshire pitchers (large and extremely rare).....25.0+

G.2 GENERAL GATES (Mc #20) Extremely rare. Probably
Wedgwood. L.
pitchers......7.5
bowls.....8.0

G.2 GENERAL GATES black transfer on a creamware bowl.

Above: **G.1a** The Gallant Defense of Stonington Aug. 9th 1814
Stonington is free whilst her heroes have one gun left black transfer on a
Liverpool creamware pitcher. Below: **G1.b** This is also known to
rarely appear on a Staffordshire pitcher as is illustrated by this
enormous (13 1/4"h) pitcher with a black transfer and applied gold
enamel. We have recorded two examples of this large piece.

G.3 Untitled - KING GEORGE II (previously unrecorded)
extremely rare. Worcester. Porcelain.
bulbous tankards.....1.5

G.3 Untitled - KING GEORGE II greyish-black transfer on a
bulbous porcelain tankard.

G.4 LONG LIVE KING GEORGE AND QUEEN CHARLOTTE
(Drakard 393) Extremely rare. Wedgwood. L.
        teapots.....1.5

G.4 LONG LIVE KING GEORGE AND QUEEN CHARLOTTE black transfer on a creamware teapot. Illustrated *Mrs. Donald Baker Collection*, Anderson Galleries, September 27, 1938.

G.5 GEORGE III KING OF GREAT BRITAIN (Drakard 394)
Extremely rare. Wedgwood. L.
        pitchers.....2.5
        teapots.....2.0

G.5 KING GEORGE III KING OF GREAT BRITAIN black transfer on a creamware pitcher, circa 1763.

G.6 Untitled - KING GEORGE III (previously unrecorded)
Extremely rare. Worcester. Porcelain.
        tankards.....2.25

G.6 Untitled - KING GEORGE III black transfer on a porcelain tankard.

G.7 GOD GRANT UNITY (Mc #184) Rarity not known. L.
        pitchers.....1.0

We have never seen this particular transfer which McCauley describes as two allegorical figures representing Britain and America with the above inscription. If the figure representing "America" is actually labelled as such, we would increase the value factor to 2.25, otherwise, it does not sound as if it is a very exciting or desirable transfer.

H.1 THE HONOURABLE JOHN HANCOCK (Mc #21) Extremely rare. Probably Wedgwood. L.

      pitchers.....19.5
      tankards.....19.5
      bowls.....20.0

H.1 THE HONOURABLE JOHN HANCOCK black transfer on a creamware tankard.

H.2 HANCOCK (previously unrecorded - see text page 58) Unique. Herculaneum Pottery. L.

      pitcher (one recorded).....17.5

H.2 HANCOCK black transfer on a creamware pitcher. The name is in applied black enamel.

H.3 HARRISON & REFORM (previously unrecorded) Extremely rare. S.

      small pitcher.....3.5

H.3 HARRISON AND REFORM green transfer on a small earthenware pitcher. Copper lustre band and highlights.

H.4 Untitled - HARRISON (previously unrecorded) Extremely rare. S.

      pitchers.....3.5
      tankards.....3.25

H.4 Untitled - HARRISON black transfer on a wide tan band surrounded by copper lustre.

H.5 HARRISON AND REFORM OUR COUNTRY's HOPE To LET IN 1841 UNION FOR THE SAKE OF UNION (previously unrecorded) Extremely rare. Staffordshire porcelain.

> tea service (each piece bearing a portion of the title)
> cups or saucers (ea).....0.50
> other items probably exist

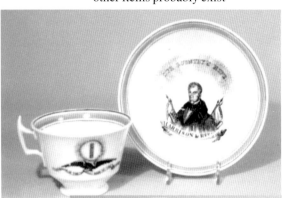

H.5 HARRISON & REFORM (saucers) UNION FOR THE SAKE OF UNION (above cup) To LET IN 1841 (right cup)

H.6 HARRISON AND REFORM UNION FOR THE SAKE OF UNION (L #745) Very rare. S.

> pitchers.....3.5

H.6 HARRISON AND REFORM black transfer within a white medallion on an overall copper lustre pitcher.

H.7 HARRISON & REFORM To LET IN 1841 UNION FOR THE SAKE OF UNION TIPPECANOE THAMES (L #746) Extremely rare. S.

> pitchers.....7.0
> creamers.....4.5

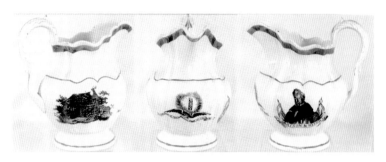

H.7 HARRISON & REFORM pitcher with a carmine transfer and pink lustre band. Log cabin has a sign To LET IN 1841. Under the spout an eagle holding a scroll with the words UNION FOR THE SAKE OF UNION. On the reverse is a bust of Harrison with the motto OUR COUNTRY's HOPE. Sometimes this has an Alexandria, D. C. importer's mark on bottom.

H.8 W. H. HARRISON THE OHIO FARMER (L #749) Extremely rare. American Pottery Manufacturing Company, Jersey City. Staffordshire-shaped earthenware.

> pitchers.....15.0+

H.8 W. H. HARRISON THE OHIO FARMER black transfer on a buff colored earthenware hexagonal pitcher. Inset: Underglaze mark located on the bottom.

H.9 GEN'l W.H. HARRISON HERO OF THE THAMES (L#
609) Extremely rare. Attributed to Ralph Wedg Wood. S.

       platters.....10.0
       plates.....3.75

G.9 GEN'l W. H. HARRISON HERO OF THE THAMES platter with
black "chickweed" border. Tams, Philadelphia importer's mark on the
reverse. One of three recorded platters with this particular border.

H.10 GEN'l W.H. HARRISON HERO OF THE THAMES (L#
609) Unique. Attributed to Ralph Wedg Wood. S.

       platter (one recorded).....10.0
       plates.....3.75

H.10 GEN'l W. H. HARRISON HERO OF THE THAMES light blue
transfer with a light blue line border on a large platter. Tams, Philadelphia
importer's mark on the reverse. Only recorded platter with this border.

H.11 HIBERNIA YE SONS OF HIBERNIA REJOICE IN THE FREEDOM OF YOUR EXTENSIVE COMMERCE. (Bundles labeled: FOR FRANCE; FOR SPAIN; FOR AMERICA). (previously unrecorded) Very Rare. L.

    pitchers.....1.0

H.11 HIBERNIA YE SONS OF HIBERNIA REJOICE IN THE FREEDOM OF YOUR EXTENSIVE COMMERCE. (Bundles labeled: FOR FRANCE; FOR SPAIN; FOR AMERICA) black transfer on a creamware pitcher.

H.12 HOPE (Mc #171) Common. Probably Herculaneum, among others. L.

    pitchers.....1.0
    bowls.....1.0
    plates.....0.20

H.12 HOPE polychromed black transfer on a creamware plate. Several potters used similar transfers and they are usually found with polychrome enamel highlights.

H.13 ESEK HOPKINS (previously unrecorded) Unique. Fell and Company. S.

    shallow bowl (one recorded).....1.0

LATE PROBABLY COLONIAL REVIVAL, 1876

H.13 ESEK HOPKINS black transfer on a rare earthenware bowl. This is probably late 19th Century manufactured during the Colonial Revival movement in America.

H.14 Untitled - HORNET AND THE PEACOCK (Mc #121) Rare. Enoch Wood and Caldwell. Also Enoch Wood and Sons. S.

    pitchers.....1.8
    plates.....1.2

H.14a Untitled - HORNET AND THE PEACOCK black transfer on (left) a pearlware plate. Pink lustre border. Above: H.14.b the same transfer on a thick walled pitcher with a broad lustre band on the collar and a pale yellow, creamy ground.

H.15 Untitled - HORNET BLOCKADING THE BON CITOYENNE (Mc #117, L #750) Extremely rare. Enoch Wood and Sons. S. pitchers.....1.75

H.15 Untitled - HORNET BLOCKADING THE BON CITOYENNE black transfer within a white oval on a Staffordshire pitcher having a green ground and a Sunderland splash lustre band around the neck, which would raise the value factor to 5.0+. Under the transfer in script is the "BENTLEY, WEAR AND BOURNE" engravers mark.

H.17 Untitled - HORNET (and unidentified vessels). (previously unrecorded) Unique. Enoch Wood and Sons. S. pitcher (one known).....2.0

H.17 Untitled - HORNET (and unidentified vessels) black transfer on a pitcher with a yellow-glazed ground and black highlights. Only recorded example of this transfer. Ex-McCauley Collection.

H.16 THE HORNET SINKING THE PEACOCK (Mc #120, L #751) Extremely rare. Enoch Wood and Sons. S. pitchers.....1.75

H.16 THE HORNET SINKING THE PEACOCK black transfer with a white octagonal vignette on a Staffordshire pitcher with an all-over green ground and a black line border. Very unusual without the splash lustre collar. This rare ground would raise the above value factor.

H.18 CAPTAIN HULL OF THE CONSTITUTION (Mc #22, L #752) Common. Enoch Wood and Sons. S. & L (rarely).
        pitchers.....1.75
        tankards.....2.25
        plates.....2.5

H.18 CAPTAIN HULL OF THE CONSTITUTION black transfer within a white oval surrounded by an extremely rare pink Sunderland splash lustre ground on a barrel-shaped pearlware pitcher. As noted in Chapter Four, this rare ground would place the value factor at 7.0+.

H.19 Untitled - HULL (previously unrecorded) Unique. Enoch Wood and Sons. S.

    pitcher - transfer polychromed (one recorded).....7.5

H.19 Untitled - HULL polychromed black transfer within a white oval surrounded by a yellow enamel ground. The neck is white.

H.20 Captain HULL of the Constitution (previously unrecorded) Unique. Probably Enoch Wood and Sons. S.

    pitchers - transfer polychromed (two recorded).....7.5

H.20 Captain HULL of the Constitution black transfer within a white oval surrounded by a green ground. Plain white collar. This transfer seems to be found only on those items where the portrait bust has been polychromed.

H.21 CAPTAIN HULL (previously unrecorded) Extremely rare. Davenport. S.

    plates.....3.5
    Liverpool pitcher (one recorded).....5.0+

H.21a CAPTAIN HULL black transfer on a blue feather edge plate. Impressed DAVENPORT.

H.21b CAPTAIN HULL black transfer on a creamware Liverpool-shaped pitcher. Unmarked, but the same transfer as above, which indicates that the Davenport pottery was making creamware in this form after 1812. Conversely, it is probable that this same firm was responsible for other Liverpool pieces that have not yet been attributed to a specific potter.

H.22 Untitled - HULL (previously unrecorded) Unique. Staffordshire shape - possible American origin.

pitcher (one recorded).....5.0

H.24 CAPTAIN HULL OF THE CONSTITUTION (previously unrecorded) Unique. S.

pitchers (one recorded).....3.5

H.22 Untitled - HULL black transfer on an earthenware pitcher. Applied blue bands. Form is typically English, but similar examples with an American pedigree are recorded.[7] The next transfer (H.23) is the reverse of this piece. This is the only recorded example of either transfer.

H.24 CAPTAIN HULL OF THE CONSTITUTION reddish-brown transfer on a creamware pitcher. This is the reverse of P.19.

H.23 COM. ISAAC HULL 1812 (previously unrecorded) Unique. Staffordshire shape - possible American origin.

pitcher (one recorded).....5.0

H.23 COM. ISAAC HULL 1812 black transfer on an earthenware pitcher. Only recorded example.

I.1 INDEPENDENCE, JULY 4TH 1776 (previously unrecorded)
Extremely rare. S.
　　　　creamer (one recorded).....1.5

I.1 INDEPENDENCE JULY 4TH 1776 black transfer on an unusual pearlware creamer/milk pitcher with a highly skilled application of light blue, ochre, red and yellow enamel.

I.2 INDEPENDENCE, JULY 4TH 1776 (previously unrecorded)
Extremely rare. S.
　　　　plate (one recorded).....2.0

I.2 INDEPENDENCE JULY 4TH 1776 black transfer on a blue feather edge pearlware plate, highlighted skillfully in light blue, red, yellow and green enamel. Quite similar to the previous transfer.

I.3 IN COMMEMORATION OF THE VISIT OF GEN^L LA FAYETTE, TO THE U.S, OF AMERICA IN THE YEAR 1824 FAYETTE THE NATIONS GUEST (L #740) Very rare in black, extremely rare in blue. R. Hall & Son. S.
　　　　pitchers.....3.5
　　　　mugs.....2.5

I.3 IN COMMEMORATION OF THE VISIT OF GEN^L LA FAYETTE, TO THE U.S, OF AMERICA IN THE YEAR 1824 FAYETTE THE NATIONS GUEST dark blue transfer on a pearlware pitcher. Extremely rare in this color.

110

J.1 MAJOR GEN'L ANDREW JACKSON (Mc #24*, L #755) Extremely rare. Davenport. S.

        pitchers (three recorded).....12.5
        plates.....6.0

J.2 GEN^L^. JACKSON HERO OF AMERICA (previously unrecorded) Very rare. Probably Enoch Wood and Sons. S.

        pitchers.....2.5

J.1a MAJOR GEN'L ANDREW JACKSON black transfer on a pearlware pitcher. Black line border and highlights.

J.2 GEN^L^ JACKSON HERO OF AMERICA black transfer on a white band flanked by copper lustre on a small pitcher. Transfer similar to L.12.

J.3 GENERAL JACKSON (previously unrecorded) Extremely rare. Probably Enoch Wood and Sons. S.

        porcelain creamer (one recorded).....1.75
        other pieces probably exist.

J.3 GENERAL JACKSON black transfer on a white porcelain creamer. May also exist on earthenware tea articles.

J.1b MAJOR GEN'L ANDREW JACKSON blue transfer on a pearlware plate with a blue feather edge.

J.4 GENERAL JACKSON THE HERO OF NEW ORLEANS (previously included with J.5 by Larsen) Rarity unknown. Enoch Wood and Sons. S.

> pitchers.....5.0
> plates (possible).....2.5
> 3 1/8"h mug (one recorded).....4.5

J.4 ANDREW JACKSON THE HERO OF NEW ORLEANS black transfer with a broad blue band and copper lustre. This also occurs in a bulbous shaped pitcher. Both forms have either a blue, canary or very rarely a rust band containing the transfer.

J.5 GENERAL JACKSON HERO OF NEW ORLEANS (L #611, L #613, L #753, L #754) Rarity unknown. Enoch Wood and Sons. S.

> plates.....2.5

J.5 GENERAL JACKSON HERO OF NEW ORLEANS rust transfer on a white pearlware plate. This transfer is also found in carmine and black.

J.6 GENERAL JACKSON (previously included with J.5 by Larsen) Rarity unknown. Enoch Wood and Sons. S.

> cup plates.....0.80
> plates (possible).....2.5

J.6 GENERAL JACKSON black transfer on a pearlware cup plate. Impressed WOOD.

J.7 JOHN JAY ESQ. LATE CHIEF JUSTICE OF THE UNITED STATES (Mc #23, L #756) Extremely rare. Davenport. S.

> pitchers.....5.0

J.7 JOHN JAY ESQ. LATE CHIEF JUSTICE OF THE UNITED STATES black transfer on a pearlware pitcher.

J.8 JEFFERSON QUOTATION - **PEACE, COMMERCE, AND HONEST FRIENDSHIP WITH ALL NATIONS - ENTANGLING ALLIANCES WITH NONE - JEFFERSON   Anno Domini - 1804** or **1802** (Mc #155) Common. Shelton Group. L.
>   pitchers.....1.0
>   plate (one recorded).....2.5

J.8 JEFFERSON QUOTATION - PEACE, COMMERCE, AND HONEST FRIENDSHIP WITH ALL NATIONS - ENTANGLING ALLIANCES WITH NONE - JEFFERSON   ANNO DOMINI - 1804 OR 1802 black transfer on a creamware plate, polychromed in red, green, blue and yellow enamel. This transfer is usually polychromed, but this is the only example recorded where it appears on a plate.

J.9 JEFFERSON QUOTATION - **PEACE, COMMERCE, AND HONEST FRIENDSHIP WITH ALL NATIONS - ENTANGLING ALLIANCES WITH NONE - JEFFERSON** (previously unrecorded) Rarity unknown. Herculaneum Pottery. L.

>   pitcher (one recorded).....1.2

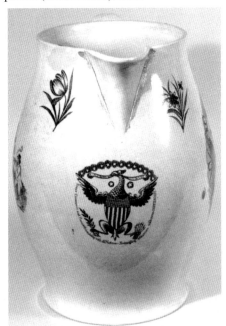

J.9 JEFFERSON QUOTATION - PEACE, COMMERCE, AND HONEST FRIENDSHIP WITH ALL NATIONS - ENTANGLING ALLIANCES WITH NONE - JEFFERSON black transfer on a creamware pitcher. Probably pirated by Herculaneum from the Shelton Group.

J.10 JEFFERSON CARTOON - **BONAPARTE   JEFFERSON   JOHN BULL** (Mc #165) Extremely rare. Herculaneum Pottery. L.
>   pitchers.....9.0

J.10 JEFFERSON CARTOON - BONAPARTE   JEFFERSON   JOHN BULL   black transfer on a creamware pitcher.

J.11 Jefferson Cartoon   **BUNOPARTE** (sic) **JEFFERSON   JOHN BULL** Mc #165) Extremely rare. Herculaneum Pottery. L.
>   pitchers.....9.0

J.11 Jefferson Cartoon - BUNOPARTE (sic) JEFFERSON JOHN BULL black transfer on a creamware pitcher.

J.12 JEFFERSON (Mc#29) Extremely rare. Probably A. or R. Stevenson. S.

> small pitcher (one recorded).....7.5+
> pitchers (heavy and crude).....5.0

J.12   JEFFERSON black transfer on a creamware footed pitcher.

J.13 THOMAS JEFFERSON **PRESIDENT** OF THE UNITED STATES OF **AMERICA** (WITH NAMES OF SIXTEEN STATES) (Mc #25) Rare. Herculaneum Pottery. L.

> pitchers.....10.0
> tankards.....12.0

J.13 THOMAS JEFFERSON PRESIDENT OF THE UNITED STATES OF AMERICA black transfer on a creamware pitcher surrounded by a flowing ribbon containing the names of sixteen States.

J.14 THOMAS JEFFERSON PRESIDENT OF THE UNITED **STATES OF AMERICA** (different arrangement of *fifteen* States) (Mc#25) Rare. Herculaneum Pottery. L.

> pitchers.....10.0
> tankards.....12.0

J.14 THOMAS JEFFERSON   PRESIDENT OF THE UNITED STATES OF AMERICA (different arrangement of *fifteen* States) black transfer on a creamware pitcher.

J.15 THOMAS **JEFFERSON PRESIDENT** OF THE **UNITED STATES OF AMERICA** (without States) (Mc#25) Rare. Herculaneum Pottery. L.

> pitchers....10.0
> tankards.....12.0

J.15 THOMAS JEFFERSON PRESIDENT OF THE UNITED STATES OF AMERICA (without States) black transfer on a creamware pitcher.

J.16 THOMAS JEFFERSON PRESIDENT of the UNITED STATES OF AMERICA (same as Mad*d*ison portrait) with a floral garland containing fifteen states (Mc #26) Rare. Herculaneum Pottery. L.
pitchers.....10.00+

J.16 THOMAS JEFFERSON PRESIDENT of the UNITED STATES OF AMERICA (same as Mad*d*ison portrait) with a floral garland containing fifteen states black transfer on a creamware pitcher.

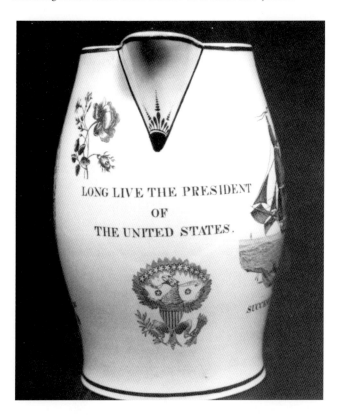

J.16a Black enamel decoration under the spout - LONG LIVE THE PRESIDENT OF THE UNITED STATES.

J.17 THOMAS JEFFERSON PRESIDENT OF THE UNITED STATES OF AMERICA - black enamel above portrait **JEFFERSON AND LIBERTY** (McC #26) Very Rare. Herculaneum Pottery. L.
pitchers.....10.0+

J.17 THOMAS JEFFERSON PRESIDENT OF THE UNITED STATES OF AMERICA black transfer on a creamware pitcher.

J.18 Untitled w/transfer - black enamel under portrait **THOs JEFFERSON PRESIDENT** (previously unrecorded) Very rare. Herculaneum Pottery. L.
pitchers.....10.0+

J.18 Untitled w/transfer - black enamel under portrait THOs JEFFERSON PRESIDENT.

J.19 THOMAS JEFFERSON PRESIDENT OF THE UNITED STATES OF **AMERICA** WE ARE ALL REPUBLICANS ALL FEDERALISTS (previously unrecorded) Unique. Probably Herculaneum. L.
pitchers.....15.0+

J.19 THOMAS JEFFERSON PRESIDENT OF THE UNITED STATES OF AMERICA WE ARE ALL REPUBLICANS ALL FEDERALISTS black transfer on a creamware pitcher.

J.20 THOMAS JEFFERSON PRESIDENT OF THE UNITED STATES OF **AMERICA 1801** WE ARE ALL REPUBLICANS ALL FEDERALISTS (Mc #28) Extremely rare. Herculaneum Pottery. L.
pitchers.....15.0+

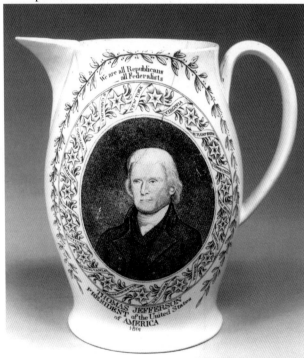

J.20 THOMAS JEFFERSON PRESIDENT OF THE UNITED STATES OF AMERICA 1801 WE ARE ALL REPUBLICANS ALL FEDERALISTS black transfer on a creamware pitcher.

J.21 Untitled - THOMAS JEFFERSON (previously recorded as Mc #28 variant ....in error) Unique. Herculaneum Pottery. L.
plaque (one known to exist).....22.0

J.21 Untitled - THOMAS JEFFERSON black transfer on an oval creamware plaque. This is the only recorded example of this transfer to date[8]. This does not have the signature under the portrait as reported by McCauley. See J.22.

J.22 Untitled - JEFFERSON (previously recorded as Mc #28 variant...this is an error[8]) Unique. Herculaneum Pottery. L.
pitcher (one recorded).....22.0
plaque (possibly one recorded)......22.0

J.22 Untitled - JEFFERSON black transfer on a creamware pitcher with the following in script beneath the portrait "I. HOPWOOD SCULPT FOR I. WYLD"[8].

J.23 Jefferson (Poem) (Mc #30) Extremely rare. Probably Herculaneum Pottery. L.

> pitchers.....15.0+
> tankards.....15.0+

J.24 Jefferson (Poem) (Mc #31) Extremely rare. Herculaneum Pottery. L.

> pitchers.....7.5
> tankards....9.5

J.23 Above: JEFFERSON POEM black transfer on a creamware pitcher. Below: detail of J.23.

J.24 Above: JEFFERSON POEM black transfer on a creamware pitcher. Below: detail of J.24

J.25 JEFFERSON (Mc #27) Extremely rare. Herculaneum Pottery. L.

pitchers.....20.0+

J.25 JEFFERSON black transfer on a creamware pitcher.

J.26 JEFFERSON (previously unrecorded) Very rare. Possibly Enoch Wood and Sons. S.

child's mug......4.5

J.26 JEFFERSON black transfer on a canary handled child's mug. Very desirable and very difficult to obtain an example in **any** condition.

J.27 THOMAS JEFFERSON (previously unrecorded) Extremely rare. Fell and Company. L.

teapots (two recorded).....1.5

LATE PROBABLY COLONIAL REVIVAL, CIRCA 1876.

J.27 THOMAS JEFFERSON greenish-black transfer on a large creamware teapot.

J.28 THOMAS JEFFERSON (previously unrecorded) Extremely rare. Fell and Company. L/S-type.

plate (one recorded).....1.0

LATE, PROBABLY COLONIAL REVIVAL, CIRCA 1876.

J.28 THOMAS JEFFERSON greenish-black transfer on a creamware, blue feather-edge plate.

118

J.29 In black enamel - **JEFFERSON** (previously unrecorded)
Unique. L.

      food warmer (one recorded).....15.0 (if period)

J.29 JEFFERSON polychrome enamel portrait bust with a black enamel title on a creamware food warmer.

J.30 THOMAS JEFFERSON (UNDERSPOUT) (previously unrecorded)
Unique. L.

      pitcher (one recorded).....2.5

J.30 THOMAS JEFFERSON red enamel inscription underspout surrounded by a wreath of leaves ending in a bowknot. Detail: The side transfers of this oddity have two humorous transfers, one of which is titled A SAILOR IN A STABLE.

J.31 CAPTAIN JONES OF THE MACEDONIAN (L #759) Common.
Enoch Wood and Sons. S.

      pitchers.....1.1
      plates.....2.5

J.31a CAPTAIN JONES OF THE MACEDONIAN black transfer within a white oval surrounded by an extremely rare pink Sunderland splash lustre ground on a barrel-shaped pearlware pitcher. The extremely rare ground raises the value of this rather common transfer to a not so common 7.0.

J.31b CAPTAIN JONES OF THE MACEDONIAN black transfer within a white oval surrounded by a maroonish-red ground. This is the only known example of this unique, but rather unattractive ground.

J.32 CAPTAIN JONES (L #758) Unique. Davenport. S.
  Staffordshire pitcher (one recorded).....3.5
  Liverpool pitcher (one recorded).....4.0
  plates.....2.5

J.33 JOHN PAUL JONES

J.32a CAPTAIN JONES black transfer on a Liverpool creamware pitcher. This is the only recorded example of this transfer on this form.

This transfer is on a large earthenware shallow Colonial Revival bowl/basin in the McCauley Collection at the Smithsonian Institution [11]

J.32b CAPTAIN JONES black transfer on a Staffordshire creamware pitcher. Illustrated originally in Barber's, *Anglo-American Pottery*, 1901 edition. This early reference is the only example of this piece that the author's record. Present location unknown.

J.34 JULY 4T 1776 AMERICA Declared Independent
(previously unrecorded) Unique. A. or R. Stevenson. L.
  wash pitcher (one recorded).....2.5

J.34 JULY 4T 1776 AMERICA Declared Independent black transfer on a creamware wash pitcher. Single medallion under the spout of PRESIDENT WASHINGTON (check-list #W.59) is the reason for the Stevenson attribution.

J.35 Untitled - JUSTICE (Figure of) (previously unrecorded)
Unique. Herculaneum Pottery. L.
        pitcher (one recorded).....4.0

J.35 Untitled - JUSTICE (figure of) black transfer on a creamware
pitcher enclosed within a typical Herculaneum Pottery black transfer wreath.

J.36 JUSTICE (previously unrecorded) Unique. Transfer on the
reverse signed T. HADLEY, STAFFORDSHIRE. L.
        pitcher (one recorded).....2.0

J.36 JUSTICE red transfer on a creamware pitcher. Transfer on
the reverse signed T. HADLEY, HANLEY, STAFFORDSHIRE.

121

K.1 MAJ. GEN. HENRY KNOX (previously unrecorded)
Unique. Fell and Company. L.
      large shallow bowl (one recorded).....1.0

LATE PROBABLY COLONIAL REVIVAL, CIRCA **1876.**

K.1 MAJ. GEN. HENRY KNOX black transfer on that unique
bowl in the McCauley Collection at the Smithsonian Institute.

L.1 LAFAYETTE (CROWNED IN GLORY) (Mc #35, L #615, L #765)
Common. Enoch Wood and Sons. S. & L.

 Liverpool pitchers (extremely rare).....2.5
 Lustre Staffordshire pitchers.....0.75
 child's mug.....1.2
 teapot (one recorded).....2.25
 saucer.....0.25
 cup plates (extremely rare).....1.75
 Lustre loving cups (extremely rare).....2.5+
 small bowl w/embossed border (one recorded).....2.25

L.1 LAFAYETTE black transfer on a Staffordshire porcelain teapot. Pink lustre highlights.

L.2 WELCOME LA FAYETTE THE NATION's GUEST AND OUR COUNTRY's GLORY (L #619) Common. R. and J. Clews. S.

 plates......1.0
 cup plates.....1.75
 platters.....3.5
 pitchers (dark blue).....2.5

L.2 WELCOME LA FAYETTE THE NATION's GUEST AND OUR COUNTRY's GLORY dark blue transfer on an embossed pearlware plate. Blue enamel rim.

L.3 GENERAL LA FAYETTE WELCOME TO THE LAND of LIBERTY ....etc (Bust facing right) (previously unrecorded) Very rare. Andrew Stevenson. S.

 plate.....2.5
 platter.....4.0

L.3 GENERAL LA FAYETTE WELCOME TO THE LAND of LIBERTY....ETC (Bust facing right) dark blue transfer on a blue feather edge pearlware plate.

L.3 detail - which shows the entire verse: GENERAL LA FAYETTE WELCOME TO THE LAND OF LIBERTY HE WAS BORN AT AUVERGNE IN FRANCE 1757 JOINED THE AMERICAN STRUGGLE IN 1777. IN 1784 HE RETURNED TO FRANCE LOADED WITH THE HONOURS AND GRATITUDE OF THE AMERICAN PEOPLE. HE RETURNED IN THE CADMUS TO NEW YORK AUG 13 1824.

This appears to be a mirror image of L.5. It also is quite crude and poorly executed.

123

L.4 WELCOME LAFAYETTE THE NATIONS GUEST Gen'l LaFayette was born at Auvergne...etc (L #762) Extremely rare. Andrew Stevenson. S.

       pitchers.....7.5
       teapots (possibly exist)

L.5 General LaFayette **WELCOME TO THE LAND OF LIBERTY** He was born at Auvergne...etc (**shorter verse**) (L #617, L # 761) Extremely rare. Andrew Stevenson. S.

       pitchers.....7.5
       plates.....3.0
       9 1/2" platter (One recorded).....6.0
       cup plates.....3.5

L.4 WELCOME LA FAYETTE THE NATIONS GUEST Gen' l LaFayette was born at Auvergne...etc medium to dark blue transfer on a pearlware pitcher.

L.5 General LaFayette WELCOME TO THE LAND OF LIBERTY He was born at Auvergne...etc medium to dark blue transfer on a pearlware pitcher.

L.4 detail - which shows the entire verse: Gen.l La Fayette was born at auvergne in France at 19 he arrived in America in a ship furnished at his own cost in 1777 and volunteered in our army as Major Gen.l at Brandywine he was wounded but refused to quit the field he assisted the army with 10000 from his own purse and kept in service until our independence was sealed and country free. In 1784 he returned to France loaded with the honours and gratitude of the amern people in 1824 the Congress unanimously offered a ship for his return he declined the honor but landed from the Cadmus at N.Y. Aug.t 13th 1824 amid the acclamations of 60000 freeman

L.5 detail - which shows the entire verse: General LaFayette Welcome to the Land of Liberty He was born at auvergne in France in 1757 joined the American struggle in 1777 and in 1824 returned to repose in the bosom of the land whose liberty he in part

gave birth to. Note that while all three of these similar portrait transfers are by Andrew Stevenson, the verses are totally different.

L.6 GENERAL LA FAYETTE **WELCOME TO THE LAND OF LIBERTY** HE WAS BORN AT AUVERGNE...ETC. (L#618) Extremely rare. Andrew Stevenson. S.
plates.....3.0

L.6 GENERAL LA FAYETTE WELCOME TO THE LAND OF LIBERTY HE WAS BORN AT AUVERGNE...etc orange-red transfer on an embossed polychromed border pearlware plate.

L.7 GENERAL LA FAYETTE **WELCOME TO THE LAND OF LIBERTY** HE WAS BORN AT AUVERGNE....ETC (previously unrecorded) Extremely rare. Andrew Stevenson. S
plates.....3.0

L.7 GENERAL LA FAYETTE WELCOME TO THE LAND OF LIBERTY HE WAS BORN AT AUVERGNE....ETC rust-red transfer on a pearlware plate which has a polychromed embossed rim.

L.6 detail - which shows the entire verse: GENERAL LA FAYETTE WELCOME TO THE LAND OF LIBERTY HE WAS BORN AT AUVERGNE IN FRANCE 1757 JOINED THE AMERICAN STRUGGLE IN 1777 AND IN 1824 RETURNED TO REPOSE IN THE BOSOM OF THE LAND WHOSE LIBERTY HE IN PART GAVE BIRTH TO.

This is the same verse as L.5, but the portrait is quite different. This time Stevenson used a portrait bust of Washington for La Fayette.

L.7 detail - which shows the entire verse: GENERAL LA FAYETTE WELCOME TO THE LAND OF LIBERTY HE WAS BORN AT AUVERGNE IN FRANCE 1757 JOINED THE AMERICAN STRUGGLE IN 1777 AND IN 1824 RETURNED TO REPOSE IN THE BOSOM OF THE LAND WHOSE LIBERTY HE IN PART GAVE BIRTH TO.

The portrait bust in this particular example is different enough from L.5 to warrant a separate listing. This has the impressed crown and circle mark used by both Clews and Andrew Stevenson.

125

L.8 GENERAL LA FAYETTE **WELCOME TO THE LAND OF LIBERTY** (previously unrecorded) Unique. Andrew Stevenson. S.

child's mug (one recorded).....4.0

L.8 GENERAL LA FAYETTE WELCOME TO THE LAND OF LIBERTY medium to dark blue transfer on a pearlware child's mug. Note that in this transfer, Stevenson deleted the entire verse.

L.9 GENERAL LA FAYETTE. **WELCOME TO THE LAND OF LIBERTY** (previously unrecorded) Extremely rare. Andrew Stevenson. S.

plates.....3.0
cup plates.....3.5

L.9 GENERAL LA FAYETTE. WELCOME TO THE LAND OF LIBERTY dark blue transfer on a pearlware cup plate impressed with the circle and crown mark used by both Clews and Andrew Stevenson.

L.10(LA) **FAYETTE THE NATIONS GUEST** IN COMMEMORATION OF THE VISIT OF GEN[L] LA FAYETTE, TO THE U.S, OF AMERICA IN THE YEAR 1824 (L #740) Very rare in black, extremely rare in blue. R. Hall & Son. S.

pitchers.....3.5
mugs.....2.5

L.10 IN COMMEMORATION OF THE VISIT OF GEN[L] LA FAYETTE, TO THE U.S, OF AMERICA IN THE YEAR 1824   FAYETTE THE NATIONS GUEST dark blue transfer on a pearlware pitcher. Extremely rare in this color.

L.11 WELCOME LA FAYETTE THE NATION's GUEST (Mc #34, L #767) Extremely rare. Andrew or Ralph Stevenson. S-type.

pitchers.....2.5

L.11 WELCOME LAFAYETTE THE NATION's GUEST black transfer on a coarse thick-walled earthenware pitcher.

L.12 WELCOME LA FAYETTE THE NATIONS GUEST(L #766) Extremely rare. Probably Enoch Wood and Sons. S.

     pitchers.....1.5
     wine (one recorded).....1.75

L.12a WELCOME LA FAYETTE THE NATIONS GUEST black transfer on a pearlware wine and small pitcher (**L.12b**), both highlighted with broad bands of copper lustre.

L.13 LA FAYETTE WASHINGTON (Mc #621, L #769) Common. Enoch Wood and Sons. S.

     plates.....1.5+
     cup plates.....0.75
     mugs.....1.0

L.13 LA FAYETTE WASHINGTON black transfer on a pearlware plate with an embossed border which has been highlighted with red, blue and green enamel.

L.14 WELCOME LA FAYETTE THE NATIONS GUEST
(previously unrecorded) Extremely rare. Probably Enoch Wood and Sons. Staffordshire porcelain.

     teapots.....1.75
     sugars.....1.5
     creamers.....1.25
     cups and saucers.....0.75+

L.14a WELCOME LA FAYETTE THE NATIONS GUEST strawberry-red transfer on a Staffordshire porcelain teapot of a rather unusual form

L.14b WELCOME LA FAYETTE THE NATIONS GUEST - another form found in Staffordshire porcelain, this time in a shape normally associated with the Wood manufactory. Black transfer on a porcelain teapot highlighted with a combination of pink enamel and pink lustre.

L.15 LAFAYETTE (previously unrecorded) Unique. Fell and Company. L.

    plate (one recorded).....1.0

LATE PROBABLY COLONIAL REVIVAL, 1876

L.15 LAFAYETTE greenish-black transfer on a blue edged plate.

L.16 LANDING OF GENERAL LAFAYETTE AT CASTLE GARDEN NEW YORK AUGUST 13, 1824. (previously unrecorded) Extremely rare. Staffordshire porcelain.

    pitchers.....5.0
    basins.....5.0
    tubs.....7.5

L.16 LANDING OF GENERAL LAFAYETTE AT CASTLE GARDEN NEW YORK AUGUST 13, 1824 magnificent polychromed scenic view on a hexagonal porcelain pitcher.

L.17 LAWRENCE DON'T SURRENDER THE SHIP (Mc #36, L #624, L #770) Common. Enoch Wood and Sons. S.

    pitchers.....1.1
    plates.....2.5

L.17 LAWRENCE DON'T SURRENDER THE SHIP black transfer on a white creamware pitcher.

L.18 JAMES LAWRENCE ESQ.ᴿ *LATE OF THE UNITED STATES NAVY* (Mc #37) Very rare. Enoch Wood and Sons. S. & L.

    Staffordshire pitchers.....2.75
    Liverpool tankards.....3.5
    Liverpool pitchers.....3.75

L.18a JAMES LAWRENCE ESQ.ᴿ *LATE OF THE UNITED STATES NAVY* reddish transfer on a creamware Staffordshire pitcher with a pale yellow ground and on a creamware Liverpool tankard (**L.18b**).

L.19 L'EPERVIER, AND PEACOCK. (previously unrecorded)
Unique. Davenport. S.
      pitcher (one recorded).....3.5

L.19 L'EPERVIER, AND PEACOCK. black transfer on a cream-ware pitcher. This transfer was not recorded until January, 1998, when it was sold in a New England auction.

L.20 LET NOT LIBERTY BE SOLD FOR SILVER NOR GOLD YOUR VOTES FREELY GIVE TO THE BRAVE & THE BOLD (previously unrecorded) Unique. S.
      small pitcher (one recorded).....1.5

L.20 LET NOT LIBERTY BE SOLD FOR SILVER NOR GOLD YOUR VOTES FREELY GIVE TO THE BRAVE & THE BOLD freehand polychrome enamels on a small creamware pitcher. This verse would work equally well for either the English or American markets.

L.21 LET NOT OUR FOES DIVIDE US OUR STRENGTH IS IN OUR UNION (previously unrecorded) Unique. S.
      plates.....0.75

L.21 LET NOT OUR FOES DIVIDE US OUR STRENGTH IS IN OUR UNION black transfer atop a green floral transfer on a pearlware plate. Shape and transfer colors typical of the 1840 - 1850 period.

L.22 LIBERTY INDEPENDENCE (without poem) (previously unrecorded) Extremely rare. Herculaneum Pottery. S.
      pitcher (one recorded).....1.75

L.22 LIBERTY INDEPENDENCE black transfer on a creamware Stafford-shire pitcher by the Herculaneum Pottery. Another example of where all "Staffordshire" is not necessarily from that district. The original of this CCI (see acknowledgements for an explanation of this acronym) had this transfer under the spout and contained the initials *BAM*.

129

L.23 LIBERTY INDEPENDENCE...ETC (Glebe poem) (M#172)
Common on Liverpool, extremely rare on Staffordshire.
Herculaneum Pottery. L.

> pitchers.....1.0
> tankards (very rare).....1.75

L.24 LIBERTY INDEPENDENCE...ETC (Glebe poem) (previously unrecorded) Unknown. Shelton Group. L.

> pitcher (one presently recorded).....2.0

L.24 LIBERTY INDEPENDENCE...ETC (Glebe poem) black transfer on a large creamware pitcher with a WASHINGTON MAP OF THE UNITED STATES (W.16) signed F. MORRIS SHELTON on the reverse.

L.23 Above: LIBERTY INDEPENDENCE As HE TILLS YOUR RICH GLEBE, THE OLD PEASANT SHALL TELL, WHILE HIS BOSOM WITH LIBERTY GLOWS, HOW YOUR WARREN EXPIRED - HOW MONTGOMERY FELL AND HOW WASHINGTON HUMBLED YOUR FOES. Below: detail.

L.25 LIBERTY 1807 (Mc #177) Extremely rare. S.

> plates.....1.0

L.25 LIBERTY 1807 medium blue transfer on a pearlware plate which has an embossed floral rim and medium blue enamel highlights.

L.26 LIBERTY **23rd DECEMBER 1801** (first view) (previously unrecorded) Unique. Herculaneum Pottery. L.
pitcher (one recorded).....2.5

L.26 LIBERTY 23rd DECEMBER 1801 (first view) polychromed black transfer on a creamware pitcher.

L.27 LIBERTY 24th DECEMBER 1801 (second view) (previously unrecorded) Unique. Herculaneum Pottery. L.
pitcher (one recorded).....2.5

L.27 LIBERTY 24TH DECEMBER 1801 (second view) polychromed black transfer on a creamware pitcher. This is the reverse of the above L.26.

L.28 Untitled - LIBERTY CAP FEDERAL FLAG (Previously unrecorded) Unique. L.
pitcher (one recorded).....+0.8

L.28 Untitled - LIBERTY CAP FEDERAL FLAG black transfer on a creamware pitcher.

L.29 Untitled - LIBERTY (previously unrecorded) Unique. S.
pitcher (one recorded).....3.5

L.29 Untitled - LIBERTY polychromed transfer on a very large pearlware pitcher.

L.30 L' I NSURGANT F RENCH F RIGATE... ETC. (Mc #106) Rare. L.
        pitchers.....2.2

L.30 *L' I NSURGANT F RENCH F RIGATE OF 44 GUNS & 411 MEN, STRIKING HER*
COLOURS TO THE A MERICAN F RIGATE C ONSTALATION, C OMMODORE T RUXTON, OF 40
GUNS, AFTER AN ACTION OF AN HOUR & A HALF IN WHICH THE FORMER HAD 75 MEN KILLED
& WOUNDED & THE LATTER ONE KILLED & THREE WOUNDED, F EB. 12TH, 1799 black
transfer on a creamware pitcher. Note how this unknown potter has
changed the spelling of the two ships and the date, plus used italics, in
comparison to the below example, which is the more common Herculaneum transfer. Also, the position of the ships has been reversed.

L.31 L' I NSURGENT F RENCH F RIGATE... ETC. (Mc #105) Scarce.
Herculaneum Pottery. L.
        pitchers.....2.0
        bowls.....2.5

L.31 L' I NSURGENT F RENCH F RIGATE OF 44 GUNS & 411 MEN, STRIKING HER COLOURS
TO THE A MERICAN F RIGATE C ONSTELLATION, C OMMODORE T RUXTON, OF 40 GUNS,
AFTER AN ACTION OF AN HOUR & A HALF IN WHICH THE FORMER HAD 75 MEN KILLED &
WOUNDED & THE LATTER ONE KILLED & THREE WOUNDED, F EB. 10TH, 1799 black
transfer on a creamware pitcher by the Herculaneum Pottery.

M.1 MACEDONIAN AND THE **UNITED STATES** (Mc #116) Rare. Possibly Wedgwood. L.

      pitchers.....2.5
      bowls.....2.75

M.1 MACEDONIAN AND THE UNITED STATES black transfer on a creamware pitcher.

M.2 Untitled - MACEDONIAN AND THE UNITED STATES GR (initials on the drum face below the transfer) (M#103... which was mistakenly listed as the *Bon Homme Richard and the Serapis)* Very rare. Wedgwood. L.

      pitchers.....1.75

M.2 Untitled - MACEDONIAN AND THE UNITED STATES GR black transfer on a creamware pitcher.

M.3 MACEDONIAN COMMANDED BY CAPT. JACOB JONES (L #773) S
      pitchers

Existence doubtful - Larsen lists this view as a yellow pitcher with a 2" purple lustre band at the neck, a form and color which sounds a bit like H.14. We do not have any record of a transfer with this title.

M.4 MADISON (previously unrecorded) Extremely rare. Possibly Enoch Wood and Sons. S.

      childs mug.....4.5

M.4 MADISON black transfer on a yellow-glaze child's mug.

M.5 JAMES MADISON (previously unrecorded) Unique. L.
      plate (one recorded).....9.0+

M.5 JAMES MADISON black transfer on a scalloped rim creamware plate. This is the only recorded example of this great rarity.

M.6 JAMES MADDISON LIBERTY INDEPENDENCE AND THE FEDERAL UNION (Mc #39)Extremely rare. Probably Shelton Group or possibly Herculaneum. L.

> pitchers.....15.0
> tankards.....15.0

M.6 JAMES MADDISON LIBERTY INDEPENDENCE AND THE FEDERAL UNION black transfer on a creamware tankard.

M.7 JAMES MADDISON PRESIDENT OF THE UNITED STATES OF AMERICA (Mc #38) Rare. Herculaneum Pottery. L.

> pitchers.....10.0
> tankards (probably exist).....12.5

M.7 JAMES MADDISON PRESIDENT OF THE UNITED STATES OF AMERICA black transfer on a creamware pitcher. This is the same transfer Herculaneum used for the JEFFERSON portraits (J.16 - J.18)

M.8 Untitled - MADDISON POEM (previously unrecorded) Unique. Herculaneum Pottery. L.

> pitcher (one recorded).....10.0+

M.8 Untitled - MADDISON POEM black transfer on a creamware pitcher. This is the only recorded example of this transfer, however close inspection by collectors and museums, should reveal more that have been missed because of the slight difference caused by the name change.

M.8 Detail: note how the engraver misspelled Maddison on this Herculaneum pitcher

M.9 A MAP OF NORTH AMERICA (previously unrecorded)
Unique. S.

      small tankard (one recorded).....3.5

M.9 A MAP OF NORTH AMERICA polychromed brown transfer on a creamware mug with a broad brown enamel band and highlights.

M.9 detail - A MAP OF NORTH AMERICA showing Louisiana, Canada and a very few American States. This dates this between 1792 (Kentucky admitted) and 1796 (Tennessee admitted).

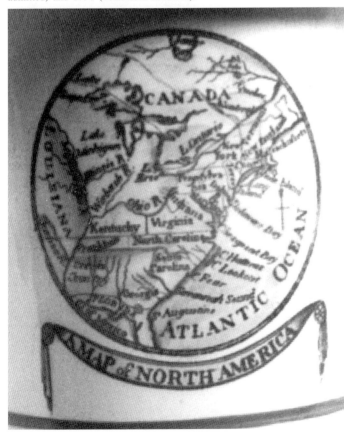

M.10 MASSACHUSETTS (previously unrecorded) Probably extremely rare. L.

      pitchers (two recorded).....1.6

M.10 MASSACHUSETTS black transfer on a creamware pitcher. Transfer printed title incorporated within the "waves" at the base of the transfer.

M.11 Untitled - MARTIAL TROPHIES (previously unrecorded) Very rare. Enoch Wood and Sons. S.

      pitchers (under spout).........add 0.1

M.11 Untitled - MARTIAL TROPHIES magenta transfer on a buff ground Staffordshire pitcher.

M.12 MAY AMERICA NEVER WANT ARTILLERY TO DEFEND HER RIGHTS (Mc #162) Very rare. Herculaneum Pottery. L.

pitchers (under spout).....+ 0.2

M.12 MAY AMERICA NEVER WANT ARTILLERY TO DEFEND HER RIGHTS black transfer beneath the spout of a creamware pitcher.

M.13 MAY COMMERCE FLOURISH (Mc #175*) Unique. L. (Note: McCauley listed this view as *May Columbia Flourish*. He had never actually viewed the transfer, but verbally describes the transfer illustrated below. This **may** exist with the McCauley title, but without firm evidence, we are deleting it and substituting the above title).

pitchers (three recorded).....1.75

M.13 MAY COMMERCE FLOURISH black transfer on a creamware pitcher.

M.14 MAY THE TREE OF LIBERTY EVER FLOURISH PEACE, PLENTY INDEPENDENCE NEW YORK (previously unrecorded) Very rare. Probably Enoch Wood and Sons. S.

pitchers.....1.75

M.14 MAY THE TREE OF LIBERTY EVER FLOURISH PEACE, PLENTY INDEPENDENCE NEW YORK black transfer on a yellow glaze ground. Silver lustre highlights. There is a 20th Century reproduction of this transfer.

M.15 THE MEMORY OF WASHINGTON AND THE PROSCRIBED PATRIOTS OF AMERICA, LIBERTY, VIRTUE, PEACE, JUSTICE, AND EQUITY TO ALL MANKIND (Mc #192, L #783) Liverpool - scarce, Staffordshire - Unique. Shelton Group. S. & L.
Staffordshire pitchers (two recorded).....6.5
Liverpool pitchers.....2.0

M.15 THE MEMORY OF WASHINGTON AND THE PROSCRIBED PATRIOTS OF AMERICA, LIBERTY, VIRTUE, PEACE, JUSTICE, AND EQUITY TO ALL MANKIND polychromed black transfer on a creamware pitcher. The two portrait busts are of John Hancock and Samuel Adams.

136

M.16 MEMORY Those PATRIOTS Who Nobly dared to Protect their rights and succeeded in Emancipating their Country from the tyranny of the Oppressors and laid the foundation of a great EMPIRE on its natural basis - LIBERTY (Mc #176) Unique. Possibly Shelton Group or Stevenson. L.
pitchers.....4.0

M.16 MEMORY Those PATRIOTS...ETC. black transfer on a creamware pitcher.

M.17 MONROE (SEAL OF UNITED STATES) (previously unrecorded. Possibly Enoch Wood and Sons. S.
child's mugs.....5.0

M.17 MONROE (SEAL OF UNITED STATES) black transfer on a yellow-glaze ground with a copper lustre band.

M.18 JAMES MONROE PRESIDENT OF THE UNITED STATES OF AMERICA (Mc #40) Extremely rare. Herculaneum Pottery. L.
pitchers.....15.0+

M.18 JAMES MONROE PRESIDENT OF THE UNITED STATES OF AMERICA black transfer on a creamware pitcher.

M.19 MOUNT VERNON THE SEAT OF THE LATE GEN.ᴸ WASHINGTON (previously unrecorded) Unique. Staffordshire porcelain.
pitcher (one recorded).....2.0

M.19 MOUNT VERNON THE SEAT OF THE LATE GEN.ᴸ WASHINGTON purple-gray transfer on a white porcelain pitcher with a satyr-head spout and brown and gray enamel highlights.

M.20 MUNROE (previously unrecorded) Extremely rare. S.
child's mug.....5.0

M.20 MUNROE red transfer on a child's
mug. This also occurs in black. Usually the
mug has a yellow-glaze ground.

M.21 MUNROE (previously unrecorded) Unique. S.
child's mug.....6.5

M.21 MUNROE medium blue transfer on a pearlware child's
mug.

N.1 Untitled - NAVAL HEROES (Mc#160, L#723) Scarce. Enoch Wood and Sons. S.
pitchers.....2.25

N.1 Untitled - NAVAL HEROES magenta transfer on a buff ground pitcher. Pink lustre highlights.

N.1 detail - showing the names: ROGERS, DECATUR, BAINBRIDGE, PERRY, WARRINGTON, STUART, BARNEY, BLAKELY, PORTER, MACDONNOUGH, LAWRENCE, JONES, HULL.

N.2 NAVAL MONUMENT Under spout (Mc #179, L #724) Extremely rare. Enoch Wood and Sons. S.
pitchers (rare).....+0.8

N.2 NAVAL MONUMENT (Under spout) black transfer on a large buff ground pitcher.

N.3 NEWBURY PORT HARBOR SUCCESS TO THE COMMERCE OF NEWBURY PORT (Mc #256) Very rare. Herculaneum Pottery. L.
pitchers.....7.5

N.3 NEWBURY PORT HARBOR SUCCESS TO THE COMMERCE OF NEWBURY PORT black transfer on a creamware pitcher.

N.4 Untitled - Nᴇᴡʙᴜʀʏᴘᴏʀᴛ Bᴀᴋᴇʀʏ (previously unrecorded)
Unique. Herculaneum Pottery. L.

      pitcher (one recorded).....15.0

N.4 Uɴᴛɪᴛʟᴇᴅ - Nᴇᴡʙᴜʀʏᴘᴏʀᴛ Bᴀᴋᴇʀʏ polychrome black transfer on a cream-ware pitcher. According to the curatorial staff at the Mattatuck Museum (which owns this piece) there is corroborating evidence to confirm the identification of this transfer.

N.5 NEW YORK, Cᴏɴғʟᴀɢʀᴀᴛɪᴏɴ, CITY OF , 16ᴛʜ Dᴇᴄᴇᴍʙᴇʀ 1835 700 Hᴏᴜsᴇs ʙᴜʀɴᴛ Aᴍᴏᴜɴᴛ ᴏғ Pʀᴏᴘᴇʀᴛʏ ᴅᴇsᴛʀᴏʏᴇᴅ 25,000,000 DOLLARS Dɪᴅ ɴᴏᴛ affect Pᴜʙʟɪᴄ Cʀᴇᴅɪᴛ (Previously unrecorded) Extremely rare. S.

      miniature pitchers.....1.2
      miniature mugs.....1.2

N.5 NEW YORK, Cᴏɴ-ғʟᴀɢʀᴀᴛɪᴏɴ, CITY OF, 16ᴛʜ DECEMBER 1835 black transfers on a miniature mug and a miniature pitcher.

N.6 Nᴇᴡ Yᴏʀᴋ (previously unrecorded) Unique. William Adams and Son. S.

      pitcher (one recorded).....1.75

N.6 Nᴇᴡ Yᴏʀᴋ red transfer within a white oval surrounded by a copper lustre ground. The two examples (N.6 and N.7) are the only two instances recorded of an American city appearing on a lustre pitcher[9]

N.7 Nᴇᴡ Yᴏʀᴋ (previously unrecorded) Unique. William Adams and Son. S.

N.7 Nᴇᴡ Yᴏʀᴋ red transfer within a white oval surrounded by a copper lustre ground. This and N.6 are the only two examples recorded. They are also the only two instances of an American city appearing on a lustre pitcher[9] .

**N.8 A NORTH VIEW OF GOV^R. WALLACEs SHELL CASTLE &
HARBOUR NORTH CAROLINA** (previously unrecorded) Unique.
S.

    large pitchers (three recorded).....20.0+

N.8 A NORTH VIEW OF GOV^R. WALLACEs SHELL CASTLE & HARBOUR
NORTH CAROLINA black transfer on a huge pearlware pitcher.

O.1 O LIBERTY! THOU GODDESS...ETC. (Poem) (Mc #173) Common. Shelton Group. L.

     pitchers.....1.0

O.2 OUR COUNTRY's HOPE HARRISON AND REFORM (previously unrecorded) Very rare. S.

     plates.....1.5
     pitchers.....3.5

O.1 O LIBERTY! THOU GODDESS...ETC. (Poem) black transfer on a creamware pitcher.

O.2a OUR COUNTRY's HOPE HARRISON AND REFORM magenta transfer on an earthenware plate. Pink enamel bands.

O.1 Detail: surrounded by an entwined ribbon containing the names of sixteen states, the poem reads: O LIBERTY! THOU GODDESS / HEAVENLY BRIGHT / PROFUSE OF BLISS / AND PREGNANT WITH DELIGHT / ETERNAL PLEASURES IN THY PRESENCE REIGN / A SMILING PLENTY / LEADS THY WANTON TRAIN.

O.2b OUR COUNTRY's HOPE HARRISON AND REFORM black transfer on a wide tan band flanked by copper lustre.

P.1 THOMAS PAINE AUTHOR OF THE RIGHTS OF MAN (Drakard #448) Extremely rare. L.

      pitchers.....4.5

P.1 THOMAS PAINE AUTHOR OF THE RIGHTS OF MAN black transfer on a creamware pitcher.

P.2 PRITHEE TOM PAINE, WHY WILT THOU MEDDLING...ETC. (Drakard #450) Extremely rare. L.

      pitchers.....2.5
      tankards.....2.5

P.2 PRITHEE TOM PAINE, WHY WILT THOU MEDDLING...ETC. black transfer on a creamware pitcher.

P.2 Detail - PRITHEE TOM PAINE, WHY WILT THOU MEDDLING BE IN OTHERS BUSINESS WHICH CONCERNS NOT THEE FOR WHILST THEREON THOU DOIST EXTEND THY CARES THOU DOST AT HOME NEGLECT THINE OWN AFFAIRS GOD SAVE THE KING (within the oval frame)

P.2 detail continued - OBSERVE THE WICKED AND MALITIOUS MAN PROJECTING ALL THE MISCHIEF THAT HE CAN WHEN COMMON POLICY WILL NOT PREVAIL HE'D RATHER VENTURE SOUL & ALL THEN FAIL

P.3 PRITHEE TOM PAINE, WHY WILT THOU MEDDLING...ETC. (Dra #450) Extremely rare. L.

      pitchers.....2.5
      tankards.....2.5

P.3 PRITHEE TOM PAINE, WHY WILT THOU MEDDLING BE IN OTHERS BUSINESS WHICH CONCERNS NOT THEE FOR WHILST THEREON THOU DOIST EXTEND THY CARES THOU DOST AT HOME NEGLECT THINE OWN AFFAIRS GOD SAVE THE KING (within the oval frame) OBSERVE THE WICKED AND MALITIOUS MAN PROJECTING ALL THE MISCHIEF THAT HE CAN black transfer on a creamware tankard that omits the last two lines of the previous transfer.

P.4 PRITHEE TOM PAINE, WHY WILT THOU MEDDLING...ETC. (Dra #451) Extremely rare. L.

tankards.....1.5

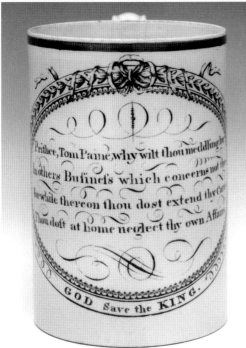

P.4 PRITHEE TOM PAINE, WHY WILT THOU MEDDLING BE   IN OTHERS BUSINESS WHICH CONCERNS NOT THEE   FOR WHILST THEREON THOU DOIST EXTEND THY CARES   THOU DOST AT HOME NEGLECT THINE OWN AFFAIRS   GOD SAVE THE KING. black transfer on a creamware tankard which omits the last four lines of the quote.

P.5 GOD SAVE THE KING.....Occasiond by TOM payne (Drakard #452) Extremely rare. L.

pitchers.....1.75

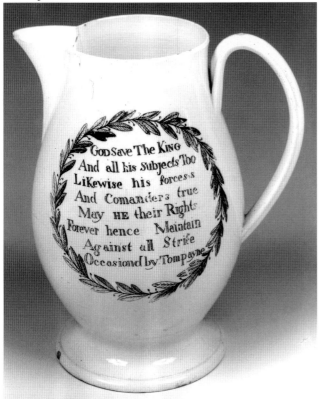

P.5 GOD SAVE THE KING.....etc. black transfer on a creamware footed pitcher.

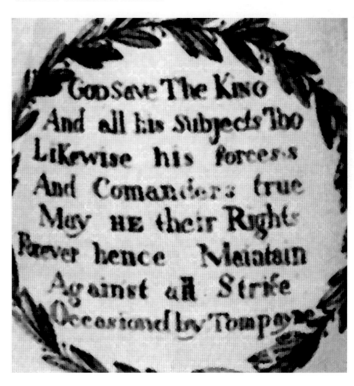

P.6 PEACE   MAY THE BLESSING OF PEACE BE EVER ATTENDED WITH PLENTY (previously unrecorded) Rarity unknown. L.

tankard (one recorded).....1.0

P.6 PEACE   MAY THE BLESSING OF PEACE BE EVER ATTENDED WITH PLENTY black transfer on a creamware tankard. This is another generic transfer which would serve both the home and export market.

P.7 PEACE AND PLENTY (previously unrecorded) Rarity unknown. L.

  beaker (one recorded).....0.5

P.7 PEACE AND PLENTY black transfer on a small creamware beaker. This is still another generic transfer.

P.9 PEACE AND PROSPERITY TO AMERICA (Mc #191, L #778) Common. Enoch Wood and Sons. S.

  pitchers.....1.0

P.9 PEACE AND PROSPERITY TO AMERICA black transfer on a yellow-glaze ground. Silver lustre bands and highlights.

P.8 PEACE AND INDEPENDENCE (Mc #186) Very rare. Probably Herculaneum Pottery. L.

  pitchers.....1.0

P.8 PEACE AND INDEPENDENCE black transfer on a creamware pitcher.

P.10 PEACE PLENTY AND INDEPENDENCE NEW YORK BOSTON (Mc # 189) Common. Herculaneum Pottery among others. L.

  pitchers.....1.0

P.10 PEACE PLENTY AND INDEPENDENCE NEW YORK BOSTON black transfer on a creamware pitcher.

146

P.11 PEACE PLENTY AND **INDEPENDENCE** NAMES OF STATES NEW YORK BOSTON (Mc #190) Fairly common. Probably Herculaneum. S. & L.

pitchers.....1.0

P.11 PEACE PLENTY AND **INDEPENDENCE** NAMES OF STATES NEW YORK BOSTON magenta transfer on a pearlware pitcher highlighted with a lovely rose-pink lustre. This unusual border would add 0.75 to the value of this transfer.

P.12 PEACE PLENTY AND **INDEPENDENCE** NAMES OF STATES BOSTON (previously unrecorded) Common. Herculaneum or Wood and Sons. L (somewhat uncommon). & S.

pitchers.....1.0

P.12 PEACE PLENTY AND **INDEPENDENCE** NAMES OF STATES BOSTON black transfer on a creamware pitcher. This transfer is normally found on Staffordshire pitchers, rarely on Liverpool.

P.13 PEACE PLENTY AND **INDEPENDENCE** NAMES OF STATES (previously unrecorded) Common. Either Herculaneum or Wood and Sons. L. & S.

pitchers.....1.0

P.13 PEACE PLENTY AND INDEPENDENCE NAMES OF STATES black transfer on a creamware pitcher. While this transfer is quite similar to P.12, there are noticeable differences

P.14 PEACE PLENTY AND INDEPENDENCE (Mc #187, L #777) Common. Probably Herculaneum Pottery. L.

pitchers.....1.0
plates...2.5

P.14 PEACE PLENTY AND INDEPENDENCE black transfer on a creamware plate. This is the only example we have seen of this transfer on a plate.

P.15 Peace, Plenty and Independence (previously unrecorded) Unique. L.

      pitcher (one recorded).....1.75

P.17 Wm. Penn, from the European Magazine (previously unrecorded) Unique. L.

      plate (one recorded).....4.5

P.15 Peace, Plenty and Independence black transfer on a creamware pitcher. Note the Seal of the United States in the oval between the two figures. The title is above this Seal, in tiny letters.

P.17 Wm. PENN, from the European Magazine black transfer on a creamware plate.

P.18 Perry (full length portrait) (L #626) S.
Existence doubtful - the plate reported by Larsen came from Alice Morse Earle's, 1892 book, *China Collecting in America*. There is no other record of this transfer.

P.19 PERRY We have met the enemy and they are ours. (previously unrecorded) Unique. S.

      pitcher (one recorded).....3.5

P.16 PEACE AND COMMERCE (French and American Flags) (Mc #185) Unique. Herculaneum Pottery. L.

      pitchers (side transfers).....2.5
      pitchers (underspout).....+20%

P.16 PEACE AND COMMERCE (French and American Flags) black transfer on a creamware pitcher.

P.19 PERRY We have met the enemy and they are ours. reddish-brown transfer on a creamware pitcher. The maker of this is unknown and there are significant differences in this transfer and those used by Wood and Davenport.

148

P.20 PERRY (L #625) Extremely rare. Davenport. S.

      pitcher (one recorded).....4.0

      plates......3.0

P.20a PERRY black transfer on a pearlware plate having an embossed blue feather edge rim. Impressed DAVENPORT.

P.20b PERRY black transfer on a Staffordshire creamware pitcher. This is the only example of this Davenport transfer on a pitcher that we have recorded. Unmarked.

P.21 PERRY WE HAVE MET THE ENEMY AND THEY ARE OURS (Mc #41, L #779) Common. Enoch Wood and Sons. S. & L. (Liverpool extremely rare).

      Liverpool pitchers.....3.5

      pitchers.....1.1

      plates......2.5

P.21 PERRY WE HAVE MET THE ENEMY AND THEY ARE OURS black transfer within a white oval surrounded by a rare green enamel ground, plain neck and black enamel highlights.

P.22 O. H. PERRY ESQ. WE HAVE MET THE ENEMY AND THAY (sic) ARE OURS HERO OF THE LAKE (Mc #42, L #627*) Extremely rare. L

      pitchers.....5.0

      plates (**existence doubtful** - reported by Larsen)

P.22 O. H. PERRY ESQ. WE HAVE MET THE ENEMY AND THAY (sic) ARE OURS HERO OF THE LAKE black transfer on a creamware pitcher. Note this transfer is "Lake", while P.23 is "Lakes".

P.23 COMMODORE PERRY WE HAVE MET THE ENEMY AND THEY ARE OURS HERO OF THE LAKES (Mc #43) Extremely rare. L. pitchers.....5.0

P.25 O. H. PERRY ESQ. WE HAVE MET THE ENEMY AND TH<u>A</u>Y (sic) ARE OURS (previously unrecorded) Unique. L. tankard (one recorded).....6.0

P.23 COMMODORE PERRY WE HAVE MET THE ENEMY AND THEY ARE OURS HERO OF THE LAKES black transfer on a creamware pitcher. Note the correct spelling of the word "they" in this transfer.

P.25 O. H. PERRY ESQ. WE HAVE MET THE ENEMY AND TH<u>A</u>Y (sic) ARE OURS black transfer on a creamware tankard.

P.24 PERRY WE HAVE MET THE ENEMY AND TH<u>A</u>Y (sic) ARE OURS HERO OF THE LAKE (previously unrecorded) Unique. L. tankard (one recorded).....6.0

P.26 COMMODORE PERRY (previously unrecorded) Unique. S. lustre pitchers (name in script...two recorded).....2.5+

P.24 (Perry) WE HAVE MET THE ENEMY AND TH<u>A</u>Y (sic) ARE OURS HERO OF THE LAKE black transfer, without the name, on a creamware tankard.

P.26 COMMODORE PERRY name in pink lustre script under the spout. Side decorations are typical scenic views executed in pink lustre.

150

P.27 Untitled - A Picturesque View of the State of the Nation (England) for Feb. 1778 (Mc #164, Drakard #409/410) Extremely rare. Herculaneum Pottery. L.

      large jug/creamer.....10.0
      pitchers.....10.0+
      plates.....7.5+

P.27 Untitled - A Picturesque View of the State of the Nation (*England*) for Feb. 1778 black transfer on a creamware plate. Over the city is the name Philadelphia. The ship is HMS Eagle, which was Admiral Howe's flagship. The two prostrate figures on the ship represent the admiral and his brother General Howe, who's troops were occupying Philadelphia. The cow is England being *milked* by a Spaniard, Frenchman and Dutchman. A variation on this theme was produced during Jefferson's presidency, however this is much earlier.

P. 28 PIKE (L #629) Extremely rare. Davenport. S.

      pitchers.....3.5
      plates.....3.0

P.28a PIKE black transfer on a pearlware plate which has an embossed blue feather edge rim. Impressed DAVENPORT.

P.28b PIKE black transfer on a creamware pitcher. Illustrated originally in Barber's, *Anglo-American Pottery*, 1901 edition. This early reference is the only example of this piece that the authors record.

P.29 PIKE Be Always Ready to Die for Your Country (Mc #44, L #782) Common. Enoch Wood and Sons. L. and S. (Liverpool extremely rare).

      Liverpool pitchers.....3.5
      Staffordshire pitchers....1.1
      plates.....2.5

P.29a PIKE Be Always Ready to Die for Your Country black transfer on a *creamware* plate with an applied border of brown and green vines and leaves, with bright red berries.

P.29b PIKE Be Always Ready to Die for Your Country black transfer within a white oval surrounded by a green enamel ground and a plain white collar.

Extremely rare. Wedgwood or Sadler. L.

     pitchers.....2.5

     tankards.....2.5

P.31 THE RIGHT HON. WILL^M PITT ESQ black transfer on a creamware tankard.

P.30 PIKE Be Always Ready to Die for Your Country (previously unrecorded) Extremely rare. Probably Enoch Wood and Sons. S.

     polychromed pitcher (one recorded).....7.5

P.32 The Right Hon^{BLE}. W^M. Pitt Esq. One of His Majesty's principal Secretaries of State and One of His Most Hon^{BLE} Privy Council J. Sadler, Liverpool (Previously unrecorded)

Very rare. Sadler. L.

     plaques.....3.5

P.30 PIKE Be Always Ready to Die for Your Country polychromed black transfer within a white oval surrounded by a green ground. Plain white neck. This transfer appears to be used only when the portrait bust is highlighted with polychrome enamels.

P.32 The Right Hon^{BLE}. W^M. Pitt Esq. One of His Majesty's principal Secretaries of State and One of His Most Hon^{BLE} Privy Council J. Sadler, Liverpool black transfer on a creamware plaque.

P.33 Untitled - WILLIAM PITT (previously unrecorded) Extremely rare. Worcester. Porcelain.

small mug.....2.5

P.33 Untitled - WILLIAM PITT greyish transfer on a porcelain mug. Right: Figure of FAME which is on both sides of this example.

P.34 W. PITT ESQ. (relief molded name and figure) (previously unrecorded) Unique. Staffordshire salt glaze.

large plate/charger (one recorded).....2.0

P.34 W. PITT ESQ. relief molded design repeated four times on the shoulder of the salt glazed plate. Circa 1760.

P.35. PLAN OF THE CITY OF WASHINGTON (Mc #265) Scarce. Herculaneum Pottery. L.

pitchers.....2.0

P.35. PLAN OF THE CITY OF WASHINGTON black transfer on a creamware pitcher.

P.36 PLURIBUS UNUM (W/LIBERTY CAP) (previously unrecorded) (Mc #151 **variant**) Very rare. Shelton Group. L.

pitchers.....1.75

P.36 PLURIBUS UNUM (W/LIBERTY CAP) black transfer on a creamware pitcher.

153

P.37 PLURIBUS UNUM (Mc #151) Scarce. Shelton Group. L.
pitchers.....1.5

P.37 PLURIBUS UNUM black transfer on a creamware pitcher.

For additional Eagles see E.7 - E.11 and S.4 - S.41.

P.38 Portland Train of Artillery (Mc #163*)

P.39 SIGNALS AT PORTLAND OBSERVATORY EASTERN STAFF
WESTERN STAFF EXPLANATION (of the signals) (Mc#260)
Extremely rare. Possibly Shelton Group. L.
pitchers.....15.0

P.39 SIGNALS AT PORTLAND OBSERVATORY EASTERN STAFF WESTERN STAFF
EXPLANATION polychromed black transfer on a creamware pitcher. This can
be quite colorful and striking.

**Existence doubtful - McCauley lists this as four men around a
cannon, with one holding an American flag. Neither McCauley
nor the authors have ever actually seen this transfer.**

P.40 Commodore Preble's personal Liverpool pitcher bearing the Preble coat of Arms and COMMODORE PREBLE'S SQUADRON ATTACKING...ETC (C.17) (previously unrecorded) Unique. Herculaneum Pottery. L.

pitcher (one recorded).....25.0

P.40 Left: THE ARMS OF PREBLE polychromed in red, black and yellow enamel

P.41 COMMODORE E. PREBLE (previously unrecorded) Unique. Herculaneum Pottery. L.

pitcher (one recorded).....+0.8

P.41 Right: Beneath the spout a wreath containing a transfer of the name and title.

In our opinion, this is probably the single most *historically* important piece of Liverpool recorded.

Right: A black transfer of COMMODORE PREBLE'S SQUADRON...ETC (check-list C.17).

P.42 COMMODORE PREBLE (Mc#45) Scarce. Herculaneum Pottery. L.

pitchers.....2.0

P.42 COMMODORE PREBLE black transfer on a creamware pitcher. Impressed HERCULANEUM.

P.43 EDWARD PREBLE (previously unrecorded) Unique. Fell and Company. S.

plate (one recorded).....1.0

LATE PROBABLY COLONIAL REVIVAL, 1876

P.43 EDWARD PREBLE greenish-black transfer on a blue feather edge plate. The plates used in this group appear to be 1780 - 1800, but the transfer is quite a bit later.

P.44 THE PRESIDENT (ship) **COMMODORE BERRY** (previously unrecorded). Unique. L.

pitcher (one recorded).....2.0

P.44 THE PRESIDENT (ship) COMMODORE BERRY black transfer on a creamware pitcher. This transfer is confusing, since our records do not list a Commodore Berry. Our records do show that neither Commodore *Barry* nor Commodore *Perry* commanded this vessel prior to her loss in January, 1815. We are still researching this transfer.

P.45 A PRIVATEER ON A CRUISE (also spelled **CRUIZE**) (Mc #132) Scarce. L.

pitchers.....1.0

P.45 A PRIVATEER ON A CRUISE red-rust transfer on a creamware pitcher. Copper lustre highlights and bands. There is an applied copper lustre anchor under the spout of this example.

P.46a THE PROPERTY OF ENGINE Nº 2 (previously unrecorded) Unique. Herculaneum Pottery. L.

      pitcher (one recorded).....+0.7 (cartouche only)

      Also See the Two Following Items

P.46a THE PROPERTY OF ENGINE Nº 2 black transfer under spout decoration found on a creamware pitcher.

P.46b Untitled - Fire Engine Pumper - **THE PROPERTY OF ENGINE Nº 2** (under spout) (previously unrecorded) Unique. Herculaneum Pottery. L.

      pitcher (one recorded).....5.0 (fire engine)

P.46b Untitled - Fire Engine Pumper - THE PROPERTY OF ENGINE Nº 2 (under spout) black enamel scene on a creamware pitcher.

P.46c Untitled - Fire Fighting - **THE PROPERTY OF ENGINE Nº 2** (under spout) Unique. Herculaneum Pottery. L.

      pitcher (one recorded).....5.0 (fire scene)

P.46c Untitled - Fire Fighting - THE PROPERTY OF ENGINE Nº 2 (under spout) black enamel scene on a creamware pitcher.

Q.1 FIRES AT QUEBEC...ᴇᴛᴄ (previously unrecorded) Extremely rare. S.

child's mug (one recorded).....0.75

Q.1 FIRES AT QUEBEC Sᴇᴘᴛᴇᴍʙᴇʀ ᴀɴᴅ Nᴏ-ᴠᴇᴍʙᴇʀ 1836 Hᴏᴜsᴇs ʙᴜʀɴᴛ Aᴍᴏᴜɴᴛ ᴏғ Pʀᴏᴘ-ᴇʀᴛʏ ᴅᴇsᴛʀᴏʏᴇᴅ 1,000,000 DOLLARS light blue transfer on an earthenware child's mug.

Q.2 QUINCY RAIL-WAY (Mc #261) Unique. S.

pitchers (two recorded).....6.0

Q.2 QUINCY RAIL-WAY black transfer on a buff ground Staffordshire pitcher. **Inset:** Title of view found in a cartouche under the spout. Note how delicate the network of glaze crackle is when compared to those fakes and reproductions in Chapter Six.

S.1 Untitled - Salem (Massachusetts) Harbor. (previously unrecorded) Very rare. Wedgwood. S.

      soups and plates.....0.80

S.1 Untitled - Salem (Massachusetts) Harbor black transfer highlighted with green and black enamel on a creamware plate. Often impressed Wedgwood.

S.3 SALLY OF BOSTON (previously unrecorded) Extremely rare. Possibly Herculaneum Pottery. L.

      plates.....2.5

S.3 SALLY OF BOSTON black transfer on an early creamware plate with an embossed green feather edge.

S.2 THE SALLY (previously unrecorded) Unique. Herculaneum Pottery. L.

      large pitcher (one recorded)......2.5

S.2 THE SALLY polychromed black transfer on a very large creamware pitcher.

SEALS OF THE UNITED STATES

The next group of transfers are all variations of the Seal of the United States as produced by the various potters during the period from 1782 through 1850. This is by no means a complete representation of the many different varieties. Our advice as to determining value of an unlisted Seal, is to find a similar listed example and use that value.

One thing should be noted: when a Seal is used as an under spout decoration, it usually has less value than if it is used as a side decoration. There are very few examples found on plates, but these do command a premium valuation.

We have listed other variations of the Seal under E PLURIBUS UNUM (E.7 - E.11) and under PLURIBUS UNUM (P.36 - P.37).

S.4 Spread eagle with shield on it's breast with a "cloud" device and stars over the head. The eagle holds a banner in it's mouth containing the motto **E PLURIBUS UNUM** (previously unrecorded) Scarce. Enoch Wood and Sons. S.

pitchers (side transfer).....1.25
pitchers (under spout).....+0.2

S.4 The same transfer used as a side decoration (left) and as an under spout decoration (above). Under the spout the value factor is +0.2

S.5 Spread (chicken-leg) eagle with a shield on it's breast and an arch of stars over the head, holding a banner containing the motto **E PLURIBUS UNUM** (previously unrecorded) Rare. L. & S.

pitchers (under spout).....1.0
pitchers (side transfer).....2.0
plates.....2.5

S.5 Very unusual Seal on an earthenware plate. Seals found on plates are extremely rare.

S.6 Spread eagle with shield on it's breast and stars arched over the head. **PLURIBUS UNUM** (previously unrecorded) Rare. L.

pitchers (under spout).....+0.2
plates.....2.5

S.6 Typical Seal which is normally found under the spout. This is extremely rare on a plate.

S.7 Spread eagle with motto **MAY SUCCESS ATTEND OUR AGRICULTURE, TRADE AND MANUFACTURES AND SAILORS RIGHTS E PLURIBUS UNUM** Related to "Arms of the United States" transfers. (Mc #150a/b/c) Enoch Wood and Sons. S.

Staffordshire pitchers (under spout - one recorded).....+0.75
plates.....1.8
child's mug.....1.5

S.7 Pearlware child's mug with a red transfer and a red enamel rim.

S.8 Spread eagle with **A PRESENT FOR MY DEAR GIRL MAY SUCCESS ATTEND OUR AGRICULTURE, TRADE AND MANUFACTURES E PLURIBUS UNUM.** Related to the "Arms of the United States" transfers. (Mc #150a/b/c) Enoch Wood and Sons. S.

child's mug.....1.5

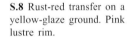

S.8 Rust-red transfer on a yellow-glaze ground. Pink lustre rim.

S.9 Spread eagle with shield on it's breast with rays and stars over the head and a banner in it's mouth with the motto **E PLURIBUS UNUM.** Beneath, the words **HERCULANEUM POTTERY LIVERPOOL** (previously unrecorded) Scarce. Herculaneum Pottery. L.

pitchers (under spout).....+0.35

S.9 Classic Herculaneum Pottery Seal of the United States on a creamware pitcher. There is a variation of this underglaze mark, which only has the words HERCULANEUM POTTERY. Note the "bumps" on the bird's shoulder.

S.10 Spread Eagle with a banner in it's mouth and stars over the head with the motto **E PLURIBUS UNUM** (previously unrecorded). Rare. S. & L.

      batter pitcher (one recorded).....1.5
      pitchers.....1.25

S.10 This Seal is rather unusual in it's design. However, the batter pitcher it is on is a heavy earthenware piece, which is the only example recorded with this type of transfer on this unusual form.

S.11 Spread eagle with a ribbon in it's mouth and the motto **E PLURIBUS UNUM.** (previously unrecorded). Rare. S.

      pebble ground pitcher (one recorded).....2.0

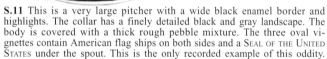

S.11 This is a very large pitcher with a wide black enamel border and highlights. The collar has a finely detailed black and gray landscape. The body is covered with a thick rough pebble mixture. The three oval vignettes contain American flag ships on both sides and a SEAL OF THE UNITED STATES under the spout. This is the only recorded example of this oddity.

S.12 Spread eagle with shield on it's breast with rays and stars over the head and a banner in it's mouth and the motto **E PLURIBUS UNUM.** Common. Herculaneum Pottery. L.

      pitchers (under spout).....+0.2

S.12 Another example of the Herculaneum Seal (note the shoulder "bumps"). Another clue to the Herculaneum origin is the transfer swag around the neck.

S.13 Spread eagle with a banner in it's mouth, stars over head and the motto **E PLURIBUS UNUM.** This surrounded by a continuous linked chain bearing the names of sixteen states, symbolizing the motto FROM MANY ONE. (Mc #154) Scarce. Probably Herculaneum Pottery. L. and S.

      Liverpool pitchers.....1.75
      Staffordshire pitchers (one recorded).....3.5
      tankards.....2.0
      plates.....2.0

S.13a Above: the Liverpool version of this transfer. **Below: S.13b** This Staffordshire example is a CCI from a poor copy in our files. Present location of this actual rarity is unknown.

S.14 Spread eagle with full Jefferson quote (see J.8): PEACE, COMMERCE, AND HONEST FRIENDSHIP WITH ALL NATIONS - ENTANGLING ALLIANCES WITH NONE - JEFFERSON - ANNO DOMINI 1802 (Mc #155) Common. Shelton Group. L.

      pitchers (under spout)......+0.2
      plates.....2.5

S.14 Please note that above we state that this occurs in a "L" form. This is an "S" form and is a recent reproduction, which we illustrate as a supplement to the information contained in Chapter Six. The quote is the full Jefferson quote, including the date 1802 or 1804 as stated in J.8.

S.15 Spread eagle with only a partial JEFFERSON QUOTATION (see J.8): PEACE, COMMERCE, AND HONEST FRIENDSHIP WITH ALL NATIONS - ENTANGLING ALLIANCES WITH (previously unrecorded) Rarity unknown. Shelton Group. L.

      pitchers (under spout)......+0.2
      plates.....2.5

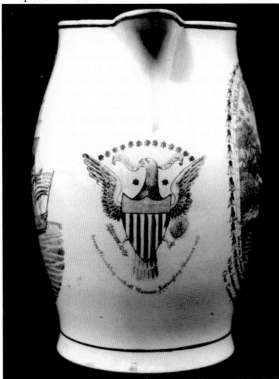

S.15 This Jefferson eagle only has a partial quote and ends with the word "with".

S.16 Spread eagle normally found with the JEFFERSON QUOTATION beneath. In this transfer the quote is entirely omitted and only has the motto found on the banner in the bird's beak **E PLURIBUS UNUM.** (previously unrecorded) Rarity unknown. Shelton Group. L.

      pitchers.....+0.2

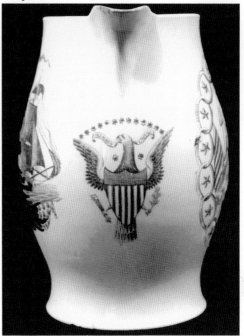

S.16 The JEFFERSON QUOTATION spread eagle without the quotation.

S.17 Spread eagle with full Jefferson quote (see J.9): PEACE, COMMERCE, AND HONEST FRIENDSHIP WITH ALL NATIONS - ENTANGLING ALLIANCES WITH NONE - JEFFERSON (previously unrecorded) Rarity unknown. Herculaneum Pottery. L.

      pitcher (one recorded - under spout).....+0.5

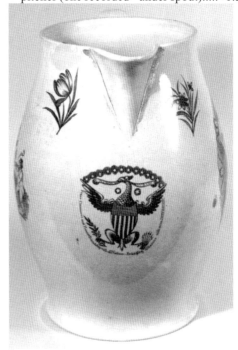

S.17 This is another example of a pottery copying the successful transfer of another. In this case, we believe, it was the Herculaneum Pottery using a Shelton Group idea.

S.18 Spread eagle with a banner in it's mouth and the motto **E PLURIBUS UNUM** over the word **AMERICA**. This is the Enoch Wood and Sons transfer usually found as an under spout transfer (See A.15). (previously unrecorded) Rare. Enoch Wood and Sons. S.

        pitchers (under spout).....+0.5
        pitchers (side transfers) 2.0

S.18 This Enoch Wood SEAL OF THE UNITED STATES is also one of the many transfers on the spectacular Albany Institute pitcher (See 2.18a).

S.19 Tiny red transfer (possibly enamel) spread eagle with a banner in it's mouth and the motto **E PLURIBUS UNUM**. (previously unrecorded) Unique. S.

        plate (one recorded).....1.5

S.19 This very early creamware plate has an enamel red line border and a tiny SEAL OF THE UNITED STATES on the rim. Unmarked, we believe it was manufactured 1782 - 1800.

S.20 Untitled - SEAL OF THE UNITED STATES. Another plate with an enamel line border and a spread eagle on the rim. (previously unrecorded). Rare. Herculaneum Pottery. L.

        plates.....1.0

S.20 Untitled - SEAL OF THE UNITED STATES - polychromed transfer (possibly enamel) on an early creamware plate impressed HERCULANEUM.

S.21 Untitled - SEAL OF THE UNITED STATES (previously unrecorded) Unique. S.

        platter (one recorded).....1.75

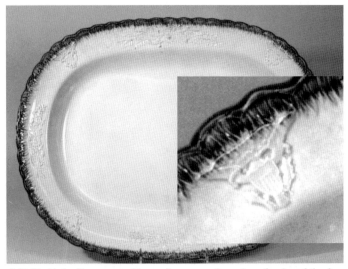

S.21 Untitled - SEAL OF THE UNITED STATES - embossed on the rim of the four corners of a 16" pearlware platter. The rim decoration has the usual embossed feather edge with large floral sprays alternating with the tiny SEALS.

S.22 E PLURIBUS UNUM (Mc #153) Scarce. Herculaneum Pottery. L.

> pitchers (under spout).....1.0
> pitchers (side).....1.75

S.22 Untitled - E PLURIBUS UNUM black transfer on a cream-ware pitcher. This identical eagle was used by Herculaneum as the under spout decoration on the JUSTICE pitcher illustrated J.35.

S.23 Spread eagle with clouds and stars. Holding a banner in it's mouth and the motto **E PLURIBUS UNUM** (previously unrecorded) Very rare. Herculaneum or Enoch Wood and Sons. L.

> pitchers (under spout).....1.0

S.23 Spread eagle with clouds and stars. Holding a banner in it's mouth and the motto E PLURIBUS UNUM black transfer on a creamware pitcher.

S.24 Untitled - SEAL OF THE UNITED STATES **E PLURIBUS UNUM** (previously unrecorded) Very rare. Herculaneum Pottery. S.

> pitchers.....1.2

S.24 Untitled - SEAL OF THE UNITED STATES E PLURIBUS UNUM magenta trans-fer on a pearlware pitcher impressed HERCULANEUM. This is virtually the same SEAL as S.22, but the shape was changed, when the transfer was applied, conforming to the sides of the pitcher. This particular method is called "bat" printing and will be discussed in Volume II of this series.

S.25 Untitled - SEAL OF THE UNITED STATES (similar to S.30) Unique. L.

> pitcher (one recorded).....2.0

S.25 Untitled - SEAL OF THE UNITED STATES black transfer on a creamware pitcher, the reverse of which is the unique FRANKLIN, ROBINSON AND COMPANY (F.15).

165

S.26 E PLURIBUS UNUM (Mc #157) Scarce. Herculaneum Pottery. L. & S.

     pitchers (Liverpool).....1.75
     pitcher (Staffordshire - one recorded).....3.0

S.26 Untitled - E PLURIBUS UNUM black transfer on a creamware pitcher.

S.28 REPUBLICANS ARE NOT ALWAYS UNGRATEFUL (L #714) Very rare (black) Extremely rare (blue). Ric^d Hall and Sons. S.

     pitchers (blue transfer)....1.75
     pitchers (black transfer).....1.0
     mugs.....1.25

Also see Chapter Six - Fakes and Reproductions

S.28 REPUBLICANS ARE NOT ALWAYS UNGRATEFUL medium blue transfer on a pearlware pitcher.

S.27 E PLURIBUS UNUM w/chain of sixteen states. (previously unrecorded) Extremely rare. L.

     pitchers.....2.0

S.27 Untitled - E PLURIBUS UNUM w/ chain of sixteen states black transfer on a creamware pitcher. The extremely rare device above the CHAIN OF STATES is a separate transfer, which is listed L.28.

S.29 E PLURIBUS UNUM (Mc #158) Common. Herculaneum Pottery. L.

     pitchers (under spout)....+0.1

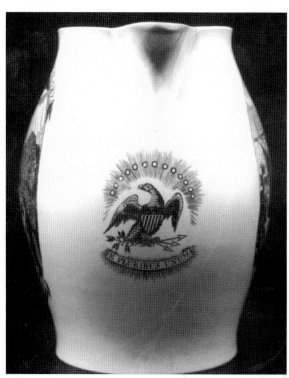

S.29 E PLURIBUS UNUM black transfer on a creamware pitcher. This is another stock SEAL used by Herculaneum.

S.30 Untitled - Spread eagle with a flat topped shield with flags, cannon and a drum below. (Mc #156) Extremely rare. L.
pitchers.....2.0

S.31b E PLURIBUS UNUM polychromed black transfer on a pearlware pitcher. Note the excellent workmanship on the silver lustre design around the neck.

S.30 Untitled - Spread eagle with a flat topped shield with flags, cannon and a drum below black transfer on a creamware pitcher.

S.31 E PLURIBUS UNUM (previously unrecorded) Possibly unique. L. and S.
Liverpool pitcher (one recorded - under spout).....1.2
Staffordshire pitcher (one recorded - side transfer).....3.5

S.32 Untitled - SEAL OF THE UNITED STATES (previously unrecorded) Extremely rare. William Adams and Sons. S.
plates.....1.75

S.32 Untitled - SEAL OF THE UNITED STATES red transfers on blue feather edge pearlware plates. The plate on the left is impressed ADAMS.

S.31a E PLURIBUS UNUM black transfer on a creamware pitcher. Note the olive branches beneath the SEAL, this is unusual.

S.33 E PLURIBUS UNUM (previously unrecorded) Extremely rare. Possibly Enoch Wood and Sons. Staffordshire porcelain.

       cup and saucer......0.85

       a single cup or a single saucer.....0.4

       teapot (probably exists)

       sugar (probably exists)

       creamer (probably exists)

       dregs bowl (probably exists)

S.33 E PLURIBUS UNUM greyish-black transfer on a Staffordshire porcelain cup and saucer. Unmarked.

S.35 Untitled - SEAL OF THE UNITED STATES (previously unrecorded) Extremely rare. S.

       cup plate.....1.2

S.35 Untitled - SEAL OF THE UNITED STATES red transfer on a 3 1/2"d pearlware cup plate. Unmarked.

S.34 Untitled - SEAL OF THE UNITED STATES (previously unrecorded) Probably extremely rare. S.

       child's mug.....0.40

S.34 Untitled - SEAL OF THE UNITED STATES light blue transfer on a pearlware child's mug.

S.36 Untitled - black enamel silhouette of THE SEAL OF THE UNITED STATES (previously unrecorded) Unique. Possibly Enoch Wood and Sons. S.

       pitcher (one recorded).....1.75

S.36 Untitled - black enamel silhouette of THE SEAL OF THE UNITED STATES on a pale-yellow ground pitcher. Side decoration is a nicely executed pink lustre maritime scene. Pink lustre is also used as a line border and to highlight the mask spout.

S.37 Untitled - SEAL OF THE UNITED STATES (previously unrecorded) Rare. Wedgwood. L.

pitchers (under spout).....1.0

S.37 Untitled - SEAL OF THE UNITED STATES black transfer on a creamware footed pitcher impressed WEDGWOOD.

S.38 Untitled - Seal of the United States **E PLURIBUS UNUM** (previously unrecorded) Rare (under spout) Extremely rare (side transfer) Enoch Wood and Sons. S.

pitchers (under spout).....1.2
pitchers (side).....2.5

S.38 Untitled - Seal of the United States E PLURIBUS UNUM black transfer on a pearlware pitcher.

S.39 Untitled - E PLURIBUS UNUM SEAL OF THE UNITED STATES (previously unrecorded) Extremely rare. Herculaneum Pottery. L.

small platter (one recorded).....2.5

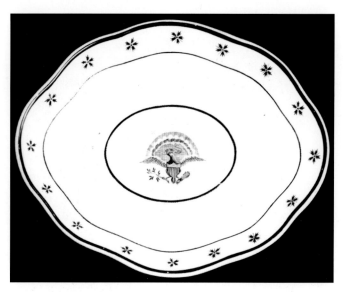

S.39 Untitled - E PLURIBUS UNUM SEAL OF THE UNITED STATES red transfer on a small creamware platter impressed HERCULANEUM.

S.40 Untitled - AMERICAN EAGLE (previously unrecorded) Unique. Enoch Wood and Sons. S.

plate (one recorded).....1.75

S.40 Untitled - AMERICAN EAGLE maroon transfer on a pearlware plate with the impressed mark of Enoch Wood and Sons.

S.41 E PLURIBUS UNUM (INTERIOR) **G. WASHINGTON MARTHA WAHINGTON MAJ. GEN. HENRY KNOX COL. WILLIAM WASHINGTON ESEK HOPKINS JOHN PAUL JONES** (EXTERIOR) (previously unrecorded - mentioned in McCauley) Unique. Fell and Company. L.

large shallow bowl (One recorded)....2.5+ (entire bowl)

S.41a THE SEAL OF THE UNITED STATES, the interior transfer of that unique shallow bowl by Fell and Company.

S.41b Overview of the entire bowl.

S.41b was supposed to be an illustration of one of two large 13"d - 14"d large earthenware shallow bowls/basins in the McCauley Collection at the Smithsonian Institution. [11] **These great rarities have the above transfer of** THE SEAL OF THE UNITED STATES **on the interior center. Around the 3"h - 4"h exterior there are the following oval portrait busts:**

> **George Washington**
> **Martha Washington**
> **Col. William Washington**
> **John Paul Jones**
> **Henry Knox**
> **Esek Hopkins**

The bowls have an impressed mark of FELL AND CO. We believe both to be later pieces made during that period known as the Colonial Revival (1870 - 1890).

S.42 SECOND VIEW OF COM. PERRY'S VICTORY (Mc #126, L #781) Scarce. Enoch Wood and Sons. S.

pitchers......2.5

S.42 SECOND VIEW OF COM. PERRY'S VICTORY black transfer on a very large pearlware pitcher. This particular pitcher has a nicely executed pink lustre decoration around the collar and is so large that the potter placed a shell-shaped handle under the spout. This was originally in the famed Arthur Sussell Collection.

S.43 Ship AMERICA Salem (previously unrecorded) Unique. Spode. L.

plate (two recorded).....2.5

S.43 Ship AMERICA Salem polychromed black transfer on a creamware plate. Title also a transfer. One of two recorded. This example, from the Peabody-Essex Museum is unmarked. Another, in the authors' collection, is impressed SPODE.

S.44 Ship WILMINGTON, Robt. Shields, Master. (previously unrecorded) Extremely rare. L.

plates......2.5

S.44 Ship WILMINGTON, Robt. Shields, Master. black transfer on a creamware plate. This transfer, as compared to S.45, serves to illustrate the English potters use of two different "stock" transfers to portray the same vessel.

S.45 Ship WILMINGTON, Robt. Shields, Master. (previously unrecorded) Extremely rare. L.

platter.....4.5

S.45 Ship WILMINGTON, Robt. Shields, Master. black transfer on a very large creamware platter.

S.46 SHIPBUILDING POEM (Mc #193) Scarce. L.
pitchers.....2.0

S.46 SHIPBUILDING POEM black transfer on a creamware pitcher.

S.47 SHIPBUILDING POEM (Mc #194) Scarce. L.
pitchers.....2.0

S.47 SHIPBUILDING POEM black transfer on a creamware pitcher.

S.47 detail -

OUR MOUNTAINS ARE COVER'D WITH IMPERIAL OAK
WHOSE ROOTS LIKE OUR LIBERTIES, AGES HAVE NOURISHED
BUT LONG E'RE OUR NATION SUBMITS TO THE YOKE
NOT A TREE SHALL BE LEFT ON THE FIELD WHERE IT FLOURISHED
SHOULD INVASION IMPEND, EVERY TREE WOULD DESCEND
FROM THE HILLTOPS THEY SHADED, OUR SHORES TO DEFEND
FOR NE'ER SHALL THE SONS OF COLUMBIA BE SLAVES
WHILE THE EARTH BEARS A PLANT, OR THE SEA ROLLS ITS WAVES

S.46 detail -

OUR MOUNTAINS ARE COVER'D WITH IMPERIAL OAK
WHOSE ROOTS LIKE OUR LIBERTIES, AGES HAVE NOURISHED
BUT LONG E'RE OUR NATION SUBMITS TO THE YOKE
NOT A TREE SHALL BE LEFT ON THE FIELD WHERE IT FLOURISHED
SHOULD INVASION IMPEND, EVERY TREE WOULD DESCEND
FROM THE HILLTOPS THEY SHADED, OUR SHORES TO DEFEND
FOR NE'ER SHALL THE SONS OF COLUMBIA BE SLAVES
WHILE THE EARTH BEARS A PLANT, OR THE SEA ROLLS ITS WAVES

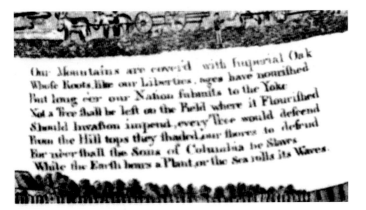

S.48 Untitled - SHIPBUILDING SCENE (previously unrecorded)
Extremely rare. Herculaneum Pottery. L.
pitchers.....3.0

S.48 Untitled - SHIPBUILDING SCENE black transfer on a creamware pitcher. Note the typical Herculaneum swag transfer around the neck. A similar transfer is known with the British Flag, rather than the American.

SHIP TRANSFERS

As a rule, a black transfer of an unnamed American flagged vessel does not effect the value of a piece. However, when the vessel is identified and it has some historical significance, the value is effected. When this hypothetical named vessel is polychromed, the value rises further. When the view of the vessel is other than just a side view, of a two or three masted vessel, the value rises. In this next section, we will illustrate just a few of the many transfers of ships found on Liverpool and Staffordshire pieces and explain the effect each has on the value of a given piece.

Before doing this, we will list the vessels of the American navy during the War of 1812, armament and the date they were launched or placed into commission. Those listed in *italics* were lost during the war. Those in **bold** were captured during the war and placed into American service. This will assist you in identifying which vessels were United States Navy vessels and which might be commercial craft.

Independence, 74, 1814	**Alert, 18, 1812**
Franklin, 74, 1815	Peacock, 18, 1813
United States, 44, 1797	Louisiana, 18, 1804
President, 44, 1797	Hornet, 18, 1805
Constitution, 44, 1797	*Wasp, 18, unkn.*
Macedonian, 38, 1812	Adams, 18, unkn.
Chesapeake, 36, 1797	Oneida, 16, unkn.
Constellation, 36, 1797	*Syren, 16, unkn.*
Congress, 36, 1797	*Argus, 16, unkn.*
New York, 32, unkn.	Enterprise, 14, 1797
Adams, 32, unkn.	*Rattlesnake, 14, unkn.*
Boston, 32, unkn.	Nautilus, 14, unkn.
Essex, 32, unkn.	*Vixen, 14, unkn.*
John Adams, 24, 1799	*Viper, 12, unkn.*
Cyane, 24, 1815	*Sch'r Vixen, 8, unkn.*

S.49 SOUTH CAROLINA (previously unrecorded) Herculaneum Pottery. L.
pitchers (two recorded).....1.75

S.49 SOUTH CAROLINA polychromed black transfer on a creamware pitcher.

S.50 PHEBE CROWELL - under spout decoration of a three masted ship above a Herculaneum Pottery, SEAL OF THE UNITED STATES.

S.50 This black transfer of a three masted ship is of interest (1) because of it's small size (2) it is polychromed (3) it is named. It would add +0.5 to the value of a piece.

S.51 LYDIA & POLLY - unusual Herculaneum Pottery polychromed transfer of a schooner-type vessel. The normal ship transfers are of the larger three masted, square-rigged merchant ships and naval warships.

S.51 This black transfer of a small ship is of interest because (1) the schooner-rigged vessel is unusual (2) the swags and wreath enclosing the view is a nice touch (3) it is polychromed and (4) named. Add +0.5 to the value of the piece. If this is the main transfer, the value factor would be 1.5.

S.52 SUCCESS TO THE CATHARINE - another unusual vessel from the Herculaneum Pottery is this two-masted, square-rigged ship.

S.52 Again, this transfer is of interest because of it's depiction of a *two*-masted, square rigged ship. Also, it is named and polychromed. Add +0.4 to the value of the piece. If this is the main transfer, the value factor would be 1.25.

S.53 THE CONSTANT - Another Herculaneum Pottery (recognize the swags?) two masted vessel with very weird rigging (a combination of square and side). While this has two of the attributes that make it interesting (named and unusual vessel), it lacks color.

S.53 An unusually rigged ship. It's name is not enough to bring this black transfer of THE CONSTANT into the realm of heightened desirability. Therefore it does not affect the value of any other transfers on this pitcher. If this is the main transfer, the value factor would be 1.0.

S.54 Untitled - however this is impressed WEDGWOOD and has a finely executed enamel border and polychrome addition to enhance the black transfer.

S.54 The Wedgwood factory produced this unusual piece which is of interest because (1) it is marked (2) polychromed and (3) an unusual two masted vessel. Add +0.3 to the value of the piece. If this is the main transfer, the value factor would be 1.5.

174

S.55 Untitled - this is your basic run-of-the-mill black transfer of a three-masted vessel that has not been polychromed or named.

S.55 Other than the American flag, this ship transfer has absolutely nothing going for it. It doesn't add anything to the value of the piece. If this is the main transfer, the value factor would be 1.0.

S.56 Untitled - same as the above, except it is just a bit more interesting since it shows a stern aspect of the ship, instead of the much more common side view.

S.56 Only the American flag and the unusual stern view of this vessel should appeal to collectors, but the value of a multi-transfer piece would not be affected. If this is the main transfer, the value factor would be 1.0.

S.57 Untitled - this is one of the many ship transfers belonging to the Shelton Group.

S.57 Once again this simple black transfer of an American flagged vessel does not add to the value of a piece. This same transfer on both sides would give the piece a nominal value factor of 0.5 to 0.7.

S.58 Untitled - This is another Ship Transfer associated with the Shelton Group. The JEFFERSON QUOTE is under the spout.

S.58 Another simple black transfer which does not effect the value.

S.59 Untitled - While very similar to the preceding Ship Transfer, this transfer is definitely by Davenport, which makes it exceedingly rare.

S.59 A black ship transfer which, while it is rather rare, still does not add to the value of a piece. It is illustrated to assist in the possible identification of a Davenport transfer on the sides.

S.60 Untitled - This is a typical stock transfer of a four-masted ship used by the Herculaneum Pottery. Note the beaded edge along the lower portion of the transfer.

S.60 Another black transfer illustrated to assist you in identifying the maker of a piece. Does not effect value. If this is the main transfer, the value factor would be 1.0.

S.61 Untitled - This rare creamware open oval vegetable dish must have been part of a dinner service, which in itself is unusual. Even more interesting is the impressed mark DIXON & AUSTIN, which brings yet another pottery into the list of those that made items expressly for the American market.

S.61 This grayish-black transfer was placed on the creamware open vegetable by the Dixon and Austin pottery. Both the form and impressed mark make this an important addition to a collection. We place a value factor of 0.5 to 1.0 on it.

S.62a Untitled - This is a small child's **TOY** high domed coffee pot with a black transfer of an American flag vessel. Impressed WEDGWOOD, this little creamware rarity is extremely rare and quite desirable.

S.62a In this instance, the transfer really has little value, however since it is of an American flagged vessel on such an unusual form, the value factor of this is placed at 1.0 to 1.5.

S.62b Untitled - This creamware footed creamer has a lovely entwined strap handle and American flagged vessels on both sides. Under the spout is a Seal of the United States. Impressed Wedgwood.

S.62b A Wedgwood piece with this form and a black transfer of a classical view has a value factor of 0.3 to 0.5. With an American flagged vessel, the value factor is 1.0+.

S.63 Untitled - This large graceful creamware soup tureen has transfers of American flagged vessels on both sides.

S.63 Creamware soup tureens with any American motif are quite rare. For that reason, the value factor is 2.0 to 3.0.

S.64 SUCCESS TO THE ALEXANDER CAPᵀ. COFFIN (previously unrecorded) Unique. Possibly Herculaneum. L. pitcher (one recorded).....2.0

S.64 A named vessel, an identified master and a vivid application of polychrome enamel on a black transfer gives this a value factor of 1.5 to 2.5, depending on what is known about the ship and it's master.

S.65 Untitled Soldiers - AMERICAN INFANTRY (Dra #428) Unique (see below). Herculaneum Pottery. L.

        pitcher (one recorded definitely for the American market).....3.5

S.65 Above: Black transfer of three infantrymen polychromed in Continental Army blue. Right: the reverse of the above, which indicates an American destination. This view is not polychromed.

S.66 THE GRATITUDE OF MASSACHUSETTS FOLLOWS CALEB STRONG TO NORTHAMPTON (Mc #46) Extremely rare. L.

        pitchers.....3.5

S.66 THE GRATITUDE OF MASSACHUSETTS FOLLOWS CALEB STRONG TO NORTHAMPTON black **transfer** on a creamware pitcher.

S.67 SUCCESS TO AMERICA (Mc #196) Rare. Herculaneum Pottery. L.

        pitchers (underspout).....+0.4

S.67 SUCCESS TO AMERICA black transfer on a creamware pitcher under the spout. Occasionally found under the handle.

S.68a SUCCESS TO AMERICA WHOSE MILITIA...ETC (Mc #178) Common. Shelton Group. L. & S.

        Liverpool pitchers.....1.5
        Staffordshire pitchers (two recorded).....5.0

S.68a SUCCESS TO AMERICA WHOSE MILITIA...ETC polychromed black transfer on a creamware pitcher. This transfer is usually polychromed.

S.68b SUCCESS TO AMERICA WHOSE MILITIA...ETC (L #724a - cancelled by Larsen)

S.68b SUCCESS TO AMERICA WHOSE MILITIA...etc extremely rare lavender transfer on a huge creamware *Staffordshire* pitcher. This is a very fine, high quality piece of transferware with lavender transfers of shells scattered over the body, which has been highlighted by medium blue enamel bands. This is the identical transfer used on S.68a, but without the addition of the enamel colors.

S.68a/b detail - SUCCESS TO AMERICA WHOSE MILITIA IS BETTER THAN STANDING ARMIES MAY ITS CITIZENS EMULATE SOLDIERS AND ITS SOLDIERS HEROES. WHILE JUSTICE IS THE THRONE TO WHICH WE ARE BOUND TO BEND OUR COUNTRYS RIGHTS AND LAWS WE EVER WILL DEFEND

S.69 SUCCESS TO THE **AMERICAN** TRADE (Mc #197) Very rare. L. and S.

  Staffordshire pitchers.....1.8
  Liverpool bowls......1.5

S.69 SUCCESS TO THE AMERICAN TRADE black transfer on a creamware bowl. Probably manufactured by Herculaneum Pottery.

S.70 SUCCESS TO OUR **NEW GOVERNOR** GENERAL BROOKS (Mc #9) Extremely rare. L.
  pitchers.....3.5

S.70 SUCCESS TO OUR NEW GOVERNOR GENERAL BROOKS black transfer on a creamware pitcher.

S.71 SUCCESS TO THE AMERICAN NAVY (previously unrecorded) Unique. L. & S.

      Liverpool pitcher (one recorded).....5.0
      Staffordshire pitcher (one recorded).....5.0

S.71 SUCCESS TO THE AMERICAN NAVY red transfer on a creamware pitcher.

S.72 SUCCESS TO THE BRITISH ARMS (previously unrecorded) Extremely rare. William Greatbach. L.

      teapot (one recorded).....2.0+ (see below)

S.72 SUCCESS TO THE BRITISH ARMS polychromed black transfer on a small creamware teapot. The reverse has a portrait bust of LORD CORNWALLIS, which was the General's title while in America. It is believed that this scene is meant to depict one of the battles of the American Revolution. It probably does, and when the source print is discovered and confirms this, the above value factor will more than double.

S.73 SUCCESS TO THE BRITISH FLEET (Drakard 299) Rare. Wedgwood and/or Herculaneum Pottery[10]. L.

      bowl (impressed Wedgwood).....2.5
      beaker.....1.5
      tobacco jar.....3.0

S.73 SUCCESS TO THE BRITISH FLEET black transfer on a covered creamware tobacco jar - an extremely rare form. This transfer dates from the French and Indian War, when the Colonies fought alongside the British.

S.74 SUCCESS TO THE CROOKED BUT INTERESTING TOWN OF BOSTON (Mc #250) Extremely rare. L.

      pitchers.....4.5

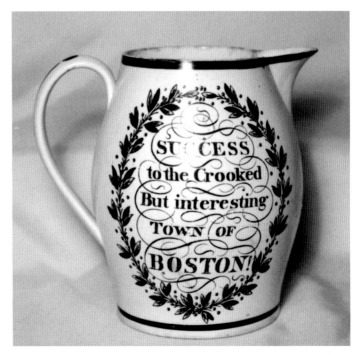

S.74 SUCCESS TO THE CROOKED BUT INTERESTING TOWN OF BOSTON black transfer on a creamware pitcher. Black enamel highlights.

S.75 SUCCESS TO THE INFANT NAVY OF AMERICA (Mc #180)
Rare. Herculaneum Pottery. L.
     pitchers.....+0.3

S.75 SUCCESS TO THE INFANT NAVY OF
AMERICA black transfer on a creamware
pitcher. Used as an under spout or under
handle decoration.

S.77 SUCCESS TO THE TRADE OF RHODE ISLAND (underspout) (previously unrecorded) Unique. Either Herculaneum or Enoch Wood and Sons. S.
     pitcher (one recorded).....2.0

S.77 SUCCESS TO THE TRADE OF RHODE ISLAND black enamel motto under the spout of this pearlware pitcher. We have notes that a SUCCESS TO THE TRADE OF NEW YORK and a SUCCESS TO THE TRADE OF VERMONT also exist. It is probably one of a group of mottos containing the name of one of the first fifteen States or important cities within those States..

S.76 SUCCESS TO THE TRADE OF BOSTON (previously unrecorded)
Unique. Either Herculaneum or Enoch Wood and Sons. S.
     pitcher (one recorded).....2.0

S.78 SUCCESS TO THE UNITED STATES America (previously unrecorded) Unique. L.
     pitcher (one recorded).....2.5

S.76 SUCCESS TO THE TRADE OF BOSTON black enamel motto under the spout of this pearlware pitcher.

S.78 SUCCESS TO THE UNITED STATES America black transfer on a creamware pitcher.

181

S.79 Success to the UNITED STATES of America (previously unrecorded) Unique. L.
> tankard (one recorded).....3.0

S.79 Success to the UNITED STATES of America black transfer on a creamware tankard.

S.80 SUCCESS to the UNITED STATES of AMERICA PLURIBUS UNUM (L #786) Common. Enoch Wood and Sons. S.
> pitchers.....1.5

S.80 SUCCESS to the UNITED STATES of AMERICA PLURIBUS UNUM magenta transfer on a buff ground pitcher. Copper Lustre bands and highlights.

S.81 SUCCESS TO TRADE   WB -TX - NO 4 (on crates) (Mc #198) Rare. Probably Shelton Group. L.
> pitchers.....1.0

S.81   SUCCESS TO TRADE   (on crates) WB - TX - NO 4 black transfer on a creamware pitcher.

S.82 initials under spout in pink lustre - **JMH   1815   Success to Trade** (previously unrecorded). Unique. Enoch Wood and Sons. S.
> pitcher (one recorded).....1.75

S.82   initials under spout in pink lustre - JMH   1815   Success to Trade. There is only one reason why this generic motto would be important to the American collector - *1815* is the year the Treaty of Ghent, which ended the War of 1812, was ratified and trade between England and America was resumed. The pottery district of England was opposed to this war and fought for its end. After trade was resumed, the labor unrest, unemployment and taxes in the area became normalized and prosperity was restored. This motto, with this date, celebrates the end of the War of 1812 and the resumption of trade with America.

S.83 SUCCESS TO THE WOODEN WALLS OF AMERICA (Mc #181)
Rare. Herculaneum Pottery. S.

        pitchers (under spout).....+0.75

S.83 SUCCESS TO THE WOODEN WALLS OF AMERICA black transfer underspout decoration on a creamware pitcher.

S.84 Surrender of Cornwallis - **CORNWALLIS RESIGNING HIS SWORD AT YORKTOWN OCT. 19, 1781** (Mc #104, L #736) Common. Enoch Wood and Sons. L. & S.

        Liverpool pitchers (extremely rare).....2.5
        Lustre Staffordshire pitchers.....0.75
        child's mug.....1.2
        teapot (one recorded).....2.25
        cup.....0.25
        Lustre loving cups (extremely rare).....2.5+

S.84 Untitled - SURRENDER OF CORNWALLIS black transfer on a pearlware teapot. Pink lustre highlights. LAFAYETTE CROWNED (L.1) on cover.

T.1 COLONEL TARLETON (Drakard #425) Extremely rare.
Herculaneum Pottery. L.
pitchers.....4.5

T.1 COLONEL TARLETON black transfer on a creamware pitcher, where the Colonel is depicted in the uniform of the British Legion.

T.2 COLONEL TARLETON (previously unrecorded) Unique. L.
pitchers (two examples recorded).....4.25

T.2 COLONEL TARLETON polychromed black transfer on a creamware pitcher.

T.3 BAN. TARLETON ESQ. COLONEL OF THE BRITISH LEGION
(previously unrecorded) Extremely rare. L.
tankard (one recorded).....4.25

T.3 BAN. TARLETON ESQ. COLONEL OF THE BRITISH LEGION polychromed transfer on a creamware tankard. The date visible on the side is 1784.

T.4 GENERAL Z TAYLOR BORN NOV 24TH 1784 Elected President of America 1848 (previously unrecorded)
Unique. S.
plate (one recorded).....2.5

T.4 GENERAL Z TAYLOR BORN NOV 24TH 1784 ELECTED PRESIDENT OF AMERICA 1848 light blue transfer on a Staffordshire earthenware plate. Polychrome floral decorations on the shoulder.

T.5 To Let in 1840 (previously unrecorded) Rarity unknown. S.

pitcher (one recorded).....3.5
mugs, tea services and plates probably exist

T.5 To Let in 1840 green transfer on an earthenware pitcher. Copper lustre bands and highlights.

T.6 Lieutenant Samuel Treat of the Castle, Boston...Etc. (Previously unrecorded) Unique. L.

pitcher (one recorded).....5.0+

T.6 Lieutenant Samuel Treat of the Castle, Boston - extremely rare presentation pitcher with an applied robins-egg blue ground inscribed in black and gold "*A gift of J. Rob to Lieutenant Treat of the Castle, 1792.*" The "castle" was Castle William in Boston Harbor, whose name was changed to Fort Independence in 1797. Samuel Treat (1750-1806) was born in Boston and held a commission in the Boston Company of Militia.

T.7 THE TRUE BLOODED YANKEE (Mc #133) Common. Probably Enoch Wood and Sons. S. & L.

pitchers.....1.0
tankards.....1.2

T.7 THE TRUE BLOODED YANKEE red transfer on a pale yellow ground. Wide band of pinkish lustre around the neck.

T.8 Tun'd to Freedom for Our Country (Mc #174*) L. Reported to exist by McCauley. This is an English subject transfer as reported by Drakard. This generic view is deleted as an American article.

185

U.1 UNITED AND STEADY IN LIBERTY'S CAUSE WEE'L EVER DEFEND OUR COUNTRY AND LAWS (linked chains with the names of sixteen states) (previously unrecorded) Unique. Enoch Wood and Sons. S.

      pitcher (under spout)(one recorded).....+0.8
      pitcher (side decoration may exist).....2.25

U.2 THE UNION OF TWO GREAT REPUBLICS (Mc #201*) Unique. Shelton Group. L.

      pitchers (three recorded).....4.5

U.2 THE UNION OF TWO GREAT REPUBLICS black transfer on a small creamware pitcher.

U.3 THE UNION SOCIETY OF CORDWAINERS OF THE CITY & LIBERTIES OF PHILADELPHIA UNITE TO MAINTAIN OUR RIGHTS INVIOLATE PROSPERITY ATTEND THE JUSTNESS OF OUR CAUSE. (Previously unrecorded) Unique. Herculaneum Pottery. L.

      pitcher (one recorded).....6.0+

U.1 detail - UNITED AND STEADY IN LIBERTY'S CAUSE WEE'L EVER DEFEND OUR COUNTRY AND LAWS magenta transfer on a pearlware pitcher. Linked chain of sixteen states, which includes W. FLORIDA and S. FLORIDA.

U.3 THE UNION SOCIETY OF CORDWAINERS OF THE CITY & LIBERTIES OF PHILADELPHIA UNITE TO MAINTAIN OUR RIGHTS INVIOLATE PROSPERITY ATTEND THE JUSTNESS OF OUR CAUSE black transfer on a creamware pitcher. Note the crown at the top of the device....was this made prior to the Revolution or did the potter forget to remove it?

U.4 UNION to the **PEOPLE** of **AMERICA** Civil and Religious Liberty to all mankind (Mc #202) Extremely rare. Shelton Group. L.

pitchers...4.25

U.4 UNION to the PEOPLE of AMERICA Civil and Religious Liberty to all mankind black transfer on a creamware pitcher.

U.5 The United States and Macedonian (Mc #115, L #788) Common. Enoch Wood and Sons. S.

pitchers.....1.1

U.5 The United States and Macedonian black transfer on a green ground pitcher that has been further decorated with a pink splash lustre band around the neck.

U.6 United States Frigate Guerriere, Comm^R Macdonnough, bound to Russia July, 1818 (Mc #134) Extremely rare. Herculaneum Pottery. L.

pitchers.....10.0+

U.6 United States Frigate Guerriere, Comm^R Macdonnough, bound to Russia July, 1818 polychromed black transfer on a creamware pitcher. This is considered by the authors as the most desirable of all the ship transfers.

U.7 UNITED STATES OF AMERICA FREE AND INDEPENDENT (previously unrecorded) Extremely rare. Probably Enoch Wood and Sons. S (porcelain).

sugar (one known - tea service probably exists).....1.5
plate (one 6 7/8"d plate known).....1.2
pitchers (two known).....1.75

U.7a Above: UNITED STATES OF AMERICA FREE AND INDEPENDENT porcelain pitcher with black transfer. English scenic views on sides. Two recorded. **U.7b** Right: Plate with green enamel border. One recorded.

188

U.8 THE UNITED STATES OF AMERICA PROSPERITY ATTEND THEM (previously unrecorded) Extremely rare. S.

       plates (two recorded).....1.0
       cup plate (two recorded).....1.5

U.8 THE UNITED STATES OF AMERICA PROSPERITY ATTEND THEM red transfer on a pearlware cup plate. One of two recorded examples.

U.9 United States and Macedonian THE VICTORY ACHIEVED IN THE SHORT SPACE OF SEVENTEEN MINUTES BY THE AMERICAN FRIGATE UNITED STATES COMMANDED BY CAPᵀ DECATUR, OVER THE BRITISH FRIGATE MACIDONIAN (sic) COMMANDED BY CAPT CARDER (previously unrecorded) Unique. Probably Enoch Wood and Sons. S. & L.

       pitchers (Liverpool - two recorded).....3.5
       pitcher (Staffordshire - one recorded).....4.25

U.9a United States and Macedonian THE VICTORY ACHIEVED IN THE SHORT SPACE OF SEVENTEEN MINUTES BY THE AMERICAN FRIGATE UNITED STATES COMMANDED BY CAPᵀ DECATUR, OVER THE BRITISH FRIGATE MACIDONIAN (sic) COMMANDED BY CAPT CARDER black transfer on a pearlware pitcher. Pink lustre decoration around the neck. Under the spout in pink lustre script is *COMMODORE DECATURE.*

U.9b UNITED STATES AND MACEDONIAN THE VICTORY ACHIEVED IN THE SHORT SPACE OF SEVENTEEN MINUTES BY THE AMERICAN FRIGATE UNITED STATES COMMANDED BY CAPᵀ DECATUR, OVER THE BRITISH FRIGATE MACIDONIAN COMMANDED BY CAPT CARDER black transfer on a creamware pitcher. One of two known examples. Present location of both unknown.

U.9c The same pitcher illustrated above, but shown with the underspout transfer of Maᴶ Genᴸ Brown under the spout. We believe the two Liverpool pitchers recorded are the only instances of an underspout use of this type transfer. Lot #379, *Clifford Kaufman Collection,* Anderson Art Assoc., October, 1931.

U.10 UNITED STATES OF AMERICA (previously unrecorded)
Unique. S.
      plate (one recorded).....1.2

U.12 U. S. (Previously unrecorded) unique. L.
      tankard (one recorded).....4.0

U.10 UNITED STATES OF AMERICA medium blue transfer on a pearlware plate. This is the only recorded example of this transfer.

U.12 U. S., black transfer of the initials within a shield device. Early federal flag. This is the only recorded example of this transfer.

U.11 UNITED WE STAND + DIVIDED WE FALL (Mc #203)
Rare. Herculaneum Pottery. L.
      pitchers.....2.7

U.11 UNITED WE STAND + DIVIDED WE FALL black transfer on a creamware pitcher.

V.1 VIEW OF COM. PERRY'S VICTORY (previously unrecorded)
Unique. Enoch Wood and Sons. S.
pitcher (one recorded).....3.0

V.1 VIEW OF COM. PERRY'S VICTORY black transfer on the "Albany" pitcher (see 2.18a/b), which is the only recorded example of this transfer variant. As you can see, the full title which starts with the word "FIRST" is missing. Whether this was a break in the transfer or a true variant, we do not know, so until we do, it receives it's own listing.

V.3 Untitled - Virtue and Valour (no Inscription) (Mc #200a) Extremely rare. Shelton Group. L. *(also see B.10 - B.12).*
pitchers.....2.25
bowls.....3.0

V.3 Untitled - Virtue and Valour (no Inscription) black transfer on a creamware punch bowl.

V.2 SIC SEMPER TYRANNIS (The Arms of the Commonwealth of Virginia surrounded by a chain of thirteen states) (Mc #263) Extremely rare. Herculaneum Pottery. L.
pitchers.....3.5
plates.....3.5

V.2 SIC SEMPER TYRANNIS (The Arms of the Commonwealth of Virginia surrounded by a chain of thirteen states) black transfer on a creamware plate.

V.4 Untitled - View of the Aqueduct Bridge at Little Falls (Mc #254, L #771) Very rare. Either Andrew or Ralph Stevenson. S-type.
pitchers.....2.0

V.4 Untitled - Aqueduct Bridge at Little Falls black transfer on a creamy pale yellow pitcher with a shortened spout and thick, heavy sides. At the base of the handle is an impressed image of a screw, which gives the appearance of the handle having been screwed on. Transfers are from the same copper plate as used by the Stevensons on dark blue Staffordshire. These pitchers are rather crude and unrefined.

V.5 VIEW OF THE AQUEDUCT BRIDGE AT LITTLE FALLS (Mc #252, L #771) Very rare. Attributed to either Andrew or Ralph Stevenson. S-type.

> heavy pitchers.....2.0

V.5 VIEW OF THE AQUEDUCT BRIDGE AT LITTLE FALLS black transfer on a thick pitcher with a creamy pale yellow ground. Title incorporated at the bottom of the transfer.

V.6 VIEW OF THE AQUEDUCT BRIDGE AT ROCHESTER (Mc #254) Very rare. Attributed to either Andrew or Ralph Stevenson. S-type.

> heavy pitchers.....2.0

V.6 VIEW OF THE AQUEDUCT BRIDGE AT ROCHESTER black transfer on a thick unusually shaped pitcher which has a pale creamy yellow ground.

V.7 A VIEW ON HUDSON RIVER (previously unrecorded) Unique. L.

> pitcher (one recorded).....5.0

V.7a A VIEW ON HUDSON RIVER a rare purple transfer on a creamware pitcher.

V.7b The original source print for V.7, as discovered by J. Jefferson Miller II, was taken from Isaac Weld's 1799 travel book, *Travel Through the States of North America, and the Provinces of Upper and Lower Canada, during 1795, 1796 and 1797*. The scene was apparently drawn by Weld during a three day trip by schooner from New York toward Albany in July, 1796.

V.8 VIEW OF LAKE GEORGE (Mc #255) Possibly unique. Either Andrew or Ralph Stevenson. S-type.
        pitchers.....2.25

V.8 VIEW OF LAKE GEORGE black transfer on a thick pitcher which has a pale creamy yellow ground.

The Many Faces
of
George Washington

Washington was the most admired public figure of his age. The English potters represented his likeness using many different source prints and paintings. Luckily, most of the portraits are actually recognizable, while some are of some other person the potter has titled "Washington" for our enlightenment. We have divided the Washington transfers into three groups:

  1. Those transfers that definitely pertain to Washington prior to his death.

  2. Those transfers which can be interpreted to have been executed either before or after his death.

  3. Transfers which were produced after his death.

1. WASHINGTON TRANSFERS PRIOR TO HIS DEATH.

W.1 G. WASHINGTON JOHN ADAMS (previously unrecorded) Unique. Enoch Wood and Sons. S.
  pitcher (one recorded).....20.0+ (see below)

W.1 G. WASHINGTON JOHN ADAMS black transfer on the "Albany" pitcher illustrated 2.18a/b. This is the only recorded example of this rare transfer, which shows the first President and first Vice-President of the United States together. The value ratio indicated above would be for a new discovery, using this transfer.

W.2 GENERAL WASHINGTON (previously unrecorded) Unique. Possibly Herculaneum. S.
  pitcher (one recorded).....6.0

W.2 GENERAL WASHINGTON black transfer on a creamware pitcher which is highlighted with a blue enamel decoration.

W.3 GENERAL WASHINGTON (previously unrecorded) Unique. L.

  plate (one recorded).....6.0

W.3 GENERAL WASHINGTON black transfer on a rather crude creamware plate. Note the decided lack of skill shown by the engraver, not only on the bust of WASHINGTON, but also on the floral sprays on the rim.

194

W.4 HIS EXCELLENCY GEN.ᴸ GEO. WASHINGTON (previously unrecorded) Extremely rare. Herculaneum Pottery or Wedgwood. L.

        tankards.....3.5

W.4 HIS EXCELLENCY GEN.ᴸ GEO. WASHINGTON black transfer on a creamware tankard.

W.5 HIS EXCELLENCY GENERAL WASHINGTON COMMANDER IN CHIEF OF THE FORCES OF THE UNITED STATES OF AMERICA & PRESIDENT OF THE CONGRESS (Mc #48) Scarce. Herculaneum Pottery and/or Wedgwood (see ⁽¹⁰⁾). L.

        pitchers.....2.5
        bowls.....3.5
        tankards.....3.5

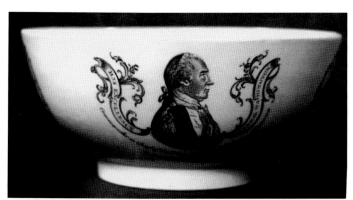

W.5 HIS EXCELLENCY GENERAL WASHINGTON COMMANDER IN CHIEF OF THE FORCES OF THE UNITED STATES OF AMERICA & PRESIDENT OF THE CONGRESS black transfer on a medium sized creamware punch bowl.

W.6 HIS EXCELLENCY GENERAL WASHINGTON COMMANDER IN CHIEF OF THE FORCES OF THE UNITED STATES OF AMERICA (L #504) Unique. Wedgwood. L.

        tea caddy (one recorded)....7.5+

W.6 HIS EXCELLENCY GENERAL WASHINGTON COMMANDER IN CHIEF OF THE FORCES OF THE UNITED STATES OF AMERICA black transfer on a tea caddy impressed WEDGWOOD. This transfer is virtually identical to the transfer used by the Herculaneum Pottery on W.5. Minor differences are found only in the shaded areas of the transfer.

W.7 HIS EXCELLENCY GEN.ᴸ GEORGE WASHINGTON (Mc #51) Extremely rare. Probably Herculaneum. L.

        octagonal plates.....2.0

W.7 HIS EXCELLENCY GEN.ᴸ GEORGE WASHINGTON black transfer on an octagonal creamware plate.

W.8 Untitled - HIS EXCELLENCY GEN'L WASHINGTON (previously unrecorded) Unique. Herculaneum or Enoch Wood and Sons (see below). S.

pitcher (one recorded).....3.5

W.8 Untitled - HIS EXCELLENCY GEN'L WASHINGTON black transfer on a broad blue band on a copper lustre pitcher. We have always thought this transfer was by the Herculaneum Pottery, but Geoffrey Godden and Michael Gibson in their work, *Collecting Lustreware*, attribute this particular form to Enoch Wood and Sons. This attribution is based on similar pieces recovered from the foundation of a church in Burslem, where Enoch Wood placed examples of his current production in the early 19th Century.

W.9 HIS EXCELLENCY GEO. WASHINGTON (previously unrecorded) Extremely rare. Probably Herculaneum, possibly Enoch Wood and Sons (see above - W.8). L.

pitchers.....4.0

W.9 HIS EXCELLENCY GEO. WASHINGTON black transfer on a creamware pitcher.

W.10 GEORGE WASHINGTON, ESQʀ GENERAL AND **COMMANDER IN CHIEF** OF THE **CONTINENTAL** ARMY IN AMERICA (previously unrecorded) Unique. Probably Herculaneum Pottery, possibly Enoch Wood and Sons. L. & S.

tankard (one recorded).....4.0

W.10 GEORGE WASHINGTON, ESQʀ GENERAL AND COMMANDER IN CHIEF OF THE CONTINENTAL ARMY IN AMERICA black transfer on a *pearlware* tankard.

W.11 HIS EXCELLENCY GENERAL GEORGE WASHINGTON MARSHAL OF FRANCE, AND COMMANDER IN CHIEF OF ALL THE NORTH AMERICAN CONTINENTAL FORCES (Mc #50) Very rare. Herculaneum Pottery or Enoch Wood and Sons. L.

pitchers.....3.25
tankards....3.5

W.11 HIS EXCELLENCY GENERAL GEORGE WASHINGTON MARSHAL OF FRANCE, AND COMMANDER IN CHIEF OF ALL THE NORTH AMERICAN CONTINENTAL FORCES black transfer on a creamware tankard.

W.12 Washington - **LONG LIVE THE PRESIDENT**(Mc #59, L #506) Unique. Ralph Wedg wood. S.
  pitchers (three known).....10.0+

W.12 Washington - LONG LIVE THE PRESIDENT olive green transfer on an embossed pitcher. Classical figure under the spout and a portrait bust of Franklin on the reverse.

W.13 Washington - **THE PRESIDENT OF THE UNITED STATES** (Mc #49) Extremely rare. L.
  tankards (four recorded).....10.0+
  small bowl (one recorded).....8.0

W.13 Washington - THE PRESIDENT OF THE UNITED STATES black transfer on a creamware tankard.

W.14 Washington - **THE PRESIDENT OF THE UNITED STATES OF AMERICA** (previously unrecorded) Unique. L.
  pitcher (one recorded).....10.0+
  tankard (one recorded).....8.0

W.14 Washington - THE PRESIDENT OF THE UNITED STATES OF AMERICA black transfer on a creamware tankard.

W.15 Washington - Map of the United States (without footnotes) (Mc #58, Mc # 58A) Common. Herculaneum Pottery. L. & S.
  pitchers (Staffordshire-extremely rare).....5.0
  pitchers.....1.75
  tankards.....2.5

W.15a Washington - Map of the United States (without footnotes) black transfer on a creamware pitcher.

197

W.15b WASHINGTON - MAP OF THE UNITED STATES (without footnotes) (Mc #58, Mc # 58A) Marked example Unique. Wedgwood. L.

pitcher (marked WEDGWOOD - one recorded).....2.25

W.15b WASHINGTON - MAP OF THE UNITED STATES (without footnotes) black transfer on a pitcher impressed Wedgwood. This raises the question of whether this transfer is Wedgwood, or did Herculaneum do the transfer on a Wedgwood blank?

W.16 WASHINGTON MAP OF THE UNITED STATES (with footnotes) (Mc #58, Mc # 58A) Rare. Shelton Group. L. & S.
pitchers (Staffordshire-extremely rare).....5.0
pitchers.....1.75
tankards.....2.5

W.16 WASHINGTON MAP OF THE UNITED STATES (with footnotes) black transfer on a creamware tankard.

W.17 WASHINGTON (Poem) (previously unrecorded) Unique. Herculaneum Pottery. L.
pitcher (one recorded).....10.0+

W.17 Above: WASHINGTON (Poem) black transfer on a creamware pitcher. Only one example has been recorded, but we expect more will be discovered as collectors and museums examine their collections more closely. Below: detail of the transfer showing the entire poem, along with the name "WASHINGTON". Present location unknown.

W.18 DEAFNESS TO THE EAR THAT WILL PATIENTLY HEAR, AND DUMBNESS TO THE TONGUE THAT WILL UTTER A CALUMNY AGAINST THE IMMORTAL WASHINGTON LONG LIVE THE PRESIDENT OF THE UNITED STATES MY FAVORITE SON (Mc #54) Rare. Shelton Group. L.

pitchers.....4.25
soup tureen.....17.5
undertray.....10.0
tankards.....5.0
bowls.....4.5

W.18a/b/c DEAFNESS TO THE EAR THAT WILL PATIENTLY HEAR, AND DUMBNESS TO THE TONGUE THAT WILL UTTER A CALUMNY AGAINST THE IMMORTAL WASHINGTON LONG LIVE THE PRESIDENT OF THE UNITED STATES MY FAVORITE SON black transfers on (a: above) a creamware bowl (b: right) an extremely rare creamware tankard (c: below) a unique creamware soup tureen.

W.19 DEAFNESS TO THE EAR THAT WILL PATIENTLY HEAR, AND DUMBNESS TO THE TONGUE THAT WILL UTTER A CALUMNY AGAINST THE IMMORTAL WASHINGTON LONG LIVE THE PRESIDENT OF THE UNITED STATES MY FAVORITE SON (Mc #55, L #793) Rare. Probably Shelton Group or possibly Herculaneum Pottery. L.

pitchers.....5.0
tankards.....5.5
bowls (possibly exist)

W.19 DEAFNESS TO THE EAR THAT WILL PATIENTLY HEAR, AND DUMBNESS TO THE TONGUE THAT WILL UTTER A CALUMNY AGAINST THE IMMORTAL WASHINGTON LONG LIVE THE PRESIDENT OF THE UNITED STATES MY FAVORITE SON black transfer on a creamware pitcher.

W.20 GEN^L WASHINGTON (previously unrecorded) Unique. L.

pitcher (one recorded).....7.5

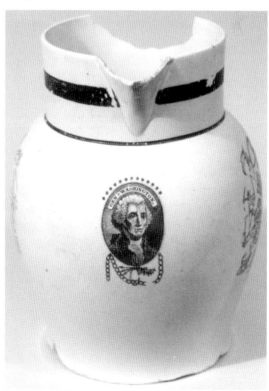

W.20 GEN^L WASHINGTON black transfer on a creamware pitcher.

W.21 G. WASHINGTON, ESQ. (Mc#47B*) Unique. Herculaneum Pottery. L.

      pitcher (one recorded).....8.5

W.21 G. WASHINGTON, ESQ. black transfer on a creamware pitcher. This is the only recorded example of this transfer, which includes the name.

W.22 Untitled - WASHINGTON (Mc #47) Scarce. Herculaneum Pottery. L. & S.

      pitchers (sometimes impressed Herculaneum).....4.0
      tankards.....4.5
      plaques.....3.5

W.22a/b Untitled - WASHINGTON black transfer on (**a:** above) an oval creamware plaque (**b:** right) a creamware pitcher.

W.22c Extremely rare tankard with a very unusual engine turned design around the upper rim.

W.23 HIS EXCELLENCY GEN.ᴸ GEO. WASHINGTON (previously unrecorded) Extremely rare. Herculaneum Pottery or Wedgwood. L.

      bowls.....4.5

W.23 HIS EXCELLENCY GEN.ᴸ GEO. WASHINGTON black transfer on a medium sized creamware punch bowl.

W.24 WASHINGTON PRESIDENT Seal of the United States. (previously unrecorded) Unique. Attributed to Joshua Heath. S. plates.....7.5

W.24 WASHINGTON PRESIDENT Seal of the United States blue transfer on a pearlware plate.

W.25 COLUMBIA'S FAVOURITE SON HIS EXCELLENCY GENERAL WASHINGTON Commander in Chief of the Forces of the United States of America & President of the Congress(same as W.5 with addition of the enamel motto. (motto and form previously unrecorded) Extremely rare. Herculaneum Pottery. L.

coffee pot......15.0+

W.25 Washington Columbia's Favourite Son HIS EXCELLENCY GENERAL WASHINGTON...Etc., black transfer and black enamel on an extremely rare creamware coffee pot.

2. TRANSFERS EXECUTED EITHER BEFORE OR AFTER WASHINGTON'S DEATH.

W.27 WASHINGTON (name only) (previously unrecorded) Very rare. Probably Enoch Wood and Sons. S.

    child's mug.....3.5

W.27 WASHINGTON olive greenish transfer on a pearlware child's mug. Brown enamel line border.

W.28 WASHINGTON (portrait bust) (previously unrecorded) Extremely rare. Probably Enoch Wood and Sons. S.

    child's mug.....6.5

W.28 WASHINGTON blue transfer on a pearlware child's mug.

W.29 WASHINGTON w/Chain of fifteen States (Mc #57) Common. Herculaneum Pottery. L.

    pitchers.....1.0

W.29 WASHINGTON w/Chain of fifteen States black transfer on a creamware pitcher.

W.30 WASHINGTON CROWNED WITH LAURELS BY LIBERTY (Mc #53) Scarce. Shelton Group. L. & S.

    Liverpool pitchers.....1.5
    Staffordshire pitcher (one recorded).....4.5

W.30a WASHINGTON CROWNED WITH LAURELS BY LIBERTY polychromed black transfer on a creamware pitcher. This transfer is usually found enhanced with polychrome enamels

W.30b WASHINGTON CROWNED WITH LAURELS BY LIBERTY lavender transfer on a very large pearlware pitcher. Blue enamel highlights.

W.31 Untitled - WASHINGTON w/chain of stars and a scroll containing the names of sixteen States (previously unrecorded) Extremely rare. Shelton Group. L.
pitchers.....2.5

W.31 Untitled - WASHINGTON w/chain of stars and a scroll containing the names of sixteen States, black transfer on a creamware pitcher.

W.32a G. WASHINGTON   AMERICA DECLARED INDEPENDENT 4TH JULY 1776 w/ scroll of fifteen States black transfer on a creamware Liverpool pitcher.

W.32b G. WASHINGTON   AMERICA DECLARED INDEPENDENT 4TH JULY 1776 w/ scroll of fifteen States black transfer on an extremely rare Staffordshire pitcher.

W.33 G WASHINGTON (AMER DECL INDEPE JULY 4 1776) (on a tablet held by the figure on the left) (fifteen states) (previously unrecorded) Unique. Shelton Group. L.

pitcher (one recorded).....2.75

W.33 G WASHINGTON (AMER DECL INDEPE JULY 4 1776) (on a tablet held by the figure on the left) (fifteen states) polychromed black transfer on a creamware Liverpool pitcher.

W.34 WASHINGTON W/CHAIN OF FIFTEEN STATES and **FIRST PRESIDENT OF THE U. S. OF AMERICA** (same as W.29, previously unrecorded with the black enamel inscription) Unique. Herculaneum Pottery. L.

pitcher (with enamel inscription).....2.5

W.34 WASHINGTON W/CHAIN OF FIFTEEN STATES and FIRST PRESIDENT OF THE U. S. OF AMERICA black transfer and enamel on a creamware pitcher.

3. Transfers Produced After Washington's Death

W.35 G. W. (on the urn) GEORGE WASHINGTON - **Born February 11, 1732, Gen.**[L] OF THE AMERICAN ARMIES 1775 - RESIGNED 1783 - PRESIDENT OF THE UNITED STATES 1789 - RESIGNED 1796. GENERAL OF THE AMERICAN ARMIES 1798 - DIED UNIVERSALLY REGRETTED 14TH DECEMBER 1799. (Mc #70) Rare. Herculaneum Pottery. L.

       pitchers.....1.75

W.35 G. W. (on the urn) GEORGE WASHINGTON - ETC. black transfer on a creamware pitcher.

W.36 GENERAL **WASHINGTON** DEPARTED THIS LIFE DEC. 14TH, **1799 AE 67** AND THE TEARS OF A NATION WATERED HIS GRAVE (Mc #72, L #790) Rare. Enoch Wood and Sons. S.

       pitchers.....3.0
       plates.....3.75

W.36 GENERAL WASHINGTON DEPARTED THIS LIFE DEC. 14TH, 1799 AE 67 AND THE TEARS OF A NATION WATERED HIS GRAVE black transfer on a creamware pitcher.

W.37 HE IN GLORY + AMERICA IN TEARS (Mc #60) Rare. Herculaneum Pottery. L.

       pitchers.....1.8
       tankards.....2.75

W.37 HE IN GLORY + AMERICA IN TEARS black transfer on a creamware pitcher.

W.38 HE IN GLORY + AMERICA IN TEARS (Mc #61) Rare. Herculaneum Pottery. L.

       pitchers.....1.8

W.38 HE IN GLORY + AMERICA IN TEARS black transfer on a creamware pitcher.

W.39 APOTHEOSIS Sacred to the memory of Washington Ob 14 Dec. A.D., 1799, Ae 68 (Mc #64A) Common. Herculaneum Pottery. L.

      pitchers.....1.0
      tankards.....2.0

W.39 APOTHEOSIS Sacred to the memory of Washington Ob 14 Dec. A.D., 1799, Ae 68 black transfer on a creamware pitcher. Note the word "Apotheosis" is white on black.

W.40 APOTHEOSIS Sacred to the memory of Washington Ob 14 Dec. A.D., 1799, Ae 68 (Mc #64B) Common. Herculaneum Pottery. L.

      pitchers.....1.0

W.40 APOTHEOSIS Sacred to the memory of Washington Ob 14 Dec. A.D., 1799, Ae 68 black transfer on a creamware pitcher. Note the word "Apotheosis" is black on white.

W.41 ASCENDING INTO GLORY (M#64c) Common. Herculaneum Pottery. L.

      pitchers.....1.0

W.41 ASCENDING INTO GLORY black transfer on a creamware pitcher with the title in very small letters near the base of the transfer.

W.42 Untitled - WASHINGTON APOTHEOSIS (previously unrecorded) Rarity unknown. Herculaneum Pottery. L.

      pitchers (probably exist).....1.25
      tankards.....2.25

W.42 Untitled - WASHINGTON APOTHEOSIS black transfer on a creamware tankard.

W.43 WASHINGTON IN GLORY AMERICA IN TEARS G * W BORN FEB 11, 1732 DIED DEC 14, 1799 (portrait facing right) (Previously unrecorded) Rarity unknown. Probably Herculaneum Pottery. L.

pitcher (one recorded).....1.25

W.43 WASHINGTON IN GLORY AMERICA IN TEARS G * W BORN FEB 11, 1732 DIED DEC 14, 1799 (portrait facing right) black transfer on a creamware pitcher.

W.44 WASHINGTON IN GLORY AMERICA IN TEARS (Mc #65) Common. Herculaneum Pottery. L.

pitchers.....1.0

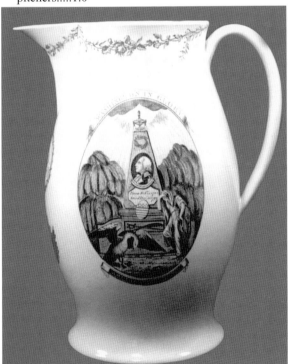

W.44 WASHINGTON IN GLORY AMERICA IN TEARS black transfer on a creamware pitcher. In this transfer, which is similar to W.43, the portrait bust is facing left.

W.45 FIRST IN WAR FIRST IN PEACE FIRST IN FAME FIRST IN VIRTUE BORN 1732 DIED - 1799 Names of the thirteen original States, with Kentucky substituted for Rhode Island (Mc #63) Common. Herculaneum Pottery. L.

pitchers.....1.0

W.45 FIRST IN WAR FIRST IN PEACE FIRST IN FAME FIRST IN VIRTUE BORN 1732 DIED - 1799 Names of the 13 original States, with Kentucky substituted for Rhode Island. Black transfer on a creamware pitcher.

W.46 WASHINGTON IN GLORY AMERICA IN TEARS BORN FEB 11, 1732 DIED DEC. 14, 1799 (Previously unrecorded) Rarity unknown. Probably Herculaneum Pottery. L.

pitchers.....1.25

W.46 WASHINGTON IN GLORY AMERICA IN TEARS BORN FEB 11, 1732 DIED DEC. 14, 1799 black transfer on a creamware pitcher.

W.47 WASHINGTON IN GLORY AMERICA IN TEARS BORN FEB. 11, 1732 DIED DEC. 14, 1799 (Mc #66) Common. L.

pitchers.....1.1

W.47 WASHINGTON IN GLORY AMERICA IN TEARS BORN FEB. 11, 1732 DIED DEC. 14, 1799 black transfer on a creamware pitcher. There are undoubtedly more variants of this popular transfer. If you obtain one which we have not listed, use the value ratio of 1.0 to 1.25 in accordance with Chapter Four.

W.48 AMERICA LAMENTING THE DEATH OF HER FAVORITE SON (Mc #62) Rare. Herculaneum Pottery. L.

pitchers.....1.75

W.48 AMERICA LAMENTING THE DEATH OF HER FAVORITE SON extremely rare polychromed black transfer on a creamware pitcher. This is the only recorded example of this rare polychrome decoration on this transfer.

W.49 WASHINGTON IN HIS GLORY (previously unrecorded) (w/o transfer, applied enamel portrait) Unique. Herculaneum Pottery. L.

pitcher (one recorded).....see below

W.49 WASHINGTON IN HIS GLORY. This piece was sold at auction in 1995. It troubled us then and still does for the following reasons (1) There is no recorded use of the motto "Washington in *his* glory" (2) the motto is a memorial, while the painted view is much earlier. Herculaneum did do a great many, well executed artistic views without transfers, and this may be one of them. We just do not feel comfortable with it.

W.50 GEORGE WASHINGTON FATHER OF HIS COUNTRY (L #630) S.

plates (two recorded).....3.5

W.50 GEORGE WASHINGTON FATHER OF HIS COUNTRY shaded blue enamel on a pearlware plate. Both examples of this portrait bust are in museums and both appear to be by the same artist.

W.51 To the Memory of the Immortal **WASHINGTON HUS-BANDRY** (previously unrecorded) Unique. Possibly Shelton Group or Stevenson. L.

pitcher (one recorded).....2.75+

W.51 To the Memory of the Immortal WASHINGTON HUSBANDRY black transfer on a creamware pitcher. This is the only example of this transfer recorded.

W.52 IN MEMORY of the IMMORTAL WASHINGTON whose **PATRIOTISM** and Military exploits in the service of his Country will be admired by Posterity (Mc #67) Unique. Possibly Shelton Group or Stevenson. L.

pitchers.....2.75

W.52 IN MEMORY of the IMMORTAL WASHINGTON whose PATRIOTISM and Military exploits in the service of his Country will be admired by Posterity black transfer on a creamware pitcher.

W.53 Heaven Has Decreed That the great **WASHINGTON...ETC.** (Mc #68*) Unique. L.

pitchers.....reported to exist

Existence doubtful - McCauley gives a detailed description of this transfer, however he indicates that he has never actually seen it. Neither have we. If it has survived destruction, there probably is one example of this hidden in some collection.

W.54 WASHINGTON HIS COUNTRY'S FATHER First in War. First IN Peace and First in the Hearts of his fellow citizens (L #791) Extremely rare. Ricᵈ Hall & Sons. S.

pitchers.....5.0 (blue transfer) 2.5 (black transfer)

Also see Chapter Six - Fakes and Reproductions

W.54 WASHINGTON HIS COUNTRY'S FATHER First in War. First IN Peace and First in the Hearts of his fellow citizens blue transfer on a pearlware pitcher.

W.55 WASHINGTON HIS COUNTRY'S FATHER (L #718)
Extremely rare. Ricᵈ Hall & Sons. S.

     pitchers.....5.0 (blue transfer) 2.5 (black transfer)

     child's mug.....1.5 (black transfer)

Also see Chapter Six - Fakes and Reproductions

W.55 WASHINGTON HIS COUNTRY'S FATHER blue transfer on a pearlware pitcher. Note the absence of the motto on the neck of the pitcher.

W.56 A MAN WITHOUT EXAMPLE A PATRIOT WITHOUT REPROACH (Mc #71) Common. Herculaneum Pottery. L.
     under spouts and handles.....+0.2

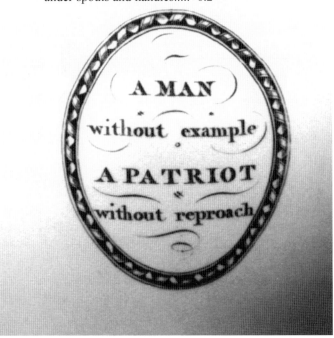

W.56 A MAN WITHOUT EXAMPLE A PATRIOT WITHOUT REPROACH black transfer under the spout of a creamware Liverpool pitcher.

W.57 TO WASHINGTON THE DELIVERER (previously unrecorded)
Rare. S.

     child's mug.....0.5

W.57 TO WASHINGTON THE DELIVERER red transfer on a pearlware child's mug.

W.58 PRESIDENT WASHINGTON (Mc #56, L #792) Unique.
Andrew or Ralph Stevenson. S.

     pitcher (creamware - one recorded).....7.5

W.58 PRESIDENT WASHINGTON black transfer on a small creamware pitcher. This is the only example we record of this transfer on fine creamware.

W.59 PRESIDENT WASHINGTON (Mc #56, L #792) Extremely rare. S.

pitchers (heavy and crude).....3.5

W.59 PRESIDENT WASHINGTON black transfer on an unrefined, heavy Staffordshire-type pitcher with a pale yellow ground.

W.61 GEO. WASHINGTON (Mc #52) Unique. S.

teapot (one recorded).......1.0

LATE PROBABLY COLONIAL REVIVAL, 1876

W.61 GEO. WASHINGTON black transfer on a creamware teapot. This teapot is a copy of a classic 18th century creamware form.

W.60 GEORGE WASHINGTON PRESIDENT OF THE UNITED STATES (within an entwined ribbon containing the names of fifteen States). (previously unrecorded) Unique. S.

plates (two recorded).....7.5

W.60 GEORGE WASHINGTON PRESIDENT OF THE UNITED STATES (within an entwined ribbon containing the names of fifteen States) black transfer on a pearlware plate.

W.62 MARTHA WASHINGTON (Mc #73) Unique. Fell and Company. L.

large shallow bowl (one recorded).....1.0

LATE PROBABLY COLONIAL REVIVAL, 1876

W.62 MARTHA WASHINGTON black transfer on a large bowl.

211

W.63 COL. WILLIAM WASHINGTON (previously unrecorded) Unique. Fell and Company. L.

    large shallow bowl (one recorded).....1.0

LATE PROBABLY COLONIAL REVIVAL, 1876

W.63 COL. WILLIAM WASHINGTON black transfer on a large bowl.

W.64 WASP AND FROLIC (Mc #114, L #794) Unique. Davenport. S.

    pitcher (one recorded).....3.5

W.64 WASP AND FROLIC black transfer on a creamware pitcher by Davenport.

W.65 THE WASP BOARDING THE FROLIC (Mc #113, L #795) Common. Enoch Wood and Sons. S.

    pitchers.....1.25

W.65 THE WASP BOARDING THE FROLIC black transfer on a pearlware pitcher.

W.66 THE WASP & REINDEER (Mc #126, L #796) Common. Enoch Wood and Sons. S.

    pitchers.....1.25

W.66 THE WASP & REINDEER black transfer on a pearlware pitcher with an extremely rare combination of a buff ground and a blue band around the neck.

212

W.67 JOHN WILKES ESQ. **THE PATRIOT** (Drakard 408) Extremely rare. Wedgwood. L.

  teapots.....1.5
  pitchers and tankards probably exist

W.67   JOHN WILKES ESQ. THE PATRIOT black transfer on an early creamware teapot. Wilkes, as Lord Mayor of London and a member of Parliament, vehemently opposed the government's policy toward America and was a champion of the Colonist's rights.

W.69 THE WORK OF MECHANICKS (sic) (previously unrecorded) Unique. Herculaneum Pottery. L.

  pitcher (one recorded).....4.0 (see below)

W.69   THE WORK OF MECHANICKS black transfer on a creamware pitcher. The identity of the building is unknown, however, the value factor above is given in the assumption that if nothing else, it depicts an American building. If it is discovered to be a historically important American building, the value factor will rise even further.

W.68 STEAMSHIP - **WILMINGTON & PHILADELPHIA** (previously unrecorded) Unique. L.

  pitcher (one recorded).....7.5

W.68 detail.

W.68   STEAMSHIP - WILMINGTON & PHILADELPHIA polychromed black transfer on a badly stained creamware pitcher. This is the only example of a steamship recorded on Liverpool.

213

Y.1 **....GIVE THE YANKEES A PLUMPER** (Poem) (Drakard 720)
Extremely rare. Enoch Wood and Sons. S.
          pitchers.....1.2

Above: ....GIVE THE *YANKEES* A PLUMPER black transfer on a pearlware pitcher
which has a buff ground and a silver lustre band around the neck. Below: detail
showing the poem: COME BRITONS REJOICE WITH HEARTS AND WITH VOICE   PEACE WITH
OLD ENGLAND AND FRANCE. THE NEWS OF THE DAY SO ENLIVENS MY CLAY, I'LL UP WITH MY
CRUTCHES AND DANCE;   CAN MORTAL FORBEAR HIS HEART FOR TO CHEAR (sic),   AND
WELLINGTON TOAST IN A BUMPER. THE DESPOT IS DOWN AND LEWIS WE'LL CROWN, SO NOW
GIVE THE YANKEES A PLUMPER. Contrary to other transfers which rejoice at the end
of the War of 1812, this transfer, which dates to that period between May
1814 (Napoleon defeated) and January, 1815 (the signing of the Treaty of
Ghent, ending the hostilities with America), wants the might of England
turned on America. The name *LEWIS* undoubtedly refers to the restoration of
Louis XVIII, misspelled by the engraver.

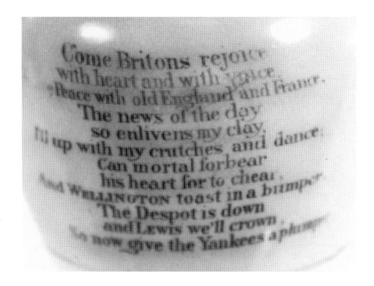

Unknown.1 Untitled - Unidentified fleet scene with American flag vessels (previously unrecorded) Unique. Enoch Wood and Sons. S.

       pitcher (one recorded).....1.0 (see below)

Unknown.1 Untitled - Unidentified fleet scene with American flag vessels black transfer on a canary ground Staffordshire pitcher. This pitcher was once in the McCauley collection and he could not identify the view. Once the transfer is identified, the value will increase dramatically.

Unknown.2 Untitled - Unidentified American Warship (previously unrecorded) Unique. Enoch Wood and Sons. S.

       pitcher (one recorded).....1.0

Unknown.2 Untitled - Unidentified American Warship black transfer on a buff ground pitcher. Gold enamel highlights. Again, once this transfer is identified, the value will appreciate dramatically.

(1) McCauley, Robert H., *Liverpool Transfer Designs on Anglo-American Pottery,* Southworth-Anthoensen Press. 1942. Page 67 states that there is another transfer without the Seal of the United States, where the two cherubs are tying up bundles, that is also signed by F. Morris. This description was printed in Earle's, *China Collecting in America,* published in 1892. He indicates he had never actually viewed this transfer. We haven't either. Therefore it is doubtful that this still exists, so we have deleted it as a separate listing and note it here for the record.

(2) Arman, David and Linda, *The China and Glass Quarterly, April/May, 1997,* The Oakland Press. On page 32 is illustrated the only recorded example of a square vegetable dish base from the Acorn and Oak Leaf Border series bearing this identical transfer in dark blue.

(3) Barber, Edwin A, *Anglo-American Pottery,* Clay Worker Press, 1899. On page 140 there is a listing for this title, however in the following ninety-eight years an example has never been re-corded, except in reference to this listing. Both Larsen and McCauley reference Barber when adding it to their own list of views. Therefore we have to believe this transfer no longer exists.

(4) Both of these transfers are listed by McCauley, who in turn lists them as appearing in Alice Morse Earle's 1892 book, *China Collecting In America.* There is no other record of these transfers, so we do not believe they still exist.

(5) This pitcher was purchased by The Mariner's Museum from Sam Laidacker in 1951. It is 13"h and polychromed over the transfer. The inventory entry for this piece states that this name had been used in catalogues, which we surmise came from the original owner's family description.

(6) Miller, J. Jefferson II, *Unrecorded American Views of Two Liverpool-Type Earthenware Pitchers,* Winterthur Portfolio #4, Winterthur, Delaware. Mr. Miller investigated the names and dates on this lengthy poem and discovered that Franklin, Robinson & Company was listed in the New York City Directory for 1797 at 279 Pearl Street, with Abraham and Samuel Robinson in partnership with Samuel Franklin. A Ralph Hodge was the Inspector of Customs and John King and Walter Heyer were officers under Hodges command. The poem refers to a dispute between the company and the United States Custom inspectors, which involved the paltry sum of two and a half cents per chest "payment or fee (legal or otherwise) given to the inspectors to clear the cargo." Obviously the firm was so incensed that they ordered this transfer placed on pitchers, which they undoubtedly distributed to other New Yorkers.

(7) Inness, Lowell, *PITTSBURGH GLASS* - 1797 - 1891, Houghlin, Mifflin and Company, Boston. 1976. On pages 18 and 19 is illustrated a similar earthenware pitcher presented to glass factory superintendent William Price in 1828. This piece, which is in the Collection of the Historical Society of Pennsylvania, was supposedly manufactured in Pittsburgh.

(8) McCauley, Robert H., *Liverpool Transfer Designs on Anglo-American Pottery.* Southworth-Anthoensen Press. 1942. Pages 76 and 135 mention a single plaque recorded with the inscription "I. Hopwood sculpt - for I. Wyld". However, he is referring to the transfer we have listed as J.20 (Mc #28). It is not that transfer, nor is it the similar portrait J.21, which is indeed a unique plaque. This inscription appears only on a third portrait (J.22), which we will assume is the same as that plaque which McCauley has noted.

(9) Biddle, James, *American History on English Jugs,* Metropolitan Museum of Art, BULLETIN (May 1964). Page 306 mentions that this piece, discovered in Newburyport, Massachusetts and one other, located in rural Pennsylvania, bear this transfer, which are the only instances of an American city appearing on lustre jugs.

(10) Drakard, David, *Printed English Pottery, History and Humour In the Reign of George III 1760 - 1820,* Jonathan Horne, 1992. On page 113 the author illustrates this transfer on a creamware bowl, which is impressed WEDGWOOD. He states that another example on a tobacco jar (which we illustrate) is printed in red. He attributes this to Herculaneum. This is not the only recorded instance of mutual use of the identical transfer by these same two potteries. For example see W.4, W.5, W.15 and W.15a, plus others. It is obvious that some interchange of product was taking place between these two potteries. It is our theory that Wedgwood was sub-contracting the production of this type of "inferior" ware to Herculaneum, as his potteries became more involved in the production of "finer" (and more profitable) enamel-decorated pieces.

(11) Our apologies for these missing illustrations. The curatorial staff of this public collection, while quite pleasant, were some-how unable to obtain several photos that we had ordered seven months earlier.

Chapter Six
Fakes and Reproductions

The collector of historical transferware is really quite fortunate in the fact that there are very few true *fakes* on the market. Although the ware has been popular for over a century, there have not been many attempts to recreate ceramic items, in this field, to defraud us. True, there are a few pesky items that pop up occasionally, but the authors hope to place a final fatal stake in the heart of these pieces with a detailed listing of how the beginning collector can avoid their snare. However, we must first define the two terms: **fakes** and **reproductions**.

A fake is a piece which was created with the intent to deceive and defraud the uninformed buyer. A reproduction was created in the style and manner of the original and should be marked accordingly. There was never any intent on the part of the manufacturer to deceive. Prime examples of reproductions are those Liverpool-shaped pitchers made to advertise Cutty Sark Liquor, or the Wedgwood reproductions in various forms, found in gift shops of museums.

The photo on the upper right illustrates a group of items that fall into the category of fakes. While it is uncertain whether these were manufactured with the intent to deceive, they are currently doing so, on a frequent basis. These turn up in auctions from Park Avenue in New York, to cornfields in Iowa. Usually the

transfer busts are crude and easily identified. Occasionally, one finds an example where the transfer is really very good, and may result in the purchase of a fake. However, one must always remember when examining these pieces, to look at the crackling of the glaze. The authentic pieces are pearlware and have a fine network of glaze crackle. The fakes appear to be a white, heavy earthenware with a very coarse network of glaze crackle. The authentic pieces are only found in a Staffordshire pitcher form and children's mugs, which come with either black or blue transfers. The fakes are recorded with only a black transfer. These fakes are found in pitchers in both Staffordshire and Liverpool form, bowls, cups, saucers and plaques.

It was only recently that we were able to determine the maker of this group of fakes. While reading Godden's and Gibson's, *Collecting Lustrewares*, we came across a section on twentieth century manufacturers. There detailed was the firm of A. E. Gray and Company, which operated in Hanley from 1913 through 1934, when they moved production to Stoke-on Trent. This operation apparently continued until the 1960's, producing a coarse earthenware decorated with a pseudo Sunderland Splash "lustre" and using black transfers such as THE SHIPWRIGHT'S ARMS and THE CONSTITUTION AND JAVA. We

6.1 Three fake pieces with black transfers of FAYETTE THE NATION'S GUEST and WASHINGTON HIS COUNTRY'S FATHER. Under the spout of the pitcher you can see the spurious SEAL OF THE UNITED STATES with the REPUBLICANS ARE NOT ALWAYS UNGRATEFUL slogan and the RICᴰ HALL & SONS mark.

6.2 Two authentic pitchers made by the R. Hall pottery to commemorate the 1824 visit of Lafayette to America. Note the detailed transfers and the lack of coarse shadows on the faces. Also note the "bamboo" handles. While not all the authentic pitchers have this feature, they all are pearlware and have a fine crackle to the glaze.

6.3a Above left: A heavy earthernware "Liverpool" pitcher with a black transfer of WASHINGTON HIS COUNTRY'S FATHER. Unmarked, this is a better than average transfer of these fakes. **6.3b** Above: A heavy earthenware white plaque with a black transfer of FAYETTE THE NATION'S GUEST. This is an excellent example of the poor quality of the engraving found on these fakes. **6.3c** Upper right: One of the mates to the FAYETTE plaque, a portrait bust of BENJ. FRANKLIN. **6.3d** The other mate to the FAYETTE plaque, with a portrait bust of WASHINGTON HIS COUNTRY'S FATHER. **6.3e** Lower left: The REPUBLICANS ARE NOT ALWAYS UNGRATEFUL transfer found on the fake bowls and pitchers.

6.4a Upper left: The fake "Sunderland Pink Lustre" bowl which assisted us in the attribution of these fakes to the Alfred E. Gray and Company of Hanley, then Stoke-On-Trent. This is a poor quality black transfer of WASHINGTON HIS COUNTRY'S FATHER. **6.4b** Above: Same bowl with the FAYETTE THE NATION'S GUEST portrait bust. Note the poor quality of the transfer as seen in the coarse shading on the faces. **6.4c** Lower left: BENJ. FRANKLIN..ETC. This time a black transfer of rather good quality. As you can note from Chapter Five, we have not recorded an authentic period transfer similar to this.

218

6.5a

6.5b

6.5a Above left: The black transfer of REPUBLICANS ARE NOT ALWAYS UNGRATEFUL copied from the Richard Hall and Sons original produced for LaFayette's visit to America in 1824. This and the transfers of WASHINGTON and (LA) FAYETTE are used on the fake pitcher illustrated 6.1. Above right: **6.5b** THE SHIPWRIGHT'S ARMS used by Gray and Company on pitchers and bowls.

carefully compared the SHIPWRIGHT'S ARMS transfer found on a fake Pink lustre bowl we had in our own collection, and to our surprise it was identical. As you can see by the various illustrations on the previous and following pages, this bowl also contained portrait medallions of FAYETTE THE NATION'S GUEST, WASHINGTON HIS COUNTRY'S FATHER, THE SEAL OF THE UNITED STATES - REPUBLICANS ARE NOT ALWAYS UNGRATEFUL - RIC^D HALL & SONS and BEN^J FRANKLIN L.L.D.F.R.S. BORN AT BOSTON NEW ENGLAND 17 JAN 1708. Of course the pseudo pink Sunderland lustre covered a heavy white earthenware body with the tell-tale coarse glaze crackle. Once again, there was no evidence of the piece ever having a makers mark. So it seems that Mr. Gray and his pottery is the culprit that has caused so many collectors so much grief.

The absence of an underglaze or impressed maker's mark indicates that these pieces must have once had a paper label with the country of origin indicated, as that requirement was made law in 1891, for all items imported into the United States. These pieces by Gray had to have been intended for the American market due to the subject matter of their decoration, so someone, somewhere, removed the labels and started the fraud process.

This brings us to the second fake which one might encounter. This is a "Liverpool" pitcher with a polychromed black transfer of the SHIP CAROLINE on one

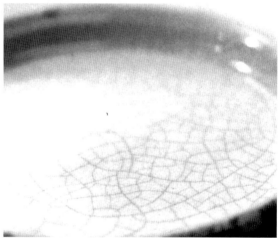

6.6 A close-up photo of the underside of the bowl previously illustrated. Note both the absence of any mark and the all-important coarse crackle of the glaze. Compare this with any 19th century antique piece of creamware or pearlware and you will be able to instantly identify any of these fakes you encounter.

6.7a/b/c/d Both sides of two "Liverpool" "Sunderland Pink Splash Lustre" pitchers manufactured by Alfred E. Gray and Company. Left to right: **6.7a** A black transfer of a drinking verse enclosed by a wreath; **6.7b** a black transfer of a British flag vessel with a verse hoping for good trade and commerce; **6.7c** a black transfer of the SHIPWRIGHT'S ARMS and **6.7d** a poem titled THE SAILOR'S TEAR. While these have little or no value as an antique, a collector might wish to include them in a collection to illustrate a fake. The transfer work on these examples is of very poor quality.

6.8a/b/c Three faces of George Washington. **6.8a** Left: Alfred Gray's version which is from the "Liverpool" pitcher illustrated 6.3a. **6.8b** Center: The authentic transfer by Richard Hall and Sons done in the 1820's. **6.8c** Right: Very poor quality transfer by Gray found on the "lustre" bowl illustrated 6.4a and 6.5a. The eyes in the two fakes are small dots, while the original are ovals. Also the scalloped border around the original seems to be better defined.

6.9a Left: The fake portrait bust of FAYETTE by Alfred Gray. Note the coarse crackle in the glaze in the area of the inner medallion. **6.9b** Right: The 1820's transfer by Hall. Once again the eyes seem to be larger, with more detail, while the fake's eyes are the same two dots found in the fake Washington transfers.

6.10a Left: The fake by Gray, which is a very good copy of the original illustrated on the right. **6.10b** Right: The original transfer. There are a few minor differences between the two transfers, but not so much as to make an identification of the fake by this transfer alone. For instance there are tiny dots in the stars of the fake and the eagle's neck is shorter than the original.

220

6.11a/b/c The three sides of the JAMES LEECH fake black transfer on an earthenware pitcher. Heavier than an authentic piece and always having a coarse crackle to the glaze.

side, a black transfer of a guild device on the other, with a black transfer of the name JAMES LEECH under a black transfer of the SEAL OF THE UNITED STATES found with and without the REPUBLICANS ARE NOT ALWAYS UNGRATEFUL slogan. This again is made of a coarse white earthenware which has the telltale coarse crackling of the glaze. We have never seen a marked example. The presence of the REPUBLICAN's slogan points toward Mr. Gray as the source.

We have **NEVER** seen a Liverpool pitcher with a transfer of the SHIP CAROLINE that is authentic. Never! Don't be fooled by this piece, it is not worth more than one to two hundred dollars, as a curiosity. It has no value to the collector of Anglo-American Historical Transferware.

However, now that we have totally

inoculated you against James Leech's "Ship Caroline", we must admit that we have seen a finely potted pearlware tankard with a black transfer of THE SEAL OF THE UNITED STATES over the name JAMES LEECH, that might be authentic. It has a lovely entwined strap handle and is sometimes impressed ADAMS. This *might* be Mr. Gray's source for the name JAMES LEECH found on his fakes, but this tankard and it's origins are still the subject of some research and much conjecture.

The next fake we will discuss is a Liverpool pitcher produced in the early Twentieth century with a red transfer concerning the Napoleonic Wars. The pitchers are somewhat heavier in weight than the originals, and have a very coarse glaze crackle. Illustrated below, these have the SUCCESS TO THE VOLUNTEERS slogan on one side and a Napoleon cartoon on the reverse titled THE GOVERNOR OF EUROPE STOPED IN HIS CAREER. These are copied from originals produced by several different potteries following England's declaration of war against France in 1803. The originals are found with red or black transfers on creamware tankards and pitchers. The source print for the cartoon was published in the London shop of Samuel Fores in April, 1803.

6.12 JAMES LEECH tankard with an impressed ADAMS mark. The SEAL OF THE UNITED STATES has fifteen stars. This appears to be authentic, but the name throws doubt upon it's authenticity.

Right: **6.13** As you can see, the transfer work is excellent but the glaze is coarse and crackle quite obvious. This is never found on a period piece, where the glaze crackle is so fine as to be invisible, except at a very close range.

Here we have illustrated four *reproductions* which should not cause any problems for the collector. All are fully identified with underglaze marks indicating the manufacturer and the country of origin that has been required on all ceramics made for import into the United States since 1891. The transfers are of good quality

6.14

6.16

and the glazes are clear and uncrackled. The weight of these pieces is a bit heavier than a period pitcher. If you find something that just doesn't seem to have the correct age, but does not have the underglaze marks on the bottom, we suggest that you examine

defraud the uninformed collector. Quite frankly, there is very little chance that even a beginning collector will be fooled by one of these. When you see them in department stores or gift shops, pick them up and examine them. Get a feel for the weight, markings and transfers. Your best protection is your own knowledge.

Hopefully, by familiarizing yourself with the illustrations in this chapter and comparing them with the original pieces illustrated throughout the check list in Chapter Five, you will be able to avoid the pitfalls that occasionally befuddle the beginning collector of Historical Transferware. If you have already pur-

6.15

6.17

the underside of the base closely to see if there is any possibility that someone used a grinder to remove the underglaze marks. Sometimes unscrupulous persons will do this with the intent to

chased one of these fakes or reproductions, you can take some solace in the fact that you now have a great learning tool at your finger-tips, to familiarize yourself with the look of a fake's transfer and glaze.

We are indeed fortunate that the really talented fakers have not invaded this field. The collectors of fine furniture and fine art are constantly reminded of the pitfalls of their respective collecting fields by the regular discovery that certain pieces, often believed to be authentic for generations, are products of a faker. With just a minimal amount of awareness and attention to detail, the collectors of transfer decorated ceramics can easily detect the few fakes that are around.

Selected Bibliography - Chapter Six

Godden, Geoffrey A. and Gibson, Michael, *Collecting Lustreware*, 1991, Barrie & Jenkins. London

Chapter Seven
Additional Information

What a person collects is often a reflection of the person himself. What interests you will normally manifest itself in the direction of your collection. So, before one is able to begin a collection, one must know what is available to collect. The very fact that you are reading this book, says that you have become aware of the fascination of historical transferware. Now that you have read to this point, you are also aware of the vast choices open to the beginning collector, as to what direction he or she wishes to take when pursuing Liverpool or Staffordshire transferware. Do you wish to collect transfers relating only to the Revolution? The War of 1812? Only Liverpool forms?

In addition to the volume that you are currently reading, there are several other fine reference works that touch upon this field. Some of the information is repetitious, since we have attempted to incorporate in this book everything that was known prior to it's publication. However, we believe a complete reference library is essential to becoming an educated collector. Below we have listed three reference books which may be of value to the collector. Also, there is a much larger list in the bibliography section of this book.

1. McCauley, Robert H., *Liverpool Transfer Designs On Anglo-American Pottery*. Out of print. Can be obtained from antique reference book sellers. Approximate cost $300.00.

2. Larsen, Ellouise B., *American Historical Views on Staffordshire China*. Out of print. Can be obtained from antique reference book sellers. Approximate cost: 1939 edition - $100.00; 1950 edition, which contains more information - $150.00; 1975 Dover reprint which contains 145 additional photos - $125.00.

3. Drakard, David, *Printed English Pottery - History and Humor in the Reign of George III 1760-1820.* Currently available from antique reference book sellers at $125.00.

After you have built your reference library, we suggest you visit some of the museums that have significant holdings of this collectible. We are aware of the pieces in the following institutions. If we have missed any, please send us a note, as we are always seeking to broaden our education in this field.

> The Peabody Essex Museum
> East India Square
> Salem, Massachusetts 01970
> 508-745-1876

The Collection numbers approximately 150 pieces, much of which is on permanent display in The East India Hall.

> The Metropolitan Museum of Art
> 1000 Fifth Avenue
> New York, New York 10028
> 212-879-5500

The size of the collection is not all that large. Depending on the current exhibitions, the number of items on display fluctuates. This institution does have a fine collection of French porcelains for the American market.

> Buffalo and Erie County Historical Society
> 25 Nottingham Court
> Buffalo, New York 14216
> 716-873-9644

We were not able to visit this museum, but they have the Spaulding Collection, which includes a great many rarities.

> The Albany Institute of History and Art
> 125 Washington Avenue
> Albany, New York 12210
> 518-463-4478

Another museum we were not able to visit personally, but they have the greatest historical pitcher in existence. (See illustration 2.18a/b)

> Philadelphia Museum of Art
> Benjamin Franklin Parkway
> Philadelphia, Pennsylvania 19101
> 215-763-8100

This institution has significant holdings in this field. The number of items on display varies.

> National Museum of American History
> Smithsonian Institution
> Washington, DC 20560
> 202-357-1300

Major holdings, including the McCauley Collection of Liverpool, the Larsen Collection of Staffordshire and the Leon Collection of Yellow-glaze (canary) earthenware. Only a small amount of the total items are on display.

The Mariner's Museum
100 Museum Drive
Newport News, Virginia 23606
757-591-7754

Another museum with major holdings of both Liverpool and Paris porcelain American historical ceramics. Very little was on display during our visit.

The Royal Pavilion Libraries and Museums
Brighton Museum and Art Gallery
4-5 Pavilion Buildings
Brighton, England BN1 1EE
0123-290000

While we were not able to visit this institution, their holdings seem to be quite large. They have the Willets Collection, which we believe to be quite extensive, with some items of American interest represented.

National Museums and Galleries on Merseyside
William Brown Street
Liverpool, England L3 8EN
0151-2070001

Another museum we were unable to personally visit. Again, as evidenced by the David Drakard book, their holdings seem to be extensive, with some items of American interest.

The Mattatuck Museum
144 West Main Street
Waterbury, Connecticut, 06702
203-753-0381

An excellent collection with many great rarities, most of which are on display.

Winterthur Museum and Gardens
Winterthur, Delaware, 19735
302-888-4600

Another excellent collection with many great rarities, which are also on display. Great curatorial staff.

We are sure there are other institutions that we have missed, but these will give you a start. Another avenue the beginning collector can pursue is antiques shows. Held with increasing frequency, you can probably find a few shows being held on any given weekend. Those that advertise themselves as having a representation of Americana will prove to be the most productive.

As we are completing this book, another avenue is in the process of providing the collector with the opportunity to learn from others with the same interest in transferware. There is presently a small group of devotees that are forming a national Transferware Collector's Club. The purpose of this organization will be to gather collectors, dealers and museum personnel under one organization to further the study and pursuit of the hobby. By becoming a member, you will have access to other collectors,

dealers and information that will deal with transferware in it's many forms. While the Club does not, as yet, have a mailing address, you can contact the authors, at the below address, for current information concerning membership.

David and Linda Arman
P O Box 39
Portsmouth, RI 02871
401-841-8403

A Final Word

The acquisition of good examples of Liverpool and Staffordshire with early transfers of American Historical interest is quite difficult. Even those items we have designated as "common" are not readily found. The thrill of obtaining an especially choice or rare transfer is the reward the collector receives for his time and effort. Patience and perseverance are needed for the hunt. We often dub those few that consistently stumble upon great "finds" as lucky. They really have made their own luck by educating themselves and going out on a regular basis, making the rounds of antiques shows, auctions and the specialist dealers. May you also be termed "lucky" in your pursuit of American Historical transferware.

Appendix I - Other English Ceramics
Appendix II - Transfers on Enamels
Appendix III - French Ceramics

Introduction

The topic of this book has been English *transfer decorated* ceramics produced for the American market during the period from 1760 through 1850. As you are probably aware, the potters of England did not limit their output to just transfer decorated creamware and pearlware. They produced many fine non-transfer decorated pieces of historical ceramics, especially for the American market. These include figural busts, jasperware plaques and brightly colored enamel decorated pieces. They also produced a group of transfer decorated *enamels* that are of a decided American interest. These are the items we will investigate in Appendix I and Appendix II. In Appendix III, we will introduce you to the products of the French potteries, which consist of individually decorated porcelain pieces, and a brief sampling of the French transfer decorated earthenwares of the Creil and other French factories.

We mentioned in Chapter One that the emerging American consumer market was a source of bitter conflict between Britain and France in the waning years of the 18th Century. Because of the once-close relationship between Britain and her North American Colonies, the English potter gained the initial advantage. With the wartime alliance between France and the Colonies during the Revolutionary War, the potters of France sought to establish the pre-eminence of their goods vis-a-vis the English. They seemed to be making some small progress toward this goal, when the French Revolution erupted and tensions grew between not only France and England, but also France and the infant United States. The

AI.1 A fine Jasperware portrait bust of LaFayette in the uniform of the American colonies, by Wedgwood, circa 1800.

Quasi-War between the United States and France in 1799, was the beginning of the end of significant amounts of French ceramics manufactured for export to North America. The end of the Napoleonic Wars in Europe, saw the French Navy and merchant fleet in shambles, unable to offer much mercantile competition to the victorious English. England quickly took advantage of the decline of French fortunes and the tremendous demand of the rapidly expanding American population's desire for European goods. Often selling items at a loss, in order to gain a foothold in these American markets, the English were also quite successful in the complete domination of any attempt by American potters to compete with the incoming flood of inexpensive ceramic wares. Exactly what did they market to the Americans?

Appendix I - Other English Ceramics

There are five groups of historical items which we will investigate in this first appendix. They are:

AI.2 Polychromed transfer of GEN LAFAYETTE on an enamel brass mirror knob. English, circa 1800-1824.

1. Plaques containing portrait busts of prominent Americans and Europeans, who had an influence on events in North America.

2. Portrait busts made for the American market.

3. Enamel decorated dinnerware for the American market.

4. English porcelains with American subjects.

5. Miscellaneous ceramic objects with American subjects.

Appendix II - Transfer Decorated Enamels

In this section, we will introduce the reader to the many transfer decorated enamels that were produced for the American market. Enamels are basically thin pieces of porcelain attached to a metal (usually copper or silver) frame. The forms normally encountered are plaques, tie-backs/mirror knobs and various sized and shaped boxes. The three main locations which produced this ware were Battersea, Birmingham and Liverpool.

Birmingham was the center of the English industrial revolution. It was there in 1751 that the engraver John Brooks applied for a patent for the process of transfer printing. In 1753 the Battersea Enamel Works were opened in the city of the same name, and it is acknowledged by most scholars that transfer printing was the main activity of that company. Although this particular company went bankrupt after only a few years of operation, the transfer printing industry became centered in these two towns (Birmingham and Battersea), producing the vast majority of this type of ceramic.

Due to the activities of Guy Green and John Sadler, the city of Liverpool joined the producers of enamels in the late 1750's. We have already discussed in Chapter Two, that the alliance of these two talented innovators, with the genius of Josiah Wedgwood, led to a revolution in the decoration of creamware and pearlware. By the early 1760's, Sadler, Green and Wedgwood were producing the first of the transfer decorated ceramic pitchers and teapots.

AI.3

AI.3 Finely executed Paris Porcelain Vase with a polychrome enamel portrait of LaFayette. French, circa 1800-1825.

intensive method of decoration, which did not survive past the first quarter of the 19th Century in the export wars between France and England. While far more beautiful, these objects were also far more expensive, so there was little to recommend them to the population as a whole. However, the products of these French factories soon became the ceramic of choice of both the new American upper class and the American Federal government. French ceramics decorated the early Republic's buildings, including the President's House.

It was only in the latter part of the 1820's, that the French factories, such as Creil, began using the transfer method of decoration on inexpensive earthenware for domestic consumption. As far as the North American export market was concerned, this effort to produce a cheap dinnerware was too little too late.

Valuation

Our method of evaluating the types of items we will illustrate in these three Appendixes will differ from that used in the first portion of this book. Since we do not have the complication of multiple historical views or artificial grounds on a single piece, we can simply assign a current price range to an object. These figures will change over a period of time, as the market for these items expands and contracts.

The prices we quote are only our opinion and assumes the piece in question is in perfect condition and the transfer or painting has the highest degree of skill in it's execution. A poorly executed painting of George Washington is worth but a fraction of the value placed on the superb examples illustrated in Appendix III.

Appendix III - French and European Ceramics

The development of transfer decoration on ceramics was basically an English phenomenon. Although a few Continental potteries experimented with the process, it's use never became widespread. Instead, the Paris Porcelain manufacturers opted for skillfully executed paintings on their ceramics. This was a labor

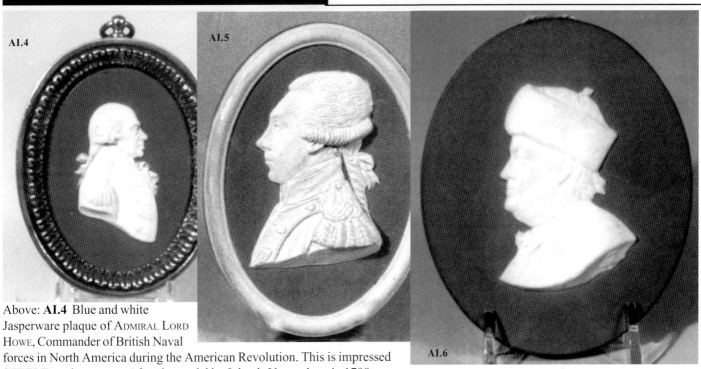

AI.4

AI.5

AI.6

Above: **AI.4** Blue and white Jasperware plaque of ADMIRAL LORD HOWE, Commander of British Naval forces in North America during the American Revolution. This is impressed STEELE on the reverse. After the model by John de Vaere, done in 1798, an identical example is recorded impressed WEDGWOOD. Circa 1800, this is extremely rare and has a value of $1,000.00 - $1,500.00. Above center: **AI.5** A very rare, blue and white Jasperware plaque of the MARQUIS LAFAYETTE in the uniform of an American Revolutionary War Major-General. Unmarked, circa 1790-1800, this has a value of $1,500.00 - $2,250.00. Above right: **AI.6** Blue and white Jasperware plaque of BENJAMIN FRANKLIN in his famous fur hat. The original source of this bust is a 1777 terra cotta bust by Jean-Baptiste Nini. Impressed WEDGWOOD & BENTLEY, it is also recorded in a 1950 reproduction, with only the WEDGWOOD mark. The value of the Wedgwood & Bentley piece is $1,250.00 - $1,750.00.

AI.8

AI.9

AI.7

Left: **AI.7** Another version of BENJAMIN FRANKLIN with the relief portrait bust on an octagonal black basalt plaque. Age and maker unknown, but probably circa 1780-1820. Value in the $1,000.00 - $1,500.00 range. Above: **AI.8** Black basalt relief bust of WILLIAM HENRY HARRISON on a circular plaque. Unknown maker, circa either 1814 or 1840. Value $750.00 - $,1250.00. Above right: **AI.9** The famous terra cotta bust of BENJAMIN FRANKLIN after a portrait by Thomas Walpole. This round plaque is inscribed B. FRANKLIN. AMERICAIN/NINI F.1777. Produced during Franklin's stay in France (1776-1785), this is valued at $1,750.00 - $2,250.00.

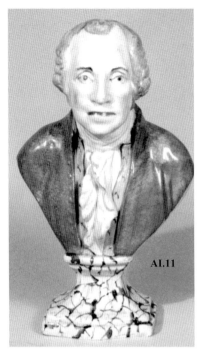

Variations of George Washington by the Wood family. Above left: **AI.10** Basalt bust of George Washington signed within a circular plaque on the reverse: WASHINGTON Born 1732 Died 1799 ENOCH WOOD SCULP 1818. This particular basalt version is more rare than the polychromed example on the far right, however it is also less desirable. Value $1,250.00 - $1,750.00. Above center: **AI.11** Polychromed enamel bust of George Washington signed Ra Wood, who was Enoch Woods' cousin and sometimes partner. Far more rare than the other two examples illustrated, it is also considered to be much earlier (1790 - 1800). These have repeatedly sold at auction in the $4,000.00 - $5,000.00 range, although an example recently sold for only $1,200.00. Above right: **AI.12** Another version of the Enoch Wood bust of Washington, this time in bright polychrome enamels. Again there is the raised circular plaque on the reverse stating the same information as that quoted for AI.10. The value of this example is $1,750.00 - $2,250.00. At this point we should add a note of caution concerning late 19th and 20th Century reproductions of this figure by William Kent Ltd of Burslem. This company was in business from 1878 to at least 1955 (we have their 1955 catalogue in our reference library). The Kent version of the Enoch Wood Washington does not have the fine detail of the original and the buttons, cravat and vest have little definition to them. The glaze has a coarse crackle. The main difference is that the reproduction does not have the circular signature disk mentioned above. These piece have only a nominal value of $50.00 - $100.00. However we have seen uneducated buyers bid several hundred dollars for these at auction.

Two great 18th century rarities. Left **AI.13** Salt glaze bust of Thaddeus Kosciuszko (1746-1817), Polish patriot and Brigadier General in the American Revolutionary Army. Around the plinth is a relief molding of martial implements and the liberty cap/ pole. Right: **AI.14** Another salt glazed bust depicting Kosciuszko's opponent during the Southern Campaign around Charleston, South Carolina in 1781, Major General Lord Cornwallis. Kosciuszko was in charge of the retreat of Greene's army, after their defeat by Cornwallis at the Battle of Guildford Court House. It was after this battle, that Cornwallis lead his victorious army to a small Virginia port named Yorktown. The rest is history. These early busts are valued at $1,000.00 to $2,000.00 each.

The many faces of George Washington and Benjamin Franklin. Above: **AI.15** Victorian figure titled FRANKLIN decorated in polychrome enamel. Circa 1860-1880, this is valued at $1250.00 - $2,000.00. **AI.16** a fine quality English porcelain figure titled WASHINGTON. Probably Worcester or Derby, circa 1850. Value $750.00 - $1,250.00. **AI.17** Superb 19th Century parian bust of Washington, probably English, but a French version is also known. Value this at $1,250.00 - $1,750.00. **AL.18** Late 19th Century bust of Washington, probably made by William Kent. Circa 1955+, this is valued at $50.00 - $100.00. **AI.19** A very rare Victorian figure of George Washington in overall white with gold highlights. Probably circa 1876, this figure of Washington, that actually resembles Washington, is rarely found. Value $1,750.00 - $2,500.00.

Below: The many faces of Franklin? Don't bet on it. To make the statement that the Staffordshire figures do not always resemble the person in question is proven beyond any doubt by the three figures below. **AI.20** Since this polychromed example is untitled, we will have to assume that it was meant to depict Benjamin Franklin. This is English, circa 1876 and due to the poor overall quality of the

piece, it is valued at $350.00 to $450.00. **AI.21** Obviously quite similar to AI.15, which is titled FRANKLIN, this example is titled *WASHINGTON* in gold script. Again, this is Victorian English, circa 1876 and is valued at $1,000.00 - $1,500.00. **AI.22** Another Victorian Franklin, this time titled *GENERAL WASHINGTON* in gold script across the base. This time the figure was highly decorated in a variety of polychrome enamels, which raises the value to $1,250.00 - $2,000.00.

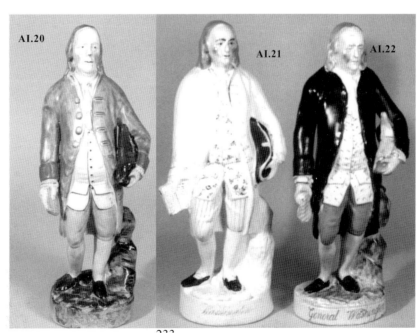

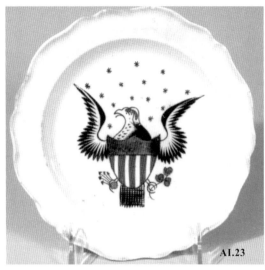

AI.23

AI.24

The variations of the Seal of the United States from the English potteries had little actual relationship to the official version, as is indicated by the examples illustrated on these two pages. The adoption by the Congress of the United States of the great Seal in 1782, provided the English ceramics industry with a much needed subject to decorate the ceramics being exported to this country. Armorial decoration had long been a staple decoration for ceramic dinnerware. Unfortunately for the potter, the new American Republic was not

AI.25   AI.26   AI.27

fertile ground for familial coats of arms. The adoption of the Seal was an armorial device that even the republican Americans would accept. Thus the factories produced many versions of the American Bald Eagle with the shield on its breast clutching the symbols of war and peace in it's talons. It was a simple matter to incorporate these designs onto the already popular blue and green "feather-edged" creamware and pearlware. This type of decoration is only rarely found on a plain piece that does not have the feather edge decoration, as is illus-

trated by **AI.23**. This is a very unusual creamware 10" diameter dinner plate with an embossed semi-scalloped rim. We have titled this version of the Seal as the "**common**" Seal, since this is the one you will encounter most frequently. Since this example is unusual, we value it at $1,000.00 - $1,500.00 and date it around 1800. The goofy looking bird found in illustration **AI.24** is extremely rare, with only three examples recorded by the authors. For what we hope is obvious reasons, we have named this creature the "buzzard" Seal and date it circa 1800 - 1820. We have seen only two of these sell, one privately at $1,700.00 and the

AI.28

AI.29   AI.30

other at auction for $1,000.00. Therefore we place the value at $1,000.00 to $1,700.00. It is a pearlware green feather edge small plate. The three Seals illustrated **AI.25** - **AI.27** have been given the name "yellow" eagles for the simple reason they are basically a yellow-ochre color. Found with both blue and green feather rims, these are somewhat more rare than the "common" variety. Manufactured between

234

1800 and 1820, these are valued at $900.00 - $1100.00 each. Somehow the decorator of the small plate **AI.28** departed from an easily recognized eagle-like bird and gave us an extremely rare bluish colored Phoenix-like Seal. The shield has been turned on it's side and there is nothing in the talons. We have only recorded one example of this version, which we date circa 1820 - 1840. The value is $800.00 - $1,200.00.

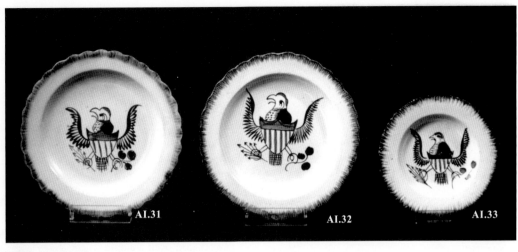

The two blue feather edge plates illustrated (**AI.29** and **AI.30**) have been named the "long-winged" Seal. These are more rare than the "yellow" eagle and are encountered infrequently. These are valued between $1,000.00 -$1,500.00. **AI.31** This is a green feather edge pearlware plate decorated with the "common" Seal. Of an unusual small 5 1/2"d size, this is probably circa 1790 - 1840 and is valued at $750.00 - $900.00. **AI.32** Another "common" eagle, this time with a blue feather edge.This is a "common" Seal with a common blue feather edge. The value ($600.00 - $800.00) is somewhat lower than the previous example for these reasons. **AI.33** Although this is another common Seal with a common blue feather edge, this is considered quite rare for two reasons: first it is a 3 1/2"d cup plate and second, it is impressed DAVENPORT. This raises the value from the $600.00 - $800.00 range to $1,000.00 - $1,500.00. Marked pieces of this type of ware are quite unusual, although it is believed that most of the potteries that produced the historical "white-ware" and dark blue for the American markets, produced specimens of this popular group. Illustrations **AI.34**,

AI.35 and **AI.36** show three "common" Seals all on green feather edge pearlware plates. Note the difference not only in the shape of the plates and the pattern of the scalloped rim, but also the variety found on the three different "common" Seals. Was this the result of different potteries or different decorators? We think a combination of both. These three are dated from 1790 - 1830 and all range in value from $750.00 - $1,200.00.

Below we have two rather special examples of the blue border pearlware plate decorated with an enamel Seal of the United States. Left: **AI.37** This is a finely detailed Seal where the decorator employed far more colors than normal and executed the decoration with a great deal of skill and detail. It is quite beautiful and extremely rare, as we only have this one example recorded. Right: **AI.38** Another special piece due to the impressed CLEWS, circle and crown mark. The rim is heavily embossed and covered with a heavy band of deep blue. The latter bird belongs to the "common" group, by reason of it's design and colors. It is also the only example we have recorded. Both are valued at $750.00 to $1,500.00.

Although the predominant

form one encounters in this ware are plates, a few pieces of authentic hollow ware are known to exist. I say authentic, because this is one area where the collector must be aware that a large group of these items were faked within the last twenty years by a china restoration specialist operating in Pennsylvania. Using pearlware and creamware plates and hollow ware of the early 19th Century, often with impressed marks, this unscrupulous, but talented person, added the "common" Seal to many pieces, causing a great deal of unhappiness in the following years. The color and style of decoration are identical to the originals. You may be able to identify one of these fakes by closely examining the decorated surface to ascertain whether any wear, such as knife marks, scratches or other defects caused by normal use, were inadvertently overpainted by the faker. A faint scratch covered by the enameled eagle indicates the eagle was applied after the scratch was made. We suggest you buy a good pocket magnifying glass for this purpose.

Right: **AI.39** This is a fine Staffordshire shaker with an early 19th Century blue decorated top and

AI.39

AI.40

AI.41

base. The Seal appears to be authentic, but we honestly do not know if it is one of the aforementioned fakes. If authentic, we would value this at $1,250.00 - $2,000.00. If not, maybe $100.00 - $200.00, for a comparison example. It's a tough call, because after years of specialization, we just can't tell. Left: **AI.40** This is an extremely rare 16" platter with a blue feather edge and a brightly polychromed "common" eagle. **AI.41** This small soup tureen and matching undertray also has the blue feather edge and both pieces are decorated with the "common" eagle. We have no doubt as to the authenticity of these pieces. Not only have they been in a famous old collection for many years, but when examined, there is no doubt that the decoration is original. Authentic platters and tureens are extremely rare and highly desirable. We believe this group dates from 1800 - 1830 and we would value the platter at $4,000.00 and the tureen set at $7,500.00+.

Left: **AI.42** This pearlware handled mug/cup was discovered by legendary New York dealer Louis Lyons in the 1980's. It has an overall green sponged decor surrounding a "common" Seal executed in the usual colors of red, ochre and blue. Naturally the main

AI.42

point of interest is the JOHN TYLER name, which makes this a "presidential" item. The entire decoration is underglaze, so there is little doubt as to it's authenticity. The Tyler association indicates the enduring popularity of the polychromed Seal of the United States decoration, which started when the Seal was adopted in 1782 and continued to at least the 1840's. This dates from the period 1832 - 1840 and is valued at $5,000.00+.

AI.43

Right: **AI.43** The shallow bowl illustrated on the right is silver resist lustre. The funky Seal of the United States was executed freehand by an artistically challenged potter . Obviously not a production item, we have only recorded two of these items. Probably made in the period 1820 - 1840, we value this at $750.00 - $1,250.00.

The items illustrated on this page probably met with little commercial success, as they are all considered extremely rare. Left: **AI.44** This is a pearlware tankard with a raised decoration of wavy vertical stripes highlighted in blue enamel, with a lovely floral band around the body in Pratt-type green, red, ochre and blue. Between these two areas of decoration, there is a narrow band containing raised letters forming the slogan AMERICA INDEPENDENT 1776. We have only recorded two of these rarities in the years we have been keeping records of such information. This dates from 1820 - 1840 and is valued at $2,500.00 - $3,500.00. Above right: **AI.45** This is a pearlware chamberpot with an exterior decoration of fruits and vines done in a brilliant blue. Tradition says that this was a "Leeds"-type decor done for the Pennsylvania Dutch market. In this case, we think tradition has it wrong, and this is strictly a Staffordshire export item, without any purposeful intent as to it's ultimate destination. The circular medallion contains a relief rendition of an eagle in flight, which many like to think is another version of the Seal of the United States. It probably is not the Seal, but more likely a scene from Greek mythology. This dates from 1820 - 1840 and has a value of $350.00 - $450.00.

AI.44

AI.45

The two pieces illustrated below have the same source, which is a 3"d patinated bronze medallion by Eccleston, done in 1805 of George Washington. Below left: **AI.46** This is an oval pearlware plaque decorated in the blue, orange-ochre, yellow-ochre and green palette called Pratt ware. For years we thought this untitled plaque was supposed to represent George II. While preparing this book, we examined both this and an original Eccleston medallion, and there is no doubt that this was taken from that source. Circa 1805 - 1815, this has a value of $2,500.00 - $3,500.00. Below right: **AI.47** Here is another version of the Eccleston Washington, this time on a heavy body brown glazed stoneware pitcher. The reverse side of this piece is decorated with The Seal of the United States. Manufactured 1830 - 1850, this has a value of $750.00 - $1,250.00. There is a reason for the seeming disparity in value between these two pieces. The plaque is not only significantly earlier, but it is quite lovely. The pitcher is not all that attractive, since the potter simply covered the entire surface with a shaded brown glaze.

AI.46

AI.47

AI.48

AI.49

The items illustrated on this page are the English counterparts to those items in Appendix III, which deal with the exquisite French porcelains made for the American market. Here are several examples of fine English porcelains made for export to that same market. Left: **AI.48** Pale green square footed compote with a central scene in natural colors depicting the HUDSON HIGHLANDS FROM BULL HILL, AMERICA. The title is on the reverse in red script. This is the type of porcelain produced by such factories as Rockingham, Masons and Ridgway during the period from 1830 - 1850. The scene uses William Bartlett's, *American Scenery* as the source. The value of this piece is $750.00 - $1,250.00. Above right: **AI.49** A much more sophisticated piece which we attribute to a more refined factory, such as Derby or Worcester. This scene is also taken from Bartlett's *American Scenery*, and is titled on the reverse ASCENT TO THE CAPITOL, WASHINGTON. The piece is basically a deep blue with gold highlights. The central scene is once again in natural colors. Also from the 1830's, this has a value of $1,500.00 - $2,500.00. Right: **AI.50** This is another exquisite example, probably manufactured by the Worcester or Derby factories in the 1830's. This is titled on the reverse CAPITOL, WASHINGTON. This footed compote has a value of $2,000.00 - $3,000.00.

Below: **AI.51** A group of seven plates from the same service as AI.48. Also done in a pale green, these Bartlett views are (from left to right) SABBATH DAY POINT, LAKE GEORGE, AMERICA; DESERT ROCK LIGHTHOUSE, MAINE; VIEW OF NORTHUMBERLAND (PENNSYLVANIA) AMERICA; NEW YORK FROM WEEHAWKEN; NEW

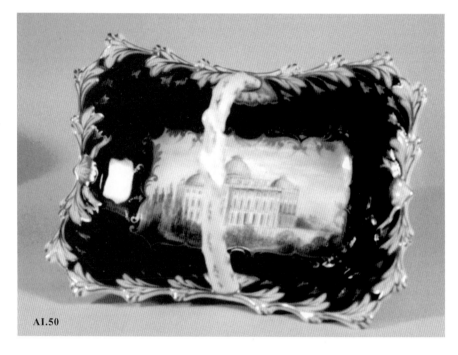

AI.50

YORK BAY FROM THE TELEGRAPH STATION; PRESIDENT'S HOUSE FROM THE RIVER, AMERICA and THE RAPIDS ABOVE THE FALLS OF NIAGARA. Once again, these were probably manufactured by one of the lesser houses in 1830 - 1850. These are valued from $300.00 to $750.00 per plate, depending on the desirability of the painted view.

AI.51

AI.52

AI.53

On this page we are illustrating another form of English ceramic termed "stoneware". The hard, porous white body is often found with a clear glaze, which gives the finished product a somewhat shiny, milky appearance. The potters also left the body unglazed, which gives it the appearance of Jasperware or parian. Those items illustrated here are recorded with either a broad chocolate enamel band, a very attractive medium blue enamel band or a tan enamel band, upon which, the potter has placed the molded white decoration. Upper left: **AI.52** This pitcher has a molded spout and an engine turned decoration around the base. Above this is a broad chocolate enamel band around the waist of the piece, and a more narrow chocolate enamel band around the collar. The lovely raised decoration was taken from an American coin. Above right: **AI.53** Under the spout, the potter has placed a relief molded generic symbol depicting PEACE & PLENTY with the overflowing cornucopias and clasped hands of friendship. Lower left: **AI.54** The reverse of this pitcher is decorated with a raised white SEAL OF THE UNITED STATES. This was manufactured for the American market in the period between 1820 - 1830. Right: **AI.55** This is another chocolate

AI.54

AI.55

enamel band pitcher that has the cornucopias under the spout and the sides decorated with portrait busts of LAFAYETTE and WASHINGTON. Both of these chocolate examples are rather rare and are valued at $1,000.00 - $2,000.00. Below left: **AI.56** This is a much more rare example with the medium blue enamel banding. On the sides are a relief portrait bust of GEORGE WASHINGTON and the same LAFAYETTE as AI.55. Below right: **AI.57** Under the spout the potter has applied a different SEAL OF THE UNITED STATES. It is obvious that this was produced to appeal to the sentiment raised in the United States by the visit of LaFayette in 1824. As we previously stated, this medium blue is much more rare and, although the date of manufacture and subject matter is basically the same, this color raises the value from $1,000.00 - $2,000.00

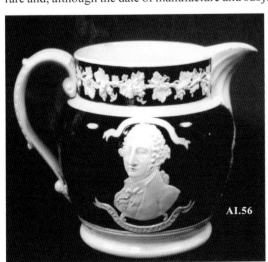

AI.56

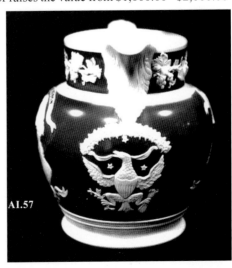

AI.57

mentioned above, to a value of $2,000.00 - $3,000.00. The value of the very rare tan examples, with the same decorations would be in the area of $1,500.00 - $2,500.00. We do not know the maker of these pieces, but would guess at Adams, Wood or Wedgwood. The forms recorded to date are, in the order of rarity, pitchers, tankards and vases, with pitchers being the most common form encountered.

Appendix II
Transfers on Enamels

Right: **AII.1** Small (11/2" - 2"w) oval enamel box with a transfer of polychromed flowers and the slogan AMERICAN INDEPENDENCE FOR EVER. Inside the cover is a tiny mirror. Note the "spider" crack on the surface. This is quite common on this type of ware and does not significantly reduce the value of the piece. However, a small piece of the enamel has broken off the upper left of the piece, which reduces the value by more than half. Circa 1780 -1820, damaged, this has a value of $400.00 - $600.00.

Left: **AII.2** AMERICA ONCE OBSCURE BUT NOW I RISE, FILL WITH JOY THE ADMIRING EYES is the black transfer printed inscription on this oval enamel box. This also has a small oval mirror inside the lid. Circa 1790 - 1820, this has a value of $500.00 - $1,000.00.

Right: **AII.3** This pendant has a lavender transfer portrait of Major General Sir Henry Clinton (1738 - 1795), who became commander in chief of the British army in North America after he succeeded Lord Howe in 1778.

Left: **AII.4** The potter used the same transfer on this small oval box, placing a smaller sized title over the reduced portrait. The smaller size of the box forced the potter to remove the lower portion of the transfer and the original title, in order to fit upon the smaller object. It worked and allowed the potter to save the cost of another engraving, used only for the box. These date from 1793 - 1795 and are valued at $1,000.00 - $1,500.00.

Left: **AII.5** This small oval box bears a full color scene of the United States frigate CONSTITUTION. Since the vessel was launched in 1797 and didn't see any significant action until 1803, this box probably dates from 1803 to 1815, the end of the War of 1812. We value this at $1,500.00 to $2,000.00.

Right: **AII.6** This mirror knob is one of a very rare series of portraits of the Leaders of the American Revolution, with this bust depicting SILAS DEANE of Connecticut (1737 - 1789). We think this was made during the period 1777 - 1790 and value it at $1,500.00 - $2,000.00.

Left: **AII.7** Another rarity from the same series, this

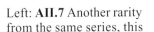

portrait bust is of John Dickenson of Pennsylvania (1732 - 1808). Labeled the "penman of the Revolution." A member of both the Stamp Act Congress and The Continental Congress, he authored several revolutionary articles urging the break from the crown. This is also valued at $1,500.00 - $2,000.00.

Right: **AII.8** From the same series, this is another portrait bust, this time depicting William H. Drayton (1742 - 1779), another American revolutionary politician from the distinguished South Carolina family that could trace it's heritage back to William the Conqueror. This too, is valued at $1,500.00 - $2,000.00.

Below: **AII.9** This pair of mirror knobs with the poly-chromed portrait busts of BENJAMIN FRANKLIN are definitely *not* common. The

portrait itself, is quite unlike any of those encountered on other English ceramics. Probably manufactured 1780 - 1810, these have a value of $2,000.00 - $3,000.00. Left: **AII.10** This small oval box is decorated with the familiar fur-hatted DR. FRANKLIN and is nicely poly-chromed. This dates from the same 1780 - 1810 period as the above mirror knobs and is valued at $1,500.00 - $2,500.00.

Left: **AII.11** This mirror knob has the polychromed Seal of the United States. This is somewhat common and is therefore valued at only $200.00 - $300.00.

Below: **AII.12** This is the first of the so-called "generic" transfers. These are slogans

that would be applicable to any English speaking market, not necessarily restricted to export to the United States. For that reason, they are priced on the low side, with this particular box having a value of $300.00 - $500.00.

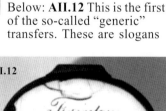

The next pair of knobs are considered extremely rare, and portray the third President of the United States, THOMAS JEFFERSON (above: **AII.13**). These could date from 1780 - 1810 and have a value of $3,500.00 - $5,000.00 for the pair.

Right: **AII.14** Another of the so-called "Leaders of the Revolution" group, this mirror knob is decorated with a black transfer portrait bust of the military secretary to George Washington and adjutant general of the Continental Army, GEN. (JOSEPH) REED (1741 - 1785) of Pennsylvania. Once again, probably made from 1777 - 1790, this is valued at $1,500.00 -$2,000.00.

Below: **AII.15** This pair of generic mirror knobs has a poly-chromed transfer of HOPE. Sometimes this is confused with the State Seal of Rhode Island, but this is one of a set of

three transfers, composed of FAITH, HOPE and CHARITY. Manufactured circa 1780 - 1820, these are valued at $200.00 - $400.00.

Left: **AII.16** This mirror knob has a nicely poly-chromed transfer of GEN. LAFAYETTE (1757 - 1834) in Continental uniform. Circa 1780 - 1810, this is valued at $800.00 - $1,200.00.

AII.17

LEFT: **AII.17** This mirror knob, which is part of the "Leaders of the Revolution" set, depicts South Carolina's HENRY LAURENS (1724 - 1792). President of the Continental Congress (1777 - 1778), he was captured by the British in 1780, while enroute to Holland to negotiate a treaty of assistance between that country and the rebellious colonies. He was exchanged for General Cornwallis, who had been captured at Yorktown, in 1782. Circa 1777 - 1790, this has a value of $1,500.00 - $2,000.00.

Right: **AII.18** MAY THE BLOSSOMS OF LIBERTY NEVER BE BLIGHTED is the patriotic motto transfer printed on this tiny box. Another generic item, it is valued at $300.00 - $500.00.

AII.18

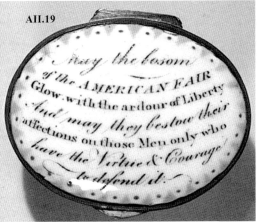

AII.19

Left: **AII.19** This box is larger than most and has a much longer patriotic verse adorning it's cover. Probably made 1790 - 1810, this is rather rare and is valued at $1,000.00 - $1,500.00.

Below: **AII.20** Almost certainly this motto is in opposition to the Jeffersonian embargo against the British in 1807, which ultimately resulted in the War of 1812. New England was very anti-war and anti-embargo and went so far as to begin the secession process from the infant United States. We value this at $800.00 to $1,200.00. The next box is probably related in both sentiment and date of manufacture.

AII.20

AII.21

Left: **AII.21** This slogan once again reflects the opposition to the growing tensions between the United States, England and France during the closing years of the 18th century and the early years of the 19th century. This is also valued at $800.00 - $1,200.00.

Right: **AII.22** This is a generic box with a patriotic sentiment of the day. It was made in the period from 1790 - 1815 and has a value of $300.00 - $500.00.

AII.22

Below: **AII.23** The rectangular shape of this box is rather unusual. While the tree of liberty might be assumed to be growing in the United States, this really isn't definite (France and Britain also had their version of the tree), so we have another generic slogan. While this is probably a bit earlier than others we have illustrated (1775 - 1800), it only has a value of $500.00 - $1,000.00.

AII.23

Below right: **AII.24** The slogan on this large oval box certainly reminds one that Britain had been fighting a global war against France and her allies for a hundred-fifteen year period from 1700 - 1815. This lovely generic box is valued at $300.00 - $500.00.

AII.24

AII.25

Left: **AII.25** Nothing generic about this mirror knob decorated with a polychromed portrait bust of COM. PERRY. This is a very unusual portrayal of the hero of the lakes, but if you examine illustration #3.51, you will see the likeness is basically correct, with the engraver showing the same forelock of hair and the prominent sideburns. Circa, 1815, this has a value of $1,500.00 - $2,500.00.

Right: **AII.26** This tiny box is transfer printed in black with the same motto often found on Liverpool and Staffordshire transfers which wish PROSPERITY TO THE UNITED STATES. Circa 1790 - 1810, this oval box, undamaged has a value of $800.00 - $1,200.00. As you can see from the illustration, a piece on the upper portion of this particular box appears to have been broken out and reattached. This would lower the value.

AII.26

AII.27

Above: **AII.27** This lovely polychromed pair of mirror knobs have a portrait bust of COM,ᴿᴱ TRUXTON the victorious commander of the U.S.S. Constellation, which defeated the French National Frigate L'Insurgent in 1799. The portrait of Truxton may actually be Admiral Nelson, renamed to appeal to the American market. The British must have exported a large number of these to the United States, because these are one of the few enamels with an American subject that are relatively common. Therefore, they are valued accordingly at $500.00 - $700.00.

Below: **AII.28** Possibly the rarest and most valuable of all the enamels we are illustrating, this is a silver box containing the transfer portrait of COL. TARLETON (1754 - 1833) commander of the British Legion during the American Revolution. This rarity is probably circa 1780 - 1785 and is valued at $3,000.00 - $5,000.00.

AII.28

AII.29

Left: **AII.29** Another of the "Leaders of the Revolution" set, this mirror knob has a black portrait bust of CHARLES THOM(P)SON (1729 -1824), a prosperous Philadelphia merchant. Recognized by Samuel Adams as a kindred spirit and a rabid revolutionary, he was Secretary of the Continental Congress. Circa 1777 - 1790, this has a value of $1,500.00 - $2,000.00.

Right: **AII.30** This mirror knob from the same set, depicts MAJ,ᴿ GENᴸ BAR. (VON) STEUBEN of Prussia (1730 - 1794), the Inspector General of the Continental Army. After the war, he continued as a military advisor to Washington, and died a citizen of the United States on his farm in Remsen, New York.

AII.30

Left: **AII.31** The transfer on this generic box has been poly-chromed with a very high degree of skill, and it resembles a tiny oil painting. Circa 1795 - 1815, it is valued at $700.00 - $900.00.

AII.31

Below: **AII.32** This polychromed box with the motto "ON WASHINGTON BOLD PLACE A CROWN OF PURE GOLD", is a very important piece of American history. Soon after the Revolution, there was a movement to replace King George III of England with King George Washington. This important box refers to this singular turning point in the history of the nation, when our present system of government was developed by our founding fathers. Circa 1780 - 1790, this is valued at $5,000.00+, whether it be poly-chromed or mono-chrome.

AII.32

Right: **AII.33** Another important box honoring GEN.ᴸ WASHINGTON. Covered in a bright blue enamel, this polychromed portrait of Washington adorns the exterior cover. Inside, where the tiny mirror is usually found, this rarity has a scene of a forested tomb with the inscription IN MEMORY OF WASHINGTON. Obviously, this is extremely rare. We believe this to be circa 1800 - 1810 and value it at $5,000.00+.

AII.33

Below: **AII.34** The first of a group of enamels celebrating the victor of the Revolution, GEN WASHINGTON.

AII.34

As in the case of transfer decorated Liverpool and Staffordshire "whiteware", the enameler found a ready export market for any item adorned with a tribute to this popular hero. The mirror knob on the left is taken from the Gilbert Stuart portrait and dates from 1797 - 1805. It is valued at $800.00 - $1,200.00.

Right: **AII.35** Another version of GEN.ᴸ WASHINGTON. This oval box dates from the period 1790 - 1810 and is valued at $800.00 - $1,200.00.

Below: **AII.36** The transfer on this oval box may be titled G. WASHINGTON, but we believe the enameler substituted a portrait of an English officer for the popular Washington. As we

AII.36

AII.35

will see a bit further along in this Washington section, this is not the only instance of this practice. We date this box 1795 - 1815 and place a value of $750.00 - $1,200.00 on it.

Below: **AII.37** This pair of mirror knobs are nicely polychromed, and once again depict Washington in uniform. These are relatively common and are valued at $500.00 - $700.00.

Below: **AII.38a** A very rare pair of mirror knobs titled GEN.ᴸ WASHINGTON, depicting the good general in a partial suit of 17th century armor. This is definitely not a portrait of the Washington we know and love. We thought this was a version of the famous painting of George II by Worlidge, but further investigation proved this to be in error. It is possible that it is taken from the 1805 Eccleston medallion (see AI.46 and AI.47). These mirror knobs are monochrome and date from 1790 - 1810. They are

AII.38a

valued at $1,000.00 - $1,500.00. Below: **AII.38b** Here is a real oddity. Presently in the Willet collection of The Royal Pavilion Museum in Brighton, England is this 1 1/2"d watch face, with the numerals on one side and this transfer of Washington on the other. The Museum dates this as 1780. As far as we know, this is unique and we value it at $5,000.00.

AII.38b

AII.37

245

AII.39

We have illustrated here three examples of different mottos with a Washington motif, used on boxes. These all date from the period 1785 - 1815 and are probably just a small representation of the variety that were probably manufactured by the English enamelers. Left: **AII.39** and below: **AII.40** are two examples of the same transfer used on two different shaped boxes. These simple boxes with a plain black transfer are valued at $500.00 - $1,000.00 each. Below : **AII.41** GREAT WASHINGTON TO THEE WE OWE OUR LIBERTY is the sentiment expressed on the small oval box. From the same

AII.40

period as the two previous Washington boxes, this is valued at $800.00 - $1,200. Below: **AII.42** The transfer inscription on this large box, once

AII.41

again reminds us of the deep feelings the Staffordshire district had in opposition to the Wars and trade embargoes between England and her former colony. This was probably manufactured in 1805 - 1815 and is valued at $800.00 - $1,200.00.

AII.42

Appendix III
French Ceramics
for the American Market

The finest pieces of American Historical ceramics are those exquisite porcelains produced in the late Eighteenth and early Nineteenth century by several manufactories in Paris, France. After the fall of the French monarchy, which had held a monopoly on the manufacture of fine porcelain, a large number of factories were opened in the Capital, many of which, established trade with the newly independent United States. The American ruling elite, such as Washington, Adams, Franklin and Jefferson, set the style for the upper class taste in French ceramics. This is evidenced by the fact that the first State Service of Presidential china, purchased by Washington, was a large service from the Sevres factory in 1790[(1)]. Tablewares, such as tea, dessert and dinner services were the main items ordered, being joined in the 1820 - 1830 period by the magnificent mantle vases, which the authors consider the ultimate in American Historical ceramics.

AIII.1

The value of these rare objects lies in not only the rarity and beauty of the form, but the degree of skill demonstrated in the execution of the portraits and topographical scenes. Some truly talented artists were employed in the decoration of these objects, but as always, there are those pieces which were mediocre when they were manufactured and remain mediocre one-hundred seventy five years later. Let us now examine a few of the exceptional pieces of ceramics the French exported to America in the period from 1780 to 1830.

Above: **AIII.1** This magnificent mantle vase has a superb portrait bust of JOHN ADAMS, PRESIDENT OF THE UNITED STATES. The decorator used a lithograph by A. or N. Maurin, which was taken from a portrait by Gilbert Stuart. Once in the collection of Gladys and Paul Richards, this portrait is identical to another vase in the collection of the Metropolitan Museum of Art[(2).] We place a value of $15,000.00 to $25,000.00 on the example illustrated because, not only is the portrait exceptional, but also the form, with the fine Sphinx handles.

AIII.2

Right: **AIII.2** This simple, rather thick, Paris porcelain plate bears a shaded black portrait bust of WILLIAM BAINBRIDGE ESQ. OF THE UNITED STATES NAVY. The source engraving (ill. 3.5), by Bance of Paris, was taken from a portrait by Gilbert Stuart. This group of eighteen small circular engravings (see **Notes - Chapter Three,** page 41)

AIII.3

were the source prints for a rare dessert service, portions of which are in the collections of The Mariner's Museum and The Henry Francis DuPont Museum, Winterthur. A few items are known in private collections, but these are quite rare, with approximately one-hundred pieces held by the two mentioned institutions. Left: **AIII.3** This is another plate from the same dessert service with a portrait bust titled MAJOR GEN.L BROWN U. S. ARMY, which used the Bance engraving taken from a portrait by John Jarvis. Both of these plates are considered extremely rare and have a value of $3,000.00 to $5,000.00.

AIII.4

Right: **AIII.4** A third view from the same dessert service with the title THE U. S. FRIGATE CONSTITUTION ISAAC HULL ESQR COMMANDER CAPTURING HIS B.M. FRIGATE GUERRIERE AUGUST 19TH 1812. This time the Bance engraving is taken from a painting by Thomas Birch. This also has a value of $3,000.00 to $5,000.00.

Left: **AIII.5** This lovely vase is decorated with a polychromed view of THE CONSTITUTION AND GUERRIERE, which used the same Thomas Birch painting as AIII.4 as a source for the view. While the various engravings produced to celebrate this particular American Naval victory outnumber those depicting other War of 1812 actions[3], the Birch source is the only version we record on French porcelain[4]. Valued by collectors at a lesser value than the form with a portrait of one of the early Presidents, this still commands a value of $8,000.00 to $12,000.00.

While on the subject of vases, we should mention another group which are more urn-like in form (see AIII .46) and are decorated with scenic landscapes or architectural views of the young United States. Usually decorated with a scene of early New York or Philadelphia[5], these are somewhat later, being of the period from 1830 to 1840. Once again, these are valued by collectors at a lesser value, depending on the skill of the decorator and the subject, and command a valuation of $4,000.00 to $8,000.00.

Below: **AIII.6** By now, you probably recognize another plate from the dessert service previously discussed. Titled STEPHEN DECATUR ESQR. *OF THE UNITED STATES NAVY*, the original Bance engraving (ill. 3.13) is taken from a painting by Gilbert Stuart.

Above: **AIII.7** is a handled mug from the same service, decorated with one of the two civilians from the Bance set, titled ROBERT FULTON ESQR. Fulton, who was an accomplished portrait painter, was also quite successful as an inventor. The French interest in him (to warrant inclusion with this set) probably occurred between 1797 and 1806, when he was in Paris testing his steamboat on the Seine. While a DECATUR mug would be valued at $2,500.00 to $3,500.00, this mug with FULTON would only have a value of half that amount.

Below: **AIII.8** The French did not produce a great quantity of transfer printed earthenware for the American market, but this plate manufactured at the Creil pottery is transfer printed with an excellent likeness of BENJAMIN FRANKLIN. This is the only example the authors record and it is valued at $3,000.00 to $5,000.00. We are not sure of the date of manufacture of this or it's companion plate of WASHINGTON (AIII.48), but we would guess it to be early 19th century. Due to the existence of a WASHINGTON gravy boat (AIII.47), there is a great probability of the existence of a full dinner service.

AIII.9

Left: **AIII.9** This is the first of several shaving mugs illustrated in this grouping of French ceramics. It is not fine porcelain, but rather a thick, heavy piece with a matte salmon band around the body and an oval vignette containing a black transfer of FRANKLIN. This and the other shaving mugs we are illustrating are from the period from 1840 - 1860. This example has a value of $1,000.00 to $1,500.00.

Below right: **AIII.10** Another first, this time a group of six saucers from what must have been a set of portrait busts of the first fourteen presidents of the United States, ranging from George Washington to Franklin Pierce. Since Pierce is the fourteenth president, that dates this group to sometime after 1852, when he won the Presidency. AIII.10 is a polychromed portrait of WILLIAM HENRY HARRISON, the ninth President of the United States. This particular saucer has a value of $2,000.00 to $3,000.00.

AIII.10

Below: **AIII.11** This is an extremely rare *pair* of porcelain vases with a polychromed scene of a naval battle titled HORNET & PEACOCK. Since the value of a single vase decorated with one of these naval battles is $8,000.00 to $12,000.00, it then stands to reason that a pair would be worth double that amount, plus a premium. We place the value of this pair at $20,000.00 to $30,000.00.

AIII.11

Below: **AIII.12** This exquisite portrait of THOMAS JEFFERSON is taken from a painting by Gilbert Stuart by way of a lithograph by A. or N. Maurin. The Brooklyn Museum of Art has a matching pair of vases, with a bust of ADAMS (see ill. AIII.1) on one and this exact portrait on the other [6]. Fully polychromed with a purple drape on the left, balanced by a chair upholstered in the same color, this is spectacular. We value this single vase at $15,000.00 to $25,000.00.

AIII.12

Below right: **AIII.13** This is a finely potted, thin-walled porcelain cup decorated with a polychromed enamel portrait bust titled THOMAS JEFFERSON. We illustrate another from the same service (AIII.37) with a portrait of ZACHARY TAYLOR. Once again, this dates this particular service to at least 1848-1850. The single cup with the JEFFERSON bust is valued at $1,500.00 to $2,500.00.

AIII.13

AIII.14

AIII.15

Above left **AIII.14** This is another plate from that rare dessert service we previously discussed, titled JACOB JONES ESQR. *OF THE UNITED STATES NAVY.* Taken from a painting by Rembrant Peale, this is another instance where the decorator used the Bance circular prints as a source. This, like the other "heroes" depicted on this service is valued at $3,000.00 to $5,000.00. Above right: **AIII.15** This Creil pottery earthenware plate has a black transfer of LE GENERAL LAFAYETTE in the uniform of the French National Guard, which he commanded at various times during the political turmoil present in France during the Napoleonic era. This particular uniform appears to be of that period during the 1830 revolution, thus dating this transfer. We value this at $1,000.00 to $1,500.00. Below right: **AIII.16** Another Creil plate that is considered somewhat common. This depicts GENERAL LAFAYETTE in the midst of a battle, with soldiers and Indians in the background and a somewhat bedraggled palm tree in the foreground. Probably meant to portray the General's role in the American Revolution, this is found with a black transfer and a black line border flanking a pale yellow band. This transfer has a value of $700.00 to $1,100.00. Below left: **AIII.17** This lovely porcelain vase is the smallest of the group illustrated in this Appendix. Decorated with a portrait bust of LAFAYETTE, with unusual unglazed porcelain heads forming the handles. As one might suspect, LAFAYETTE was a favorite with the decorators of French porcelain, so it is his countenance that we encounter most frequently. We value this at $3,000.00 to $5,000.00.

AIII.17

AIII.16

250

AIII.18a

AIII.18b

AIII.18c

AIII.18d

AIII.19a

AIII.19b

Above left: **AIII.18** This is a grouping of a place setting of the dessert service we have been discussing, decorated with a portrait of JAMES LAWRENCE ESQR. *LATE OF THE UNITED STATES NAVY.* There are two plates (9 1/2"d and 6 1/2"d), plus a cylindrical mug and a cup shown without it's saucer (which is decorated only with the gold bands - no portrait). We have been placing a value of $3,000.00 to $5,000.00 on the plates. When evaluating these pieces with a <u>military</u> figure portrayed, both plates will be valued the same, while the mug and a cup with saucer, should be worth $2,500.00 to $3,500.00, a cup alone, would be reduced in value to $2,000.00 - $3,000.00 .

Above right: **AIII.19** some of the same forms, but these busts portray JAMES MONROE, *PRESIDENT OF THE UNITED STATES* (1817 - 1825), which effectively dates this service. Due to the political nature of this portrait, the value rises dramatically to $6,000.00 to $9,000.00 for the plates and $4,000.00 to $6,000.00 for the cups and mugs. Below left: **AIII.20** Perhaps the most valuable ceramic piece illustrated in this book is this exceptional Paris porcelain tall vase, with delicate handles formed by figures of swans and having a most attractive band of rose-pink enamel, with gold highlights, around the body, containing an oval vignette with a finely executed polychrome portrait titled JAMES MONROE, PRESIDENT OF THE UNITED STATES. We place a conservative valuation of $20,000.00 to $30,000.00+ on it and realize that if it was ever placed at auction, it would most likely command a record price for this type of ware. This piece is outstanding in every way. Below right: **AIII.21a/b** Another large plate and a mug from the dessert service with a portrait bust of OLIVER H. PERRY EQSR. *OF THE UNITED STATES NAVY.* The plate is valued at $3,000.00 to $5,000.00 and the mug at $2,500.00 to 3,500.00.

AIII.20

AIII.21a

AIII.21b

AIII.22

AIII.23

AIII.25

Above left: **AIII.22** One of the six saucers previously discussed, this one with a polychromed portrait bust of JOHN TYLER, the tenth President of the United States. Ceramic items pertaining to this presidency are quite rare and highly desirable. This is valued $2,500.00 to $3,500.00. Above center: **AIII.23** The third saucer is a portrait bust of JAMES K. POLK, the eleventh President of the United States and the successor to JOHN TYLER. Also considered rare and desirable, this is valued at the same $2,5000.00 to $3,500.00. Below left: **AIII.24** Another large plate from the dessert service we have been discussing, in this instance decorated with a portrait bust of GENERAL PIKE *LATE OF THE UNITED STATES ARMY.* Using the Bance engravings as a source, this reflects the death of the General during the assault on York (Toronto) in April, 1813.

Above right: **AIII.25** This very rare mug shown with a saucer from the dessert service has a portrait bust of DAVID PORTER *OF THE UNITED STATES NAVY.* This Bance engraving was taken from the Gilbert Stuart painting of the Captain of the U.S.S. Essex. The saucer is decorated with only the gold band and does not have a portrait. This is valued at $2,500.00 to $3,500.00. Below right: **AIII.26a/b** This plate and mug are decorated with portrait busts of a young MAJOR GEN^L WINFIELD SCOTT *OF THE UNITED STATES ARMY.* The painting by Joseph Wood was used by Bance as a source for the engraving and thus the ceramics. The mug is valued at $2,500.00 to $3,500.00, while the plate is valued at $3,000.00 to $5,000.00.

AIII.24

AIII.26a

AIII.26b

AIII.27

AIII.28

Above left: **AIII.27** It is obvious that the source of this extremely rare vase was the same Bance engraving used on the previous two items from the dessert service. Also titled MAJOR GEN[L] WINFIELD SCOTT OF THE UNITED STATES ARMY, this polychromed portrait is surrounded by a wide band of light pink, highlighted with green and gold. It is spectacular. We value this at $15,000.00 to $25,000.00. Above right: **AIII.28** The reverse of the SCOTT vase contains an oval vignette decorated with a version of the SEAL OF THE UNITED STATES. If this SEAL alone, were to be found on a vase, we would value it at $3,000.00 to $5,000.00. Below left: **AIII.29** This is the fourth saucer from that group of six we have been discussing, decorated with a polychromed portrait of an older WINFIELD SCOTT, probably meant to portray him during his unsuccessful campaign for the presidency in 1852. We value this at $2,000.00 to $4,000.00. Below center: **AIII.30** This finely potted creamer is decorated with another version of the SEAL OF THE UNITED STATES flanked by two Indians, all of which are polychromed. This was probably part of a dessert service. It is valued at $1,000.00 to $1,500.00. Below right: **AIII.31** An exceptionally fine cup and matching saucer decorated with still another version of the SEAL OF THE UNITED STATES. Very finely potted, the decoration reflects the high skill of the artist who applied the gold, black and red enamels. Probably made to order for an American embassy, this is valued at $1,500.00 to $2,500.00.

AIII.29

AIII.30

AIII.31

Left: **AIII.32** This cup and saucer dates from the second half of the 19th century and is decorated with a pair of crossed American flags and another version of the Seal of the United States, in polychrome enamels. Fifty years later and with a much less impressive decoration, this is valued at less than half of AIII.31. Right: **AIII.33** This cup with a polychromed portrait of General Z. Taylor is from the same set as AIII.13. This is the piece which dates the set, as it portrays Taylor as a General, and was therefore made prior to or during the presidential campaign of 1848. This is the latest presidential figure in the set. Extremely rare and highly desirable, because it is a period piece, this is valued at $3,000.00 to $4,000.00. Below left: **AIII.34** This medium sized plate has been decorated with two different versions of the Seal of the United States. Done in a palette of purple and black, it has a similar type of central device as the cup and saucer illustrated in AIII.32. Probably manufactured during the second half of the 19th century, this has a value of $400.00 to $800.00.

Bottom left: **AIII.35** This large cylindrical earthenware prune jar is decorated with still another version of the Seal of the United States. At one time, it no doubt had a lid. Once in the Collection of Gladys and Paul Richards, this appears to be Liverpool creamware to the casual observer, but it is French. Since the French potteries were able to produce an inexpensive, transfer-decorated "creamware", it makes one wonder why they did not challenge the English dominance of the export trade to North America, with this cheaper, more saleable product. This prune jar is valued at $1,500.00 to $2,500.00 and is the only example of French transfer printed creamware that the authors record. Bottom right: **AIII.36** This ornate vase clearly reflects the Victorian romance with "gingerbread" forms. Manufactured for the presidential campaign of Zachary Taylor in 1848, the polychromed portrait of the General in uniform is titled Rough & Ready. This is an extremely rare, if not unique piece, highly desirable to political collectors, yet it lacks the grace and beauty of the earlier vases we have illustrated and the cartoon-like portrait of Taylor lacks the beauty and skill shown in the earlier French porcelains. For those reasons, it is valued at $3,000.00 to $5,000.00, instead of the five figure values placed on the vases portraying Washington, Jefferson, Adams and Scott.

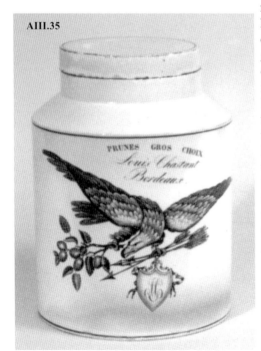

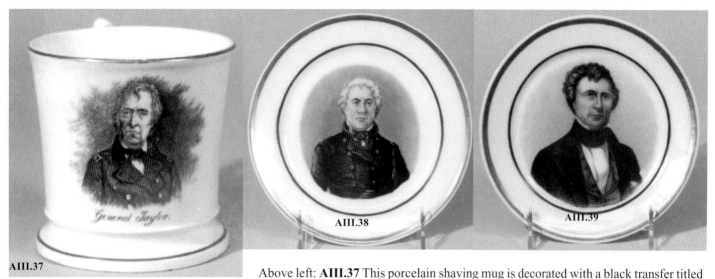

AIII.37   **AIII.38**   **AIII.39**

Above left: **AIII.37** This porcelain shaving mug is decorated with a black transfer titled GENERAL TAYLOR and was probably manufactured for the presidential campaign of 1848. Sometimes these are found with both the General's portrait and another of WASHINGTON (see below) on the same mug. In most instances, the mug will be decorated with a single portrait. In the case of GENERAL TAYLOR, we value this at $2,000.00 to $3,000.00. Above center: **AIII.38** This is the fifth of six saucers we have been discussing, with this example having a polychromed portrait of ZACHARY TAYLOR. Again made for the presidential campaign of 1848, this has a value of $2,500.00 to $3,500.00. Above right: **AIII.39** The sixth saucer from the group is the

AIII.41

rarest and most valuable since it is decorated with a polychromed portrait of FRANKLIN PIERCE, the fourteenth President of the United States (1853 - 1857). This is the piece which dates this group to the election of 1852, when PIERCE defeated the Whig candidate, WINFIELD SCOTT. Period ceramic items for this president are extremely rare, which accounts for it's valuation of $4,000.00 to $5,000.00. Left: **AIII.40** This simple shaving mug decorated with TAYLOR'S nickname of ROUGH AND READY is considered unique. For this reason, it is desired by political collectors and commands a valuation of $1,500.00 to $2,500.00. Right center: **AIII.41** While this small porcelain bowl/saucer is reminiscent of

AIII.40

the group of six saucers we have already discussed, it is of much higher quality and an extremely rare, finely executed portrait of MARTIN VAN BUREN, the eighth President of the United States (1837 - 1841). From a group of six, discovered by the legendary Connecticut antiques dealers Rockwell and Avis Gardiner in the early 1980's, these are related in all respects to those fabulous vases, which we have been illustrating in this Appendix. The VAN BUREN is considered the best of the group, since it is the period piece and is valued at $4,000.00 to $5,000.00. Those decorated with the portraits of WASHINGTON,

AIII.42

FRANKLIN, MADISON and MONROE are valued at $1,000.00 to $2,000.00, while the recorded example of JAMES POLK is valued at $2,000.00 to $4,000.00. Left: **AIII.42** This shaving mug is the companion to the TAYLOR mug (AIII.37) and has a transfer of WASHINGTON. Made almost fifty years after his death, it is valued at $500.00 to $1,000.00, while the large plate from the dessert service (right: **AIII.43**) has a valuation of $3,000.00 to $5,000.00 for the decoration of GEORGE WASHINGTON ESQ. *LATE PRESIDENT OF THE UNITED STATES*.

AIII.43

255

AIII.44

AIII.45

Left: **AIII.44** Once in the Collection of Paul and Gladys Richards, this fine Paris Porcelain vase bears a polychromed bust of GEORGE WASHINGTON using the famous Gilbert Stuart painting as a source. Right: **AIII.45** Another vase decorated with a portrait bust also identified as WASHINGTON, but this could also be ADAMS. If it is WASHINGTON, then either vase would be valued at $8,000.00 to $12,000.00. If AIII.45 is in fact ADAMS, then the value is $15,000.00+. Below left: **AIII.46** Here is a pair of Urn-shaped vases with poorly executed portraits of GEORGE WASHINGTON and MARTHA WASHINGTON. While this shape was used by the French in the 1830's, decorated with skillfully executed landscapes and architectural views, there is little skill evident in the painting decorating these two vases, which we estimate were manufactured after 1850. If these were of the form and quality evident in AIII.44, this pair would be valued at over $25,000.00, but both the form and decoration are of such an inferior quality that we value these at only $1,000.00 to $3,000.00 (or less). As you can see, the artistic quality of both the form **and** decoration are extremely important to the valuation of these French porcelains. Below right: **AIII.47** and **AIII.48** Both of these pieces of earthenware are from the Creil factory and are decorated with a black transfer of GEORGE WASHINGTON. We believe the date of manufacture of these fine pieces to be between 1800 and 1820, which is quite early for most transfer decorated earthenware. Perhaps this was the French response to English creamware and pearlware. These are both considered extremely rare and are valued at $3,000.00 to $5,000.00 each.

AIII.46

AIII.47

AIII.48

256

AIII.49

AIII.50

Above left: **AIII.49** This is an early plate (1800 - 1815) from a service with a history of ownership in Baltimore, Maryland. Featuring musical instruments and classical figures in the border, this was the height of fashion in the new republic at the turn of the 19th century[7]. The central motif is an olive branch crossed with a thirteen star American flag. The decoration is done in a sophisticated palette of coppery-peach and black. The plate is valued at $1,000.00 to $2,000.00.

The remaining pieces illustrated on this page are all products of the Meissen factory and all were manufactured in the late 18th and early 19th centuries for the American market. Above right: **AIII.50** This fine saucer has an overall dark blue ground surrounding a quatrefoil vignette, highlighted in gold, containing a polychromed portrait of JAMES MADISON. This has the underglaze crossed swords mark on the base, identifying the factory. At one time this must have had a cup, which might have also had a portrait decoration. This saucer, which is the only one the authors record, is valued at $3,000.00 to $5,000.00. Below left: **AIII.51** This is a similar saucer also attributed to the Meissen factory with an overall dark blue ground surrounding a circular vignette containing a polychromed portrait of THOMAS JEFFERSON. This also has the crossed swords underglaze mark in blue and is the only example the authors record. It too, is valued at $3,000.00 to $5,000.00. Below right: **AIII.52** Probably manufactured fifty years earlier than the two preceding Meissen pieces, this fine cup and saucer with a highly skilled portrait of BENJAMIN FRANKLIN is exceptional in every way. Once in the Collection of Gladys and Paul Richards, it is obvious to even the casual observer that the quality of this 18th century piece is far superior to those items manufactured at the same factory fifty years later. If this portrait was of a president in office, during it's manufacture, the value would be far higher than the $3,000.00 to $5,000.00 placed upon this portrait of inventor/writer/diplomat FRANKLIN.

AIII.51

AIII.52

Below: **AIII.54a/b** These are two late arrivals, which must be placed out of order at the end of this Appendix. Another portrait bust from the dessert service, this time of Isaac Hull Esq. *of the United States Navy.* Both pieces are valued at $2,500.00 to $3,500.00.

AIII.54a

AIII.54b

(1) Detweiler, Susan G., *George Washington's Chinaware,* Abrams, 1982, pages 119 - 134.

(2) Frelinghuysen, Alice C., *Paris Porcelain in America,* The Magazine Antiques, April, 1998, Plate XVI, page 562.

(3) Olds, Irving S., *Bits and Pieces of American History,* Olds, 1952, page 105.

(4) Frelinghuysen, plate XI, page 559, there is illustrated a superb vase with a naval battle which is incorrectly identified as The Constitution and Guerriere. The scene portrayed is actually The Constitution Capturing the Java off the Coast of Brazils (Olds #185, page 162) after a *"drawing under the direction of a witness by W.G."* Neither the artist, engraver nor publisher are named in this English version. However, there is a French copy of the exact scene titled Le Combat Naval - Gloire Americaine (Olds #186, page 162) published by M. Guerin in Paris, naming Garneray as the engraver. Who copied who is unknown, but this most probably was the source of the view on the vase in the Metropolitan.

(5)*Ibid,* page 561.

(6)*Ibid,* plate XVI, page 562.

(7) *Ibid,* page 559. The author illustrates a similar plate and a tureen from this service on page 557, plate VII and VIII, where she states that this is attributed to the Dihl et Guerhard factory, circa 1800 - 1815. The classical figures in the border of the illustrated plate are all different from the example illustrated AIII.49.

Addendum One
Herculaneum Pottery

These are the transfers which we now attribute to the Herculaneum Pottery. The views are (using the numbering system from Chapter Five):

A.7. JOHN ADAMS PRESIDENT...ETC
A.13. THE FRIGATE ALLIANCE
A.17. AMERICAN MANUFACTURES..ETC
A.21. AN EMBLEM OF AMERICA
A.34. AUT VINCERE AUT MORI BOSTON FUSILEER
B.4. BALTIMORE MARGARET DELANY
B.10. BY VIRTUE AND VALOUR...ETC
B.11. BY VIRTUE AND VALOUR...ETC. (POSSIBLE)
B.13. BY VIRTUE AND VALOUR...ETC. (POSSIBLE)
C.12. COLUMBIA - UNTITLED
C.17. COMMODORE PREBLE'S SQUADRON ATTACKING ...ETC
C.18. CONSTITUTION
C.28. MARQUIS CORNWALLIS
C.30. CUMBERLAND, ENGINE, NO 8, SOCIETY....ETC.
D.10. DEUS NOBIS HAEC OTIA FECIT
D.11. J. DICKENSON ESQR....ETC (PROBABLY)
D.12. A DROLL SCENE IN NEWBURYPORT
E.1. EASTON POINT - UNTITLED
F.5. BENJAMIN FRANKLIN L.L.D. F. R. S. BORN AT BOSTON..ETC
F.6. BENJ. FRANKLIN BORN AT BOSTON..ETC. (PROBABLY)
F.7. BENJ. FRANKLIN L.L.D.F.R.S. BORN AT BOSTON ...ETC.
F.8. DR. FRANKLIN
F.9. BENJ. FRANKLIN L.L.D.F.R.S. BORN AT ...ETC.
F.19. FREEPORT ARTILLERY
G.1. THE GALLANT DEFENSE OF STONINGTON
G.2. GENERAL GATES
H.1. THE HONOURABLE JOHN HANCOCK
H.2. HANCOCK
H.12. HOPE
J.9. JEFFERSON QUOTATION
J.10. JEFFERSON CARTOON
J.11. JEFFERSON CARTOON
J.13. THOMAS JEFFERSON PRESIDENT OF THE UNITED STATES OF AMERICA
J.14. THOMAS JEFFERSON PRESIDENT OF THE UNITED STATES OF AMERICA
J.15. THOMAS JEFFERSON PRESIDENT OF THE UNITED STATES OF AMERICA
J.16. THOMAS JEFFERSON PRESIDENT OF THE UNITED STATES OF AMERICA
J.17. THOMAS JEFFERSON PRESIDENT OF THE UNITED STATES OF AMERICA
J.18. UNTITLED - JEFFERSON
J.19. THOMAS JEFFERSON... WE ARE ALL REPUBLICANS..ETC.
J.20. THOMAS JEFFERSON... WE ARE ALL REPUBLICANS..ETC.
J.21. UNTITLED - THOMAS JEFFERSON
J.22. UNTITLED - JEFFERSON
J.23. JEFFERSON POEM
J.24. JEFFERSON POEM

J.25. JEFFERSON
J.35. JUSTICE
L.22. LIBERTY INDEPENDENCE
L.23. LIBERTY INDEPENDENCE (GLEBE POEM)
L.26. LIBERTY 23RD DECEMBER 1801
L.27. LIBERTY 24TH DECEMBER 1801
L.31. L'INSURGENT FRENCH FRIGATE....ETC
M.6. JAMES MADDISON LIBERTY, INDEPENDENCE..ETC. (PROBABLY)
M.7. JAMES MADDISON PRESIDENT OF THE...ETC. .
M.8. UNTITLED - MADDISON POEM
M.12. MAY AMERICA NEVER WANT ARTILLERY
M.18. JAMES MONROE PRESIDENT OF THE UNITED STATES
N.3. NEWBURYPORT HARBOR
N.4. UNTITLED - NEWBURYPORT BAKERY
P.8. PEACE, PLENTY, INDEPENDENCE
P.10. PEACE PLENTY AND INDEPENDENCE NEW YORK BOSTON
P.11. PEACE PLENTY AND INDEPENDENCE STATES NEW YORK BOSTON
P.12. PEACE PLENTY AND INDEPENDENCE STATES BOSTON (POSSIBLE)
P.13. PEACE PLENTY AND INDEPENDENCE STATES (POSSIBLE)
P.14. PEACE PLENTY AND INDEPENDENCE
P.16. PEACE AND COMMERCE
P.27. UNTITLED - A PICTURESQUE VIEW OF THE STATE OF THE NATION 1778
P.35. PLAN OF THE CITY OF WASHINGTON
P.40. ARMS OF PREBLE
P.41. COMMODORE E. PREBLE
P.42. COMMODORE PREBLE
P.46A. THE PROPERTY OF ENGINE NO 2
P.46B. UNTITLED - FIRE ENGINE PUMPER
P.46C. UNTITLED - FIRE FIGHTING
S.2. THE SALLY
S.3. SALLY OF BOSTON (POSSIBLE)
S.9. SEAL OF THE UNITED STATES
S.12. SEAL OF THE UNITED STATES
S.13. SEAL OF THE UNITED STATES
S.17. SEAL OF UNITED STATES - JEFFERSON QUOTE
S.20. SEAL OF THE UNITED STATES
S.22. SEAL OF THE UNITED STATES
S.23. SEAL OF THE UNITED STATES
S.24. SEAL OF THE UNITED STATES
S.26. SEAL OF THE UNITED STATES
S.29. SEAL OF THE UNITED STATES
S.39. SEAL OF THE UNITED STATES
S.48. UNTITLED - SHIPBUILDING
S.49. SOUTH CAROLINA
S.50. SHIP
S.51. SHIP
S.52. SHIP
S.53. SHIP

S.60. Ship
S.64. Success to the Alexander (possibly)
S.65. Untitled - Soldiers
S.67. Success to America
S.69. Success to the American Trade (probably)
S.73. Success to the British Fleet
S.75. Success to the Infant Navy of America
S.76. Success to the Trade of Boston (possible)
S.77. Success to the Trade of Rhode Island (possible)
T.1. Colonel Tarleton
U.3. Cordwainers Society
U.6. United States Frigate Guerriere Bound for Russia
U.11. United We Stand, Divided We Fall
V.2. (Virginia) Sic Semper Tyrannis
W.2. General Washington
W.4. His Excellency Gen^L Geo. Washington
W.5. His Excellency General Washington...etc.
W.6. His Excellency General Washington
W.7. His Excellency Gen^L George Washington
W.8. His Excellency Gen^L Washington (possible)
W.9. His Excellency Geo. Washington (possible)
W.10. George Washington Esqr General and Commander...etc
W.11. His Excellency General George Washington..etc

W.15. Washington - Map of the United States
W.17. Washington Poem
W.21. G. Washington, Esq.
W.22. Untitled - Washington
W.23. His Excellency Gen^L. Geo. Washington (probably)
W.25. Columbia's Favorite Son His Excellency General...etc.
W.29. Washington
W.34. First President of the U. S. of America
W.35. Washington Funeral Urn
W.37. He In Glory America In Tears
W.38. He In Glory America In Tears
W.39. Washington Apotheosis
W.40. Washington Apotheosis
W.41. Ascending Into Glory
W.42. Untitled - Apotheosis
W.43. Washington in Glory (probably)
W.44. Washington in Glory
W.45. First in War...etc.
W.46. Washington In Glory
W.48. America Lamenting The Death of Her Favorite Son
W.49. Washington In His Glory
W.56. A Man Without Example A Patriot Without Reproach
W.69. The Work of Mechaniks

Addendum Two
The Shelton Group

Below, we have listed the transfers which we now attribute to the "Shelton Group". Using the numbering system from Chapter Five, they are:

A.8. John Adams, President of the United States
A.10. Adams Map of United States
A.18. America Declared Independent (probably)
B.12. Untitled - By Virtue and Valour....etc. (signed "T. Fletcher, Shelton").
F.4. The Foederal Union (possible)
J.8. Jefferson Quote - Anno Domini...etc.
L.24. Liberty Independence (Glebe poem)
M.6. James Maddison..etc. (possible)
M.15. The Memory of Washington and the Proscribed Patriots
M.16. Memory Those Patriots..ect (possible)
O.1. O Liberty! Thou Goddess...etc.
P.36. Pluribus Unum
P.37. Pluribus Unum
P.39. Signals at Portland Observatory
S.14. Seal of the United States
S.15. Seal of the United States
S.16. Seal of the United States

S.57. Ship
S.58. Ship
S.68. Success to America Whose Militia...etc.
S.81. Success to Trade
U.2. Union of Two Great Republics (possible)
U.4. Union to the People
V.3. Untitled - Virtue and Valour
W.16. Washington Map of the United States
W.18. Deafness to the Ear...Immortal Washington
W.19. Deafness to the Ear...Immortal Washington (also recorded signed "T. Fletcher Shelton")
W.30. Washington Crowned With Laurels by Liberty
W.31. Untitled - Washington
W.32. Washington America Declared Independent
W.33. G. Washington
W.51. To the Memory of the Immortal Washington (possible)
W.52. In Memory of the Immortal Washington..etc (possible)

Addendum Three
Enoch Wood and Sons

We attribute the following views to the Wood firm (using the numbering system from Chapter Five):

A.2. ADAMS (PROBABLY)
A.3. ADAMS (PROBABLY)
A.14. AMERICA
A.15. AMERICA E PLURIBUS UNUM
A.20. FISHER AMES
A.23. ARMS OF THE UNITED STATES
A.24. ARMS OF THE UNITED STATES
A.25. ARMS OF THE UNITED STATES
A.30. ARMS OF THE UNITED STATES (PROBABLY)
A.31. ARMY HEROES
B.1. COMMODORE BAINBRIDGE
B.7. MAJOR GEN'L BROWN NIAGARA
C.16. COMMODORE MACDONNOUGH'S VICTORY ON LAKE CHAMPLAIN
C.20. CONSTITUTION'S ESCAPE FROM THE BRITISH
C.23. (UNTITLED) CONSTITUTION IN CLOSE ACTION W/THE GUERIERRE
C.24. CONSTITUTION IN CLOSE ACTION WITH THE GUERIERRE
C.25. CONSTITUTION TAKING THE CYANE AND THE LEVANT
D.3. STEPHAN DECATUR, ESQ. OF THE UNITED STATES NAVY
D.7. DECATOR
E.4. THE ENTERPRISE AND BOXER
F.3. FIRST VIEW OF COM. PERRY'S VICTORY
F.16. FREE TRADE AND SAILORS THEIR RIGHTS
F.17. FREE TRADE AND SAILORS THEIR RIGHTS
F.18. FREE TRADE AND SAILORS RIGHTS
H.14. UNTITLED - HORNET AND THE PEACOCK
H.15. UNTITLED - HORNET BLOCKADING THE BON CITOYENNE
H.16. THE HORNET SINKING THE PEACOCK
H.17. UNTITLED - HORNET
H.18. CAPT. HULL OF THE CONSTITUTION
H.19. UNTITLED - HULL
H.20. CAPT. HULL OF THE CONSTITUTION
J.2. GENL. JACKSON HERO OF AMERICA (PROBABLY)
J.3. GENERAL JACKSON
J.4. GENERAL JACKSON THE HERO OF NEW ORLEANS
J.5. GENERAL JACKSON HERO OF NEW ORLEANS
J.6. GENERAL JACKSON
J.26. JEFFERSON
J.31. CAPTAIN JONES OF THE MACEDONIAN
L.1. LAFAYETTE CROWNED IN GLORY (PROBABLY)
L.12. WELCOME LAFAYETTE THE NATION'S GUEST
L.13. LAFAYETTE WASHINGTON
L.14. WELCOME LAFAYETTE THE NATION'S GUEST
L.17. LAWRENCE DON'T SURRENDER THE SHIP
L.18. JAMES LAWRENCE ESQ. LATE OF THE UNITED STATES NAVY
M.4. MADISON
M.11. UNTITLED - MARTIAL TROPHIES

M.14. MAY THE TREE OF LIBERTY EVER FLOURISH
M.17. MONROE
M.20. MUNROE
N.1. UNTITLED - NAVAL HEROES
N.2. NAVAL MONUMENT
P.9. PEACE AND PROSPERITY TO AMERICA
P.12. PEACE PLENTY AND INDEPENDENCE (POSSIBLE)
P.13. PEACE PLENTY AND INDEPENDENCE (POSSIBLE)
P.21. PERRY WE HAVE MET THE ENEMY AND THEY ARE OURS
P.26. COMMODORE PERRY (POSSIBLE)
P.29. PIKE BE ALWAYS READY TO DIE FOR YOUR COUNTRY
P.30. PIKE BE ALWAYS READY TO DIE FOR YOUR COUNTRY
S.4. SEAL OF THE UNITED STATES
S.7. SEAL - MAY SUCCESS ATTEND OUR AGRICULTURE TRADE AND MANUFACTURES, ETC.
S.8. SEAL - A PRESENT... MAY SUCCESS ATTEND OUR AGRICULTURE, ETC.
S.18. SEAL OF THE UNITED STATES
S.33. SEAL OF THE UNITED STATES (POSSIBLE)
S.36. SEAL OF THE UNITED STATES (POSSIBLE)
S.38. SEAL OF THE UNITED STATES
S.40. UNTITLED - SEAL OF THE UNITED STATES
S.42. SECOND VIEW OF COM. PERRY'S VICTORY
S.76. SUCCESS TO THE TRADE OF BOSTON (POSSIBLE)
S.77. SUCCESS TO THE TRADE OF RHODE ISLAND (POSSIBLE)
S.80. SUCCESS TO THE UNITED STATES OF AMERICA
S.82. SUCCESS TO TRADE 1815
S.84. SURRENDER OF CORNWALLIS- CORNWALLIS RESIGNING HIS SWORD
T.7. THE TRUE BLOODED YANKEE (PROBABLY)
U.1. UNITED IN LIBERTY'S CAUSE...ETC
U.5. UNITED STATES AND MACEDONIAN
U.7. UNITED STATES OF AMERICA FREE AND INDEPENDENT
U.9. UNITED STATES AND MACEDONIAN - THE VICTORY...ETC
V.1. VIEW OF COM. PERRY'S VICTORY
W.1. WASHINGTON JOHN ADAMS
W.8. UNTITLED - HIS EXCELLENCY
W.9. HIS EXCELLENCY GEO. WASHINGTON (POSSIBLE)
W.10. GEORGE WASHINGTON, ESQR...ETC. (POSSIBLE)
W.11. HIS EXCELLENCY GEORGE WASHINGTON (POSSIBLE)
W.27. WASHINGTON
W.28. WASHINGTON (PROBABLY)
W.36. GENERAL WASHINGTON DEPARTED THIS LIFE, ETC.
W.65. THE WASP BOARDING THE FROLIC
W.66. THE WASP AND THE REINDEER
Y.1. GIVE THE YANKEES A PLUMPER
UKN.1. UNIDENTIFIED FLEET SCENE
UKN.2. UNIDENTIFIED AMERICAN WARSHIP

Addendum Four
Davenport

The following fourteen transfers have been attributed to the Davenport firm:

A.32. ATTACK ON FORT OSWEGO
B.8. BROWN (above portrait) HERO OF NIAGARA (below portrait)
C.19. CONSTITUTION AND GUERIERRE
C.22. CONSTITUTION AND JAVA
E.3. ENTERPRISE AND BOXER
H.21. CAPTAIN HULL

J.1. MAJOR GEN'L ANDREW JACKSON
J.7. JOHN JAY, ESQ. LATE CHIEF JUSTICE OF THE UNITED STATES
J.32. CAPTAIN JONES
L.19. LEPERVIER AND PEACOCK
P.20. PERRY
P.28. PIKE
S.59. SHIP
W.64. WASP AND FROLIC

Selected Bibliography

Articles

Biddle, James, *American History on English Jugs*, The Metropolitan Museum of Art Bulletin, May, 1964.

Hill, Nola O., *American History on Liverpool and Staffordshire*, The Magazine Antiques, October, 1953.

Frelinghuysen, Alice C., *Paris Porcelain in America,* The Magazine Antiques, April, 1998

Keyes, Willard E., *The Cow and the Sleeping Lion,* The Magazine Antiques, January, 1941.

The Magazine Antiques, September, 1945.

Miller, J. Jefferson, *Unrecorded American Views on Two Liverpool-type Earthenware Pitchers,* Winterthur Portfolio #4, Winterthur Museum, Library and Gardens, Winterthur, Delaware.

Nelson, Christina H., *Transfer-printed Creamware and Pearlware for the American Market,* Winterthur Portfolio, #2, Winterthur Museum Library and Gardens, Winterthur, Delaware.

Reference Books

Arman, David and Linda, *Historical Staffordshire; An Illustrated Check-List*, 1974, Arman Enterprises, Inc., Danville, Virginia.

Arman, David and Linda, *First Supplement to Historical Staffordshire; An Illustrated Check-List,* 1977, Arman Enterprises, Inc., Danville, Virginia.

Arman, David and Linda, *The China and Glass Quarterly Volume I, Numbers 1-4*, 1997, Oakland Press, Portsmouth, Rhode Island

Barber, Edwin Atlee, *Anglo-American Pottery*, 1901, 2nd Edition, Patterson and White, Philadelphia, Pennsylvania.

Bowen, Abel, *Naval Monument,* 1816, Bowen, Boston, Massachusetts.

Drakard, David, *Printed English Pottery - History and Humor in the Reign of George III*, 1992, Horne, London.

Ewins, Neil, *Supplying the Present Wants of Our Yankee Cousins*, 1997, City Museum and Art Gallery, Stoke-On-Trent, England.

Gaylord, Charles, *American Naval Battles*, 1837, Gaylord, Boston, Massachusetts.

Godden, Geoffrey A. and Gibson, Michael, *Collecting Lustreware*, 1991, Barrie & Jenkins. London.

Henrywood, R. K., *An Illustrated Guide to British Jugs*, 1997, Swan Hill, Shrewsbury, England.

Klamkin, Marian, *American Patriotic and Political China*, 1973, Scribners, New York, New York.

Larsen, Ellouise Baker, *American Historical Views on Staffordshire China,* 1939, 1950 (E. B. Larsen) and 1975 (Dover).

Lockett, Terrence A. and Godden, Geoffrey A., *Davenport - China, Earthernware & Glass 1794 -1887.* 1989. Barrie & Jenkins. London

McCauley, Robert H., *Liverpool Transfer Designs on Anglo-American Pottery*, 1942, Southworth-Anthoesen Press, Portland, Maine.

Niles, John M., *The Life of Oliver Hazard Perry,* 1821, Cooke, Hartford, Connecticut.

Olds, Irving S., *Bits and Pieces of American History*, 1951, Olds, New York, New York.

Polan, Sandra, et al, *Nineteenth-Century Transfer-Printed Ceramics From the Townsite of Old Velasco, Brazoria County, Texas*, 1996, U. S. Army Corps of Engineers, Galveston, Texas.

Smith, Edgar Newbold, *American Naval Broadsides*, 1974, Philadelphia Maritime Museum, Philadelphia, Pennsylvania.

Spero, Simon, *18th Century English Transfer-Printed Porcelain and Enamels*, 1991, Mulberry Press, Carmel, California.

Tattersall, Bruce, et al, *Wedgwood Portraits and the American Revolution*, 1976, National Portrait Gallery, Washington, District of Columbia.

Printed by Pacific Rim, International Printing
Los Angeles, California